Chinese Cooperative-Harmonious Democracy

I0121810

After several decades of reform and opening up, China has come to a critical period of transformation and development. How to deepen political reform for this country has once again attracted the world's attention.

This book proposes a new democracy model for China's political reform – "cooperative-harmonious democracy". Absorbing the core values of democracy, this model draws on Chinese traditional "harmony and cooperation" and "people-oriented" thought, as well as modern cooperative game theory. More importantly, this book adopts the new model to analyse some present practice cases in China. This book is a valuable theoretical innovation and a significant achievement in promoting the interdisciplinary research of political science and public management. It strategically reflects on how to promote the development of cooperative-harmonious democracy from the perspective of high-level design. The policy suggestions it proposed will be a valuable reference for policy-makers.

Dr. Zongchao Peng is a professor and associate dean of School of Public Policy & Management, and director of Center for Crisis Management Research, Tsinghua University.

Dr. Ben Ma is a professor and associate dean of School of Political Science & Public Management, Shandong University, and a part time researcher in Center for Crisis Management Research, Tsinghua University.

Dr. Taoxiong Liu is a professor and associate dean of School of Social Sciences, and executive director of Center for Strategy and Policy, Tsinghua University.

China Perspectives series

The *China Perspectives* series focuses on translating and publishing works by leading Chinese scholars, writing about both global topics and China-related themes. It covers Humanities & Social Sciences, Education, Media and Psychology, as well as many interdisciplinary themes.

This is the first time any of these books have been published in English for international readers. The series aims to put forward a Chinese perspective, give insights into cutting-edge academic thinking in China, and inspire researchers globally.

For more information, please visit https://www.routledge.com/series/CPH

Forthcoming titles:

Contemporary Chinese Diplomacy
Qu Xing, Zhong Longbiao

Technology Experts and Scientific Decision
Ru Peng

Creative Involvement: a New Direction in China's Diplomacy
Wang Yizhou

Creative Involvement: the Evolution of China's Global Role
Wang Yizhou

China: Tackle the Challenge of Global Climate Change
Hu Angang, Guan Qingyou

Chinese Cooperative-Harmonious Democracy

Zongchao Peng
Ben Ma
Taoxiong Liu

Routledge
Taylor & Francis Group
LONDON AND NEW YORK

清華大学出版社
TSINGHUA UNIVERSITY PRESS

First published 2017 by Routledge

2 Park Square, Milton Park, Abingdon, Oxfordshire OX14 4RN

52 Vanderbilt Avenue, New York, NY 10017

Routledge is an imprint of the Taylor & Francis Group, an informa business

First issued in paperback 2020

British Library Cataloguing in Publication Data
A catalogue record for this book is available from the British Library

Library of Congress Cataloging in Publication Data
A catalog record for this book has been requested

ISBN: 978-1-138-90017-2 (hbk)
ISBN: 978-0-367-51899-8 (pbk)

Typeset in Times New Roman
by Apex CoVantage, LLC
Sponsored by National Social Science Fund of China

Contents

Figures and table

Figures

Table

Foreword I

China's political science, after three decades of recovery and development, really needs to take on the challenge to face the strategic choice of China's political reform and, on the foundation of outstanding achievements in political science, to think about a genuine democratic model with Chinese cultural characteristic by taking a perspective from the fine traditional Chinese thinking and culture. This project, supported by the National Social Science Fund with the contribution of Professor Peng Zongchao and other scholars, proposes a new model for China's future socialist cooperative-harmonious democracy through exploring the differences and similarities of Chinese and Western cultures and adopting the perspective of the thoughts of "harmony and cooperation" and "people-oriented", and the modern cooperative game theory; this model surpasses not only the Western liberal democracy, which places too much emphasis on individual rights and the democratic process, but also traditional socialist democracy, which pays too much attention to collective interests and centralized authority; this new model tries not only to retain the advantages of the socialist democracy, but also to achieve a greater degree of civil liberty and improvements in the democratic process, so that under the protection of the relevant institutions various conflicts can be continuously resolved, unnecessary social unrest and its devastating consequences can be avoided, and ultimately a harmonious coexistence of all parties can be attained.

This project is strong in theoretical analysis and empirical study; the analytical framework is well defined and the logical reasoning is solid; the content is rich with in-depth demonstration, and the proposed design of institutional development is clear and practical; all these make this study a valuable reference for policymakers.

Overall, the research result is a very important contribution to the field of political science. Therefore, it is my pleasure to recommend this achievement to the society and the readers. I anticipate seeing further studies to address this research topic, and expect the desired success of related reforms and innovative practices.

Ning Sao
Professor, Director
Public Policy Institute
School of Government, Peking University
January 30, 2013

Foreword II

Today, after the reform and opening up, China has come to a critical period of transformation and development, facing the difficult task of deepening reform as well as the serious challenges of social conflicts. The issue of how to further promote political reform has been put on the agenda and drawn attention from all walks of life. However, what is the direction for China's political reform? What is the model of a socialist democracy with Chinese characteristics? How can the political construction be promoted in a way that not only makes sure that socialist democracy continues to improve, but also avoids or reduces unnecessary social strife and conflict in China? How can the conflicts and contradictions in social progress be solved through the reform of the political system, while the harmony and stability of the society can be maintained? These are important research topics and practical issues for the academia and the administrators to ponder and explore.

Professor Peng Zongchao and other scholars undertake this academic and historical mission. After years of collaborative research, they propose a cooperative-harmonious democracy that draws on cooperative game theory and Chinese traditional thoughts: "harmony and cooperation" thought and "people-oriented" thought. This concept is not only theoretically innovative, but also practically valuable to improve China's democratic reality. The study caught my attention when it commenced several years ago, and now I am very pleased to see its overall results. The study is a valuable theoretical innovation, and a significant achievement in promoting the interdisciplinary research of political science and public management; the study contains in-depth analyses on several cases of political reform and innovative public management practices, and the policy suggestions proposed is a valuable reference for policymakers. I'm very much looking forward to seeing the publication of the research result to advance related researches and reforms and make a valuable contribution to the democratic development of China.

Xue Lan
Professor, Dean
School of Public Policy and Management
Tsinghua University
January 31, 2013

Preface

Democracy seems to be an unfathomable and intriguing topic, but it is manifested in everyday life. When friends get together at a restaurant, a common question is: Who should place the order? The norm in China is that the one who pays the bill orders for everyone, and to whose decision all the other participating friends would not have objections. While in Western culture, everyone at the table orders and pays for himself/herself. Which is more democratic? Obviously, the Western way is more democratic from the perspective of direct participation. The Chinese style seems to be centralized and authoritarian but is not completely undemocratic – because the one who pays the bill or places the order may have had all the participants' automatic or temporary authorizations to place the order on behalf of everyone, which can also be regarded as a representative democracy. If this person knows each friend's meal preference, is conscious of food nutrition and familiar with the menus, then his/her decision may be more in line with everyone's need. Since China's reform and opening up, a good deal of culture and different ways of life from the West have been introduced into this country, including the manner of paying a dinner bill. Thirty years later, has our convention on this type of occasion been changed? There is no fundamental change. This is very intriguing. On one hand, in terms of the level of democracy, some part of our culture is not democratic enough, but not necessarily undemocratic if seen from another angle; on the other hand, once a custom is formed and stays for long, it is often very difficult to be completely changed. Even when a change is required, the influence of cultural traditions needs to be taken into consideration.

Since 1996, the development of democracy in China has been my research interest, and the comparative study of the direct election system of the People's Congress is the focus of my doctorate study at Peking University; although my postdoctoral research with Tsinghua University in 1999 was then primarily in the areas of public management and the policymaking process centering on the policy hearing system, China's democratic decision making remains a focus of my research. Comparisons between the East and West are deemed necessary in these studies, from which I gradually realized that the difference between the systems itself is important, but behind the system the difference in ideologies and cultural traditions cannot be ignored. For example, to introduce practices of campaigns into the electoral process and debate the hearing system will be faced with the barriers created by the inherent culture which appreciates reservation over pub-licity. Therefore, the democratic system of a country must be integrated with its cultural traditions to really take root and effect in operation.

In the spring of 2006, I was fortunate to participate in a new MPA course, "Chinese Traditional Governance Thought and Practice," organized by the school I'm affiliated with. Despite that I had taken similar courses in college, such as the history of ancient Chinese political thought, and history of the Chinese political system, I am, after all, not a history major and with no further specialized training in these areas. As a result, this course proved to be a real challenge to me, and I had no choice but to stay with it. In any case, this course pressured me to revisit Chinese traditional governing theories and practices from the perspective of public management, and from there to discover China's cultural advantages, such as the "people-oriented" and "harmony and cooperation" thoughts.

In the academic year from 2006 to 2007, I was even fortunate to receive the scholarship "Young Educator 1:1 Project", funded by the China Scholarship Council and Tsinghua University, and joined the Asia Program of the John F. Kennedy School of Government at Harvard University as a visiting fellow. I was then mainly engaged in research projects on emergency and crisis management in the US and China. Dr. Liu Taoxiong was then also a visiting fellow there, and is an expert in economics and game theory. We had many opportunities to share our thoughts on various research issues, and even had a collaborative research on planning strategies for the pandemic crisis. I have to mention that we both sat in on an MPA course, "Democratic Theory", led by Ms. Jane Mansbridge, a famous politics professor of John F. Kennedy School of Government. It is this course that gave us the opportunity to systematically study various types of Western demo-cratic theory. Therefore, in view of a strong demand for democratic theory in China's democratic politics development, together we applied for funding from the National Social Science Fund to support our project "Chinese Cooperative-Harmonious Democracy: Reform Strategies for a Future Cooperative-Harmonious Chinese Democracy", a research on the Chinese democratic model from the per-spective of traditional Chinese thinking and cooperative game theory. This col-laborative research was approved as a 2007 Special Project. After returning to China, we immediately began our research in this specialized area. Dr. Ma Ben joined the team for his postdoctorate research right after his graduation. It was his participation and the support from many relevant parties that have made this research project successfully executed and completed as scheduled.

Today, how to improve the development strategies to effectively promote Chi-na's democratic politics indeed has once again attracted the world's attention – can China really formulate a genuine political model of socialist democracy with local cultural characteristics? At present, more and more scholars are soberly aware that China's democratization cannot simply copy Western liberal democracy, which overemphasizes individual rights and freedom and multiparty competition. Meanwhile, China's democratic development can no longer be confined in tra-ditional socialist democracy. While conventional socialist democracy has many advantages, such as centralized power for grand construction, less responsibility abdication, and high efficiency, the biggest limitation is the excessive concentration of power in the Party, the upper management, levels and the leaders. Since the implementation of reform and opening up, this type of democracy has undergone continuous reforms and improvements, with more Chinese characteristics added to relevant content, and evidences of improved governance. However, this model still needs a theoretical generalization that truly speaks Chinese cultural characteristics. For example, the predominant model of Western capitalist democracy is generally known as "liberal democracy". Then, what type of democracy is the socialist democracy with Chinese characteristics? How to achieve it in reality? We cannot satisfy with generalization by the fundamental principles, such as "democratic centralism" and "an organic unity of the Party's leadership, people's sovereignty, and the rule of law". This is but a generalization at a basic level, and we should have our own theory characterized by our cultural features.

At present, an innovative idea is much needed in China's democratization; how to define a democratic model from the macro level of democratic theory has its theoretical and practical significance in the future development of democracy in China, as we need a model that not only breaks the shackles of our existing model but also goes beyond the democratic model that worships liberal democracy. John Naisbitt (2010) proposed in his book on China's megatrends that China's democracy is a "vertical democracy". This generalization is certainly innovative, but it does not seem to identify the cultural characteristics in our model of democracy.

This book suggests that the future model of Chinese socialist democracy should be a "cooperative-harmonious democracy": which takes into account the core values of democracy, such as the state power comes from the people, fully leverages the spiritual resources from the "people-oriented" and "cooperation and harmony" thoughts in Chinese tradition, and employs the modern forefront theory and methods of cooperative game for a systematic examination and empirical research when constructing China's future democratic model.

Based on the actual needs of China's democratization and the progress in related academic research, we proceeded with a comparative analysis on the theories and institution development of both liberal and socialist democracies; we then have detailed discussions on the implication of traditional Chinese "people-oriented" and "harmony and cooperation" thought to cooperative-harmonious democracy, as well as on the value and inspiration of cooperative game theory to cooperative-harmonious democracy; we employ cooperative game theory to explore the historical experience (such as Spain's experience) of transition to democracy, and advance to present our vision on the fundamental aspects of cooperative-harmonious democracy, such as its basic ideas, principles, content, forms, and steps. Next, we conduct case studies from the fresh theoretical perspective of cooperative-harmonious democracy on the practices related to typical democratic reforms – the case of Honghe, Wenling, and Ya'an, and finally draw conclusions and make suggestions for policymaking.

From the researches, we believe that China's democratization should fully leverage the intellectual resources – the "people-oriented" and "harmony and cooperation" thoughts – in Chinese tradition as well as modern cooperative game theory and methods, and truly focus on the organic integration and unity of the Party's leadership, people's sovereignty, and the rule of law. We should vigorously promote the development of democracy within the Party, but also gradually improve the political status of democratic parties and their participating members' ability and level; especially the democratic parties may take part in exercising governance under the Party's leadership so as to strengthen and improve the multiparty cooperation and political consultation under the leadership of the Communist Party of China (CPC); we should be more active in promoting electoral democracy with the People's Congress as the core system as well as the system development in which citizens could orderly participate in a deliberative democracy, so as to develop Chinese-style socialist cooperative-harmonious democracy in a steadily progressive manner.

Our study touches upon a grand topic, of which the research goal can definitely not be completed by a small group like ours, and on which only a preliminary and not quite matured study was conducted. Today we would like to share the relevant research findings with the academia and the friends in this profession; our purpose is to take the initiative and hope for generous feedback; we are also eager to have more colleagues join us to advance this research project and the continuous development of the relevant reforms and practices.

Peng Zongchao
Professor, Associate Dean
School of Public Policy and Management, Tsinghua University
January 28, 2013 in Tsinghua Yuan

Acknowledgements

We are greatly indebted to the National Social Science Fund of China (NSSFC) for its support to and funding of this research project, "Chinese Cooperative-Harmonious Democracy: Strategic Research on China's Future Political Reform toward Cooperative-Harmonious Democracy", since 2007.

We are deeply grateful to Tsinghua University's Humanities Publication Fund for its sponsorship and Tsinghua University Press for its strong support for the publishing of its Chinese version and the translation of its Chinese version into the English version.

Our special thanks go to the members of the Research Team for their active participation and hard work. Ma Ben's postdoctoral research between October 2007 and September 2009 laid a good foundation for this book. After that, he continued to participate in follow-up research of this project, the publication of results, the field study in Honghe Prefecture and Ya'an City, and the co-writing of Chapters 1–3 and Chapters 6–10 of this book; he also undertook to oversee coordination and contact between the Team members. Liu Taoxiong took part in the initial development and feasibility study of the project and the field study in Honghe and Team discussions, and wrote Chapter 4. He Jianyu took part in Team discussions and the field study in Honghe, and wrote Chapter 5. Li Ming took part in Team discussions and wrote the part on budgetary participation in Chapter 8. Peng Zongchao, as the project chief expert, participated in the field studies in Honghe and Ya'an as well as the co-writing of Chapters 1–3 and Chapters 6–10, and was responsible for overall coordination of the project and the finalization of this book. Xu Jiajun contributed a lot to data collection, the writing of Chapter 3, and the writing of papers for international symposiums. Xue Lan, Cui Heping, Zhong Kaibin, Shen Xuhui, and Zou Beibei participated in the feasibility study, internal discussions, the collection and sorting out of information, and the search for international academic resources.

We are very grateful to our project advisors, Prof. Cao Deben, Prof. Ning Sao, Prof. Peng Xingye, Prof. Hu Chirui, and Mr. Fu Kui, for their valuable scholarly advice on project application, feasibility study, and implementation as well as their constant encouragement and support. Our special thanks go to Prof. Xue Lan and Prof. Ning Sao, who have written the forewords to this book despite their tight schedules.

We also highly appreciate the lasting care and selfless help from many colleagues of our School of Public Policy and Management, Tsinghua University, including Prof. Su Jun (also the former Director of the Humanities Division of Tsinghua University), Prof. Fang Huijian, Prof. Hu Angang, Prof. Yu An, Prof. Meng Qingguo, Prof. Yang Yongheng, Prof. Wang Yahua, Associate Prof. Zheng Zhenqing, and Miss Wang Xuran and Ms. Chen Jinghong (Administrative Assistants at the Center for Crisis Management Research). We also thank the PhD candidates of our school for their discussions on the early results of this research during Public Policy II lectures and my supervised PhD candidates, Ms. Cheng Jiaxu and other students for their editorial checking efforts in the final stage of this English version publishing period.

The results of this project have been presented at some academic conferences at home and abroad, including: the symposium on "Chinese Public Policy Process: Theory and Practice" co-sponsored by the Chinese Public Administration journal and Nankai University in March 2008 (second-prize winner of the "excellent paper"); the 64th International Forum on China's Reform at China Institute for Reform and Development in Hainan in November 2008; the Theoretical Symposium for the 60th Anniversary of CPPCC in September 2009; the workshop on Conceptualizing Global Democracy in Cairo in December 2009; the symposium on "Greater China's Reform and Transformation of Public Administration: Theory and Practice" at Hong Kong University in February 2010; the symposium on democracy within the Party at Shandong University in May 2010; the symposium on "Political Development in East Asia from China's Perspective: Experience and Enlightenment" co-sponsored by *Beijing Cultural Review* magazine and the Political Science Institute of the Chinese Academy of Social Sciences. We are very grateful to the hosts and attendees of these conferences for their criticism and suggestions, thanks to which our project has been deepened and improved.

We are also much obliged to newspapers and journals such as *People's Daily*; *Comparative Economic and Social Systems*; *Reform, Study and Exploration*; *Shandong Social Sciences*; and *Theoretical Research* for having published results of this project before this book.

Our thanks also go to the Standing Committee of the People's Congress of Honghe Prefecture, the Organization Department of the Municipal Party Committee of Ya'an City, and the Publicity Department of the Municipal Party Committee of Wenling City as well as their leaders for their strong support to us during our field studies.

Last but not least, we thank Ms. Zhou Jing of Tsinghua University Press for the enormous effort she put into the editing, translation, and publishing of this book.

1   Introduction

Today's China is still under the spell of the millennium autocracy . . . democracy should not be delayed any longer.

– Sun Yat-sen

China is not perfect; its most prominent disadvantage, simply put, is non-democracy. Chinese people are in need of democracy . . . only with democracy, China can move on.

– Mao Zedong

Without democracy, neither socialism nor socialist modernization could be realized.

– Deng Xiaoping

Developing socialist democracy and establishing a socialist political civilization are an important goal for building a well-off society in an all-round way.

– Jiang Zemin

People's democracy is a brilliant banner that has always been held high by our Party. Since the policy of reform and opening up was introduced, we have reviewed our experience, both positive and negative, in developing socialist democracy and reaffirmed that people's democracy is the life of socialism. We have ensured that all power of the state belongs to the people and worked to steadily promote reform of the political structure. As a result, we have made major progress in developing socialist democracy and opened up and kept to the socialist path of political development with Chinese characteristics, thus charting the correct course for achieving the most extensive possible people's democracy in China.

– Hu Jintao

Proposition

No country in today's world dares to oppose democracy openly; even authoritarian countries have to rely on the cloak of democracy in order to obtain justification, legitimacy, and authority. Amartya Sen once stated that throughout the nineteenth century, it was not surprising to see national debates for democracy. However, in the twentieth century, questioning democracy itself was wrong. Democracy is no longer a political system of choice; on the contrary, democracy is a developmental course to follow for every country and any society.[1] Moreover, in the twenty-first century, there is no reason to deny the universal value of democracy. It can be said that democracy is the root of power for all modern nations, the foundation of all political powers, and the key concept to distinguish ancient from modern politics. Therefore, democracy is the core content and fundamental goal of modern political progress from a traditional society to a modern society.

Although democracy has become an iron rule for a modern society and politics, the incessant controversy over democratic politics indicates that there is never a consensus view on democracy, which includes a broad range of different ideas. Why do people have so diversified an understanding of democracy? This is because democracy itself is an "essentially contested"[2] and "interpretive"[3] concept; that is, the extensive disagreement and interpretation of democracy fail to establish a neutral and appropriate concept.

Different understanding of democracy influences a country's choice of political system and actual operation model. As no two leaves are exactly the same in the world, no democratic countries share the same political system. In another word, each country has its distinctive model of democracy. However, a successful democratic model is not only the product of a nation's social environment, but also deeply rooted in the country's traditions. "Any successful democratic nation has its democracy based on its level of economic development, political system and cultural environment. Therefore, democracy is an exclusive political model of a nation."[4]

Ancient China has no tradition of democracy, while modern China has not established a standardized democracy. For China, a country with a long history of authoritarian regimes, democracy is often but a fancy word. Since the late Qing Dynasty, a variety of democratic systems, such as constitutional monarchy and multiparty governance, had been implemented, but they were often short-lived and unable to withstand the trial in practice. The establishment of new China, which is a new socialist democracy, changed China's political operation profoundly. "Democracy, just like any other truth, must undergo the test of practice. Practice is the ultimate assessment in determining the condition and the level of democracy for any country or region."[5] The initial implementation of this model had contributed to a stable and consolidated regime of new China. However, it was still immature and thus unable to avoid the erroneous policymaking and the huge disaster of ten years of the Cultural Revolution. Yet the significance is that since the beginning of reform and the opening up policy, this evolving socialist democratic model that features Chinese cultural values has promoted the position of the people as masters of the country and ensured stable and rapid socioeconomic growth. The achievement is noteworthy and has basically sustained the practical trial as of today.

But whether China's democratic model has been established is still debatable.[6] The reform and opening up policy introduced in 1978, by breaking away from a previous traditional model of socialist democracy, has propelled progress and put many serious challenges in China's path to democracy. This is because in traditional socialist era that featured a planned economy, society did not have any independent resource to form an independent interest demand. Therefore, the country was devoid of the political pressure that comes from diverse competing interest groups. However, as the reform and opening up deepens, traditional political structure of a highly integrated state and society begins to loosen up; pluralism is gradually replacing the old single-interest pattern and further diversifying the social structure.[7] Coupled with people's growing awareness of civil participation and the increasingly intensified aspirations to realize democracy,[8] the development of democracy in China is a pressing business to be finished.

Today, after thirty years of reform and opening up, how to promote China's development of democracy more effectively and how to build its future model of democracy is really a complex problem. Without doubt, even facing strong pressure from Western countries, China's democratic development should not simply choose a way of Western-style liberal democracy, especially given the performance of "third wave" democracy from the liberal countries. As of now, the results of "third wave" democratization that rose in the late twentieth century are not satisfactory. Although some countries obtained liberal democracy at a great cost, the vicious competition among political parties weakens the governing mechanism, independence, and imparity of national institutions, deprives the possibility for the people to enjoy fair governance,[9] and sees serious crises in administration; the myth of liberal democracy has begun to subside.

Western liberal democracy is a democracy developed from the concept of individualism, that is, the individual is the basic unit of democracy. This means that under the supremacy of individual rights, democracy is not *collectively* given. In order to reflect individualistic democracy, its prominent features are to advocate individual freedom – people have the power to oppose the government, and the government must be chosen by the people. The overall system emphasizes the implementation of a representative system, a free and competitive election, a system of multiple parties, and a decentralized autonomy to ensure the implementation of such liberal democracy. Therefore, in contrast to feudalism, Western liberal democracy is a very advanced political model, but the biggest limitation is that the overly emphasized individual rights and freedom, competitive elections, and government decentralization, as well as prioritized individual freedom and power, are sometimes at the expense of the collective public interest.

Similarly we should also review the pros and cons of China's socialist democracy, traditional political model of China. Traditional Chinese socialist democracy originated from Marxist-Leninist political thought and the practice of the international communist movement and is influenced by the despotism of China history; it can be generally regarded as a collectivist democracy, in which groups rather than individuals are the basic units. That means that democracy is not attained from personal right, but a right granted by a collective or society to an individual. The collectivist democracy is characterized by the integration of centralism and democracy. The overall system depends on the centralized democracy to ensure the implementation of the political idea. "There is no impassable gulf between democracy and centralism, both of which are essential for China."[10] Therefore, the greatest strength of our traditional democratic model is the collective power for greater undertakings with higher efficiency, but its key limitation is that the related institutionalization is often prone to collective interests and concentration of power, and the power excessively concentrates within the Party, the upper management levels and the leaders. Therefore, we sum it up as traditional model of socialist democracy.[11]

In terms of conflict management and cooperation, liberal democracy and traditional socialist democracy have respective practical reasons, but their problem-solving processes are both based on non-cooperative game theory. In other words, the design of both democracy models is based on the assumption that the participants in the democratic process are likely to be uncooperative. Following the premises, more emphasis is placed either on the protection of individual rights or on the defense of collective interests. Then the conflict is solved through a democratic mechanism or through a centralized mechanism, transforming the situation from a non-cooperative game to a cooperative one. Considering China's current political development, it is impossible to choose a path of liberal democracy or simply copy traditional socialist democracy in history. In fact, as long as the democracy is not perceived as a fixed model, and the inadequacy in the democratic practice is recognized, it is possible to explore a new model of socialist democracy. Political reform is different from economic reform. The development of democracy somehow needs an overall theoretical guidance. A blueprint is more critical than the caution in "trial and error". That is, there should be a validated top-level design based on an advanced theory of democracy development. Otherwise, fragmented reforms without guidance only have limited effect, or even become an obstacle hindering the further development of democracy.

Of course, a democracy of a macro-theoretical design does not necessarily imply a radical political reform. In fact, the principle of incrementalism is still one of the basic strategies to follow in China's democratic reform. How can a specific model of democracy that meets China's political outlook be created from a macro-democracy theory? In our opinion, the construct of China's future democratic model should incorporate the core values of democracy, such as a nation of the people and state power from the people, fully leverage the intellectual resources of traditional "harmony and cooperation" thought and "people-oriented" thought, and employ the innovative cooperative game theory so as to conduct a comprehensive, systematic, and in-depth analysis.

Therefore, we believe that to see true ideological emancipation, the direction of China's democracy development is neither a simple continuation of the existing traditional socialist democracy (a democratic model with more emphasis on the development of collective right and the concentration of power, see discussion later) nor a mechanical copy of the Western liberal democracy (a democratic model focusing more on individual freedom and decentralization), but a "cooperative-harmonious democracy" characterized by its own history, culture, and social conditions. The focus of the model is to leverage Chinese intellectual heritage, such as "harmony and cooperation" thought, and "people-oriented" thought with the existing collective rights for development, to enhance the institutional advantage by keeping moderate concentration of powers, and to take into account a moderate expansion of personal freedom and rights as well as public power control mechanism in order to achieve the organic unity between the individual and the collective, democracy and centralism; by employing principles of modern cooperative game theory in relevant system design, to promote a maximized integration of interests, to resolve conflicts, to eliminate confrontation, and to achieve cooperation and harmonious development among social parties, even in the event of possible conflict. Its core value is not only to maximize the citizens' freedom and rights, but also to realize the best collective interests through the centralized and institutionalized authority, so as to achieve harmonious coexistence between individual rights and the collective rights as well as between major political parties.[12]

Literature review

Reviews of the liberal democratic model and studies of alternative models

In his *Patterns of Democracy: Government Forms and Performance in Thirty-Six Countries*, Arend Lijphart defines two major types of democracy: the Westminster, or majoritarian model of democracy and the consensus model of democracy – majoritarian democracy is characterized by competition, exclusion, and confrontation, while the consensus model of democracy features negotiation, inclusion, and cooperation. The author suggests that consensus democracies significantly outperform majoritarian systems in every democratic country. This argument breaks away from traditional belief that majoritarian democracy is the best model.[13] Early in the 1960s, Lijphart proposed the concept of Consociational Democracy[14]; in 1977, he attested this concept in his case studies with Belgium, the Netherlands, Switzerland, and Austria[15]; since 1984, Lijphart used the term *consensus democracy* more often to describe a certain type of democracy; based on his study of the democratic practices in 21 countries, he examined the characteristics and performance of consensus or majoritarian democracies and concluded that both consociational democracy and consensus democracy stress non-competitive cooperation, a feature distinguished from majoritarian democracy.[16] In 1999, Lijphart broadened his study to cover 36 countries; he not only had in-depth analyses and classifications of the majoritarian and consensus democracies, but also explored different designs and patterns of democratic institutions. Lijphart's empirical study reveals that the universal values of democracy must be in accordance with the specific situations of each country, and the best democracy for a country is developed correspondingly to its political, economic, cultural, and traditional realities. Lijphart's consensus democracy expands our understanding of the design of democratic institutions and bears significant implication to the development of Chinese democracy by showing us a new perspective in deciding a model that meets the democratic principles as well as China's national conditions.

In *Beyond Liberal Democracy,* Daniel A. Bell argues that Western-style liberal democracy developed entirely from the norms and practices in Western society but its theory is regarded as universally applicable. However, East Asia has morally legitimate theories that are quite different from those of the Western liberal democracies. Therefore, a right choice for East Asia is not simply implementing the Western-style model when the time seems ripe, but absorbing those appropriate elements found in the region's political realities and cultural traditions. If a democracy is to take root in East Asia and be effective, modification needs to be made in order to be more appropriate for the contemporary political and economic realities in this region.[17]

In his 1997 journal article "The Rise of Illiberal Democracy" published in *Foreign Affairs*, Fareed Zakaria pointed out the rise of non-liberal democracies was evident in places from Peru to Palestine, from Sierra Leone to Slovakia, or from Pakistan to the Philippines. Many countries have seen their leaders who came to office through competitive elections abuse of political power and limiting the rights of the people. Therefore, rash and hasty liberal democratization only brings to people the pain of illiberal democracy instead of happiness.[18] *The Future of Freedom: Illiberal Democracy at Home and Abroad*, another book by Zakaria, published in 2003, provides a more detailed analysis of the illiberal democracy, in which the elected regime that claims to represent the interests of the people actually violates the rights of the people, horizontally or vertically. This phenomenon, to different degrees, has been seen in various countries, such as India, Pakistan, Russia, Ukraine, and the Philippines, and prevails in the countries of Latin America.[19] Zakaria's analyses illustrate that "Western liberal democracy might prove to be not the final destination on the democratic road, but just one of many possibilities [that exists]."[20]

In *World on Fire: How Exporting Free Market Democracy Breeds Ethnic Hatred and Global Instability*, Amy Chua illustrates the big difference in the process of democratization and privatization between non-Western and Western countries; the former's sudden, swift, and aggressive development of universal suffrage and privatization contrasted to the gradual emergence of the electoral mechanism and market economy in the latter summons a serious damage to the nation's governance and development. Especially in those impoverished countries or the countries where the minority dominates the market, the democracy and market – at least judged by their current implementation – are in intense confrontation. The simultaneous pursuit of the market economy and liberal democracy only provokes constant ethnic conflicts and leads to disastrous consequences, namely, violent genocide or political and economic subversion. This is because in a country with market-dominant minorities, the market and democracy still favor different people, different classes, and even different ethnic groups. These market-dominant minorities amass a lot of wealth, while democracy grants the impoverished majority political power. In this case, the pursuit of democracy and a market economy would spark the potentially catastrophic ethnic nationalism. The majority of the "native" populace incited by ballot-seeking politicians would unleash their violent hatred toward the rich minorities. Therefore, market economy/democracy is not a valid prescription to improve the governance of the developing countries.[21] The implication of Chua's research is that we should pursue a moderate democracy; any radical promotion or implementation of democratization will not bring about democracy but lead to chaos, even riots, which will further hinder the realization of democracy.

Deliberative Democracy – Essays on Reason and Politics, co-edited by James Bohman and William Rehg, is a collection of articles by contemporary Western scholars on deliberative democracy. This anthology, an important work of contemporary Western research on deliberative democracy, discusses the basic concepts and contents of this democratic theory systematically and summarizes various criticisms.[22] In his book *Deliberative Democracy and Beyond – Liberals, Critics, and Contestations*, John S. Dryzek points out that the deliberative turn of democracy shows people's continuing concern in the democratic authenticity, which means the extent to which the democratic control (the implemented popular sovereignty) is substantive rather than symbolic, as well as the capacity of citizens' participation in democracy. The book evolves on expounding fourteen questions, such as whether the deliberation is a decisive and more effective approach to solve the social problems; whether deliberation is a means to reach consensus or merely a prelude before voting; whether the deliberation should stop at a representative system or advance to the social sphere. These are questions addressed in order to facilitate the understanding of the form of deliberative democracy.[23]

James Berman, in his book *Public Deliberation: Pluralism, Complexity and Democracy*, highlights that since most research on deliberative democracy is basically normative – established and derived from ideals rather than realities – it is difficult to make possible connections between these political theories and the actual practices and reforms of democracy, thereby increasing the skepticism about the feasibility of deliberative democracy. Responding to the skepticism, Berman examines the three major challenges: multiculturalism, inequality, and social complexity, and concludes that these are not insurmountable obstacles for a deliberative democracy.[24]

Democracy as Public Deliberation – New Perspectives, a collection of critical writings edited by Maurizio Passerin d'Entreves, offers, first of all, specific evaluations of the major normative theories of deliberative democracy; second, analyses of this democratic system design; third, empirical investigation into the relationship between deliberation and decision making; fourth, case studies on the effect of public deliberation in religious and cultural conflicts. The essays collected in this volume are reviews and criticisms on previously published theories of deliberative democracy. Combined with the social reality, this book provides a fresh and original perspective on the normative theories and institutional development of public deliberation. Although scholars still hold different opinions on its essence and institutional construction, deliberative democracy is regarded as a theoretically strong and institutionally viable model of democracy.[25]

In his paper "Different Areas of Deliberative Democracy: Deliberative Democracy and Local Democracy in China" for the Hangzhou International Conference, John S. Dryzek argues that for deliberative democracy, the legitimacy of the political decision making depends on the rights and capabilities of the people who participate in the process and will be influenced by the public policies, particularly when a large number of citizens are to be affected by the decision. For this reason, the authors believe deliberative democracy can be used in many areas, where the deliberative democratic practice can be established, for example, at the national institutions, among ordinary citizens, or in the public domain. As for the application of public deliberation in China, the author believes that China does not have the correspondingly liberal democratic systems; therefore, more attention needs to be paid to the deliberation employed in the public domain and grassroots governments, so as to increase its legitimacy. The author also recognizes the innovative form of deliberation in China's grassroots governance.[26]

John Keane believes that some common political trends, emerging in the United States, France, and Germany, indicate the decay of old democracy. For example, Parliament has lost a lot of its previously established powers; the number of party members has dropped sharply; citizens' distrust of political leaders has significantly heightened; politics often bears a dirty reputation and is constantly associated with corruption. All of these trends suggest that there is something wrong with electoral democracy. The goal of democracy has shifted to monitoring the public service sector that is related to societal welfare, such as health care and education. That is, the growing monitory democracy causes the decay of electoral democracy. The monitory democracy means every aspect of social and political life is subject to public scrutiny, and the standard practice is operated not only in representative democracy but also in the state government, intergovernmental, or international levels, by institutions with no party or parliament involvement, or even unelected institutions. The monitory democracy has the following advantages:

1   It provides the public with better information and diverse views regarding the operations and performance of government.
2   It is more transparent, as it is operated by the populace instead of a top-down supervision.
3   It is more in line with the nature of democracy, which is reflected not only in the political landscape but also in broader areas.
4   As electoral democracy leads to political apathy, monitory democracy can further strengthen the voices of ordinary citizens and motivate public participation in policymaking.
5   It is one of the most dynamic forms of democracy and one of the most sensitive democratic model to powers.

Therefore, Keane believes monitory democracy represents the trend of contemporary democracy development.[27]

Chinese traditional thought and democracy research

Du Weiming, in his "Cultural Implications of the Rise of Confucianism in East Asia," stressed that while democratization is an inevitable trend, election doesn't equal democracy. In England, traditional pragmatism, empiricism, and gradualism significantly affect the form of democratic practice; France's democracy is marked with rationalism, culturalism, and revolutionary spirit; Germany's democracy features romanticism and nationalism; America's democracy is powered by a strong civil society; the democratic concept exemplified in East Asia illustrates that democratization is an evolutionary process and is compatible to the ideas of administrative meritocracy, an elite education system, and a special social network. We can say that the Confucian culture provides a wealth of resources for East Asia to develop its own unique style of democracy.[28]

In *Chinese Political Thoughts – Confucianism and Democratization,* Tan Yuanping has the following thematic discussions: in discussing the democratization of China, it is equally important to have an in-depth knowledge of Western democracies and to respect traditional values rooted in the Chinese cultural system and the important guiding role of our cultural roots in finding a path to democracy. Tan illustrates the relationship between traditional "people-oriented" thought and democracy; he also highlights the moral principle of "all-embracing harmony" in the Chinese tradition, that is, "the cardinal spirit of Chinese culture lies in harmony and moderateness."[29] Under the principle of "all-embracing harmony", the relations between Heaven and man, between people, and between people and things are mutually conducive and beneficial so that they can all be natural and harmonious. Confucius grasped this principle and underscored the ideas of a "middle ground" and "harmony", which were then embedded in the Chinese mentality. In addition, Tan also sheds new light on the relationship between democracy and traditional political thoughts (rules of rites). He argues that the relationship between the individual and society is manifested through the rules of rites and refutes the theory of "ignorance of the individual in traditional Chinese society". In Confucianism, the individual is valued not as a fighter for his own rights but as a vital instrumentation to promote benevolence so as to fulfill both individual and collective values. "Integrating self into the others" creates a harmonious relationship between individuals and the community. Therefore, traditional relationship between the individual and the collective is not anti-democratic but rather valuable in promoting democracy.[30]

He Xinquan in his *Confucianism and Modern Democracy* mentions that the theoretical links between Confucianism and modern democracy pave the path not only for Chinese civilization and politics but also for the future of the entire Confucian East Asia. Centering on the theme of Confucianism and modern democracy, the author analyzes in detail the democratic views presented by various Confucian scholars, including Liang Shuming, Xiong Shili, Mou Zongsan, Tang Junyi, Xu Fuguan, and Zhang Junmai. Except for Liang Shuming, the other leading Neo-Confucian scholars agree upon the possibility of building a liberal democracy within a reconstructed framework of Confucian moral philosophy. Confucianism can be applied in modern democratization, in which "Confucianism leads to spiritual excellence and a new practical success in liberal democracy." In fact, since the late Qing Dynasty, Confucianism has been less favored than liberal democracy, which has become a gauge in determining the value and rationality of Confucianism. Neo-Confucianism is only a new interpretation of

Confucianism that aims for a liberal democracy. Theoretically speaking, the Neo-Confucian perspective has its implication in the Confucianism construct. Yet, as liberal democracy has been gradually losing its glory in review, if we continue to confine our investigation in a possible Confucianism-born liberal democracy, we are not taking full advantage of Chinese traditional culture. If the Confucians can take liberal democracy as a base to grow on instead of a goal to attain, and focus on constructing a pluralistic democracy, their argumentation could be more valuable. "If China chooses to move towards a modern democratic politics, without giving up the precious value system in cultural traditions, there seems no other choice but to mediate and reconcile the two with every effort."[31] Chinese democracy, with mediation and reconciliation, is to develop independently on the foundation of the Confucian tradition, but also to absorb the experience and strength of liberal democracy, so as to create a model of democracy in line with Chinese traditions.

Studies on Chinese traditional "harmony and cooperation" and "people-oriented" thought

Zhang Liwen in his *Theory of Harmony and Cooperation* states that "harmony and cooperation refer to the summation of the new structures, new things, and new life after a dynamic transforming process of numerous conflicts and integrations between or within the tangible and the intangible worlds, such as nature, society, mankind, souls and civilization." Harmony and cooperation embrace conflicts and integration and transcend the initial conflicts into a new conceptual realm after integration, which gives value and justifies the existence of conflicts. We can say that harmony and cooperation dwell in all worldly phenomena and in all thinking. The thought of "harmony and cooperation" is the essence and the core value of the humanities in Chinese culture; it gives life to the Chinese culture. To resolve the five challenges facing humanity (man and nature, man and society, man and man, the human mind, different civilizations), harmony and cooperation can be the best cultural choice, which is the cultural tradition to be inherited and applied creatively to solve the current problems of China.[32]

In his *On People-Oriented Governance*, Xu Yatang argues that the fundamental goal of political rationality established by people-oriented governance is not to accomplish or meet the private interests of those in power but to safeguard the social welfare and ethical education of the populace. Thus, there are three requirements in this governance:

- Responsibility – to establish the sense of responsibility of those who are in power and are held responsible for the success or failure of the government
- Honesty and righteousness – according to the benevolence of human nature, to seek the governor's honesty, righteousness, and propriety in governing people
- Meritocracy – the governors should take it as their main responsibility to elect the wise and the capable.

We can say that modern values can be found in Chinese traditional "people-oriented" thought, which should not serve as a vassal of Western democracy but have its own independent values in theory and practice.[33]

Research on the development model of Chinese democracy

There is voluminous research on the democracy of China conducted by domestic and foreign scholars, whose theoretical approaches fall into three general categories.

The first approach is to explore the values and institutional models of socialist democracy, among others, from the early Marxist literature and the actual international communist movements. Professor Gao Fang, for example, based on his years of comprehensive and in-depth research on Marxist literature and the practices of the international communist movement, combined with his studies on the international experience of democratization, conducted systematic examinations on the development of Chinese democracy and the reform of political institutions (such as intra-Party democracy, inter-Party democracy, people's democracy, the relationship between democracy and centralism, and the political party system).[34] Li Tieying also has done systematic studies of Marxist theory of democracy and three generations of leaders' related discussions on socialist democracy with Chinese characteristics, and proposes that China should actively and steadily push forward the construction of socialist democratic politics with ingenious characteristics in the new century.[35]

The second approach is to explore the democratic elements from Confucianism and political traditions and realities in East Asia and China; some research is pessimistic,[36] while some is relatively optimistic.[37] The central argument in *The Democracy of the Dead: Dewey, Confucius, and the Hope for Democracy in China*, by David Hall and Roger Thomas Ames, is that China has always been and will continue to be a communitarian society. To realize a Chinese democracy means to promote a democratic form of a communitarian society, which is at odds with liberal democracy that currently predominates in the Western countries. Therefore, it can be said that the core conventions of liberal democracy are not suitable for China's national conditions. Traditional Confucianism contains several elements that can be completely transmitted into a communitarianist democracy; these elements can be developed into an orderly democratic model full of vitality and humanity. This model, on the one hand, agrees with traditional Chinese communitarian thought, and on the other hand avoids many drawbacks of the liberal democratic model, which is built on the basis of individual rights.[38] David Hall and Roger Ames, both famous Western Sinologists, believe that China will move toward some form of democracy, which is not modeled on liberal democracy. The challenge ahead for China's democratization is "how to clearly demonstrate a communitarianist democracy model that matches the deepest values of traditional Chinese society". This undoubtedly provides room in the construction of a Chinese "cooperative-harmonious democracy". Although the author's reflection is out of Western-centrism, the research approach, by demonstrating that "denial of traditional Chinese culture is refusing to offer the best opportunity for China's democratization," provides a theoretical basis to construct a model of "cooperative-harmonious democracy".

Suzanne Ogden, in *Inklings of Democracy in China*, starts out with explanation on how to define democracy. In her view, democracy is a social construct, which is not like a car being objective, concrete, and tangible but is subjective and varying. Therefore the concept of democracy is constantly evolving. Any country that desires democratization should re-interpret democracy based on its own needs, development, values, culture, and systems. Ogden also questions the universal value of liberal democracy, by emphasizing that never has a single model of democracy won recognition for all times and all places throughout history. On China's democratic process, Ogden holds different views from most Western scholars. She believes that democratization is progressing at a fair pace in China and that the leaders are determined to create a society with more equality and justice, which are much appreciated and emphasized in Chinese people's understanding of democracy and different from the Westerners' political ideas. China's democratization is certainly modeled on liberal democracy, with more focus on deliberation and harmony, and influenced by the cultural value of "harmony" in the model selection. Currently the political model is moving toward a unique Chinese democracy different from Western liberal democracy. Maybe someday this model with Chinese characteristics will be more influential than the Western liberal model of democracy.[39]

Ranjoo Seodu Herr notes that Confucian democracy seems to be a contradictory concept, because Confucianism advocates social hierarchy, which is in disagreement with the idea of equality that democracy upholds. In fact, Confucianism presupposes a concept of equality, such as everyone is equal across the gentleman level. Herr believes that Confucian democracy, differently from Western democracy, is conceptually possible and morally justifiable.[40]

In the preface to *Dilemma and Development of Chinese Democracy* and *Construction of Chinese Democracy – Exploration of a New Model*, Jin Yaoji proposes that to establish democracy in China, we should consider three questions at different levels:

1   What is democracy, that is, to clarify the nature of democracy
2   What is the desired democracy, that is, to refine our subjective expectation of democracy
3   What is the possible democracy, that is, under certain conditions of time and space, to what objective extent democratization can achieve.

These three questions are interrelated but independent of one another; if they are mixed up in seeking democratization, the established democracy will become utopian or vulgar. Based on a clear understanding of these three inquiries, he believes the construction of democracy in China is a huge, multifaceted project that involves politics, economy, culture, education, and legislation and cannot be accomplished in a rush. This democracy bears the universal character of democracy and a distinct mark of Chinese traditional culture. As can be seen, the author's notion of "Chinese Democracy" emphasizes the growth and operation of democracy in Chinese culture and society, where the democracy has to interact with the social and cultural context; the institutional design will not be nor need be the same with Western democracy.[41]

Some Chinese scholars explore the approaches to construct a Chinese-style democracy in accordance with the actual needs of democratic development in China. Yan Jirong once proposed three paths to a Chinese democracy: "to explore the theoretical resources of Chinese democracy from the ideological origin of democracy; to expand the space possible for a Chinese democracy from the perspective of the democratization process; to interpret and to enrich the features of Chinese democracy with the experiences gained from reforms".[42] Liu Xirui, by comparing Western representative democracy, puts forward that a preliminary model of socialist democracy has been formed; he named this model *integrated democracy*, which exhibits the integrated characteristics of elitism and populism as well as representative democracy and direct democracy.[43]

The third approach is mainly examining the ideas and experience of Western liberal democracy. Many democratic models have been formed in human history, but traditional model of liberal democracy and its variations still prevail in the Western world. This model is based on individual liberalism and game theory, and the core idea is of individual rights, free elections, party competition, separation of political powers, the rule of law, etc.

Since the 1980s, a new model or school of democracy, namely deliberative democracy, has emerged in the West; this model tries to go beyond the liberal or pluralist democracy with more attention to the decision-making process, which involves full communication, negotiation, and rational judgment regarding the interests of all parties in the public domain so as to achieve democratic agreement and be conducive to a society with more diverse or heterogeneous cultures. This theory not only sees growing impact in the Western countries in recent years but also draws the close attention of Chinese scholars.[44] It was also known as *negotiation democracy*, including corporatist democracy, consociational democracy, and democracy with veto power, which are actually similar to consensus democracy.[45]

Most of the theories mentioned above emphasize seeking democracy and the subsequent cooperation through a conflict-negotiation model, rather than a democracy through cooperation. The international community already has a few discussions on cooperative democracy and calls for the regeneration of primitive tribalist democracy.[46] China also has similar discussions,[47] which are basically about democratic cooperation through democracy, rather than democracy through cooperative negotiation.

China has made it a point not to follow the Western liberal democratic model, and for a long time has adhered to democratic centralism, of which the main content includes multiparty cooperation under the leadership of the Communist Party of China (CPC), the unitary system and the combination system of legislative and executive powers. Because of its emphasis on collective and social values and a centralized, authority-led democracy, this model is often criticized as an authoritarian political system. This view is not objective. Indeed, there was one historical period when individual leaders and the central government had overly concentrated political powers. However, over the past thirty years of reform and modification, China has seen democratization trends in an established collective leadership, separation of Party and government, increased participation of non-communist parties, an enhanced function of the National People's Congress (NPC) and decentralization of economic control, which do not, in an absolute sense, constitute a totalitarian or authoritarian regime, but a socialist democracy. In fact, many developing countries that promote electoral democracy also recognize the strength of this system in China, as democracy does not solve all the problems of these countries. China's political system cannot replace Western-style liberal electoral democracy, but China's reform experience does suggest that a governance model also can be successful as long as the political system is in line with the culture and history of the country.[48]

The distinctive advantages seen in China's political system, such as collective power for grand undertakings and rapid economic growth, deserve continued support. Yet some key issues still exist: the emphasis on meeting the essential requirements of a democratic state system while ignoring the significance of building democratic institutions in the governing system remains a deficit democracy with overly centralized powers. Then, how can China's political reform advance steadily in the future? In this regard, the national leaders have had some thoughts and scholars have also had a lot of discussions, mostly pertaining to some specific aspects, including the administrative reform, community-level democracy, intra-Party democracy, the rule of law, development of the NPC, the electoral system, etc.[49] There are some but very limited studies on the long-term strategic planning of political reform.[50] In recent years, scholars have recognized that the long-term strategic planning to develop democracy in China must combine its political culture to have a different design. The reasons are, first, the Chinese people want a democracy more in line with the "people-oriented" thoughts advocated by Confucius and Mencius rather than a democracy by the Western definition, even though they use the word "democracy" to describe their ideals. Second, the people have different standards in evaluating the government, and this evaluation cannot be met by a simple electoral democracy. Third, for the government and the scholars of political science, the questions are: What is the desired democracy when we design the system? What kind of system design can meet the demands of the people? If the intellectuals and the people have different ideas for democracy, should the demands of the people or the ideals of the intellectual elite be fulfilled first?[51]

Therefore, this book will meticulously uncover the essence of "people-oriented" and "harmony and cooperation" thoughts in Chinese political and cultural tradition, with an approach employing cooperative game theory and methods, combined with China's reality and national conditions, especially taking into account its future development trends (such as modernization, globalization, informatization, and electronic democracy). Then it will fully absorb proper contents from different democratic thoughts and models, including liberal democracy, socialist democracy, and contemporary deliberative democracy, attempting to really go beyond the existing model of democracy, put forward an innovative proposal, and explore a future socialist cooperative-harmonious democracy, a political model, and development strategy with unique Chinese characters. The theoretical signifi- cance is to conduct an innovative and comprehensive research on the core values of China's future socialist democracy and on the construct of fundamental institu- tions and institutional development, from the cooperation-negotiation perspective that goes beyond traditional conflict-negotiation perspective as seen in most of the existing democratic theories, combined with the cultural advantages found in people-oriented and harmony-valued Chinese tradition. Its practical implica- tion is to provide solid support for multidisciplinary research and valuable policy recommendations for the core direction of China's socialist democratic political reform, for the choices of strategic policies, for building a harmonious society in China, and for realizing the Chinese dreams of prevailing peace and rejuvenation.

Research framework and methods

Based on the actual needs of China's democratization and the progress in related academic research, we proceed with a comparative analysis of the theories and institution development of both liberal and socialist democracies; we then have detailed discussions on the implication of traditional Chinese "harmony and coop- eration" and "people-oriented" thoughts as well as the value and inspiration of cooperative game theory for cooperative-harmonious democracy; we employ cooperative game theory to explore the history of political transition to democracy (such as Spain's experience), and present our vision on the fundamental aspects of cooperative-harmonious democracy, such as its basic ideas, principles, content, forms, and steps. Next, we conduct case studies from the fresh theoretical perspec- tive of cooperative-harmonious democracy on the domestic practices related to typical democratic reforms – such as the cases of Honghe, Ya'an, Wenling, and Xinhe, and conclude the research with recommendations for policymaking. The basic framework of the research is shown in Figure 1.1.

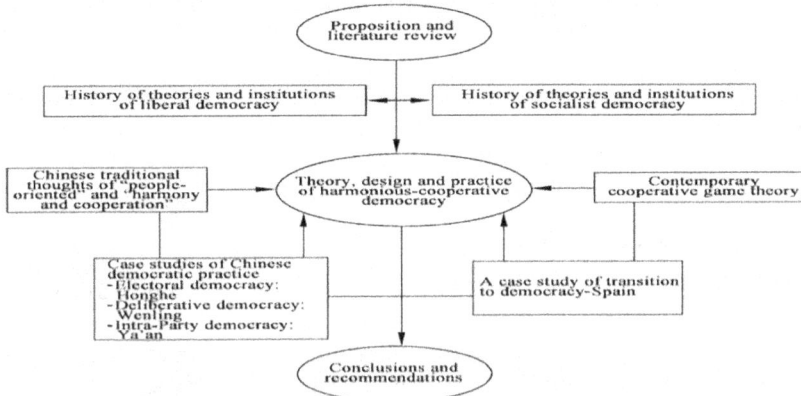

Figure 1.1 Research framework and analysis

The research method is a tool by nature, which constrains scope, breadth, and depth when studying the subject during the research. Before choosing the tool, the research topic and subject should be identified. To address the issues mentioned above, this research employs the following methods:

1   *Literature review.* This is a research method to discover the essence of things through consulting, analyzing, and organizing the literature. Literature review is the most commonly used method and is the first step of almost all research. The sources for a literature review are mainly related works, research papers, journal articles, and dissertations. Much of the research in this book employs this approach.
2   *Normative research method.* This book approaches the theoretical study of cooperative-harmonious democracy mainly from two aspects: one is from the "people-oriented" and "harmony and cooperation" perspectives, which are derived from traditional Chinese political thought, to illustrate the indigenous ideology and cultural roots of cooperative-harmonious democracy; the second is from the perspective of modern game theory to explore how the democratic model can improve cooperative game, and to offer contemporary thinking in constructing a cooperative-harmonious democratic system.
3   *Case study.* This method conducts in-depth, comprehensive and systematic empirical analysis on a specific subject; the primary purpose is to provide an explanation and reasoning through the description of a case. This book aims to deepen the understanding of cooperative-harmonious democracy through analyzing specific cases, such as the direct election system in Honghe Prefecture, Yunnan, democratic deliberation in Wenling, Zhejiang, the budget reform of Foshan, Guangdong, the practice of intra-Party democracy in Ya'an City, Sichuan, as well as the international case of Spain's transition to democracy.
4   *Historical study.* This method describes, explains, and analyzes events that have occurred through a systematic collection of data so as to understand the past events. We also conduct some historical studies to compare and analyze the development of Western and Chinese democratic theory and practice.

In addition, we value firsthand information and have conducted field research and interviews on some local cases mentioned above, hoping to provide reliable support for study-related issues.

Contributions and limitations

With full leverage on traditional Chinese "people-oriented" and "harmony and cooperation" thought as well as the ideas and methods of modern cooperative game theory, the possible contribution of this book is the proposed concept of "cooperative-harmonious democracy" with Chinese characteristics, the visionary design of its basic institution, and a preliminary normative analysis and empirical research on the theory and practice of this democratic model. Hopefully these discussions can make a modest contribution to the theoretical and practical development of democracy in China.

Because of the limited time and other constraints in reality, it is very difficult for us to present a deeper and more systematic theoretical discussion on the research subject. At present, the institutional design and empirical case study of "cooperative-harmonious democracy" are not very detailed and substantial, which speaks the limitations of this book. It is hoped that in the future, there will be chances to make this research more complete.

Notes

1 Amartya Sen, "Democracy as a Universal Value", *Contemporary China Studies*, 2000, 2.
2 W. B. Gallie, "Essentially Contested Concepts", *Proceeding of the Aristotelian Society*, 1955–1956, 56: 167–198.
3 Dworkin categorized concept into "criterion concept," "natural-kind concept", and "interpretive concept." The criterion concept is people's shared concepts, of which the definition attains a (roughly) clear consensus. For example, we can clearly define that a bachelor is an unmarried man; such a definition is clear, universal, and common. Therefore, all "bachelors" are all "unmarried men" and all "unmarried men" are all "bachelors." "Natural-kind concept" refers to an object of particular physical or biological structure, such as rocks, trees, lions, and so on. "Interpretive concept" refers to a concept derived from the reflection and interpretation of a particular social practice. See Ronald Dworkin, "Hart's Postscript and the Character of Political Philosophy", *Oxford Journal of Legal Studies*, 2004, 24(1): 1–37.
4 Zheng Yongnian, "Rethinking China's Democracy for a Faster and Better Democracy", Zaobao.com, http://www.zaobao.com/special/forum/pages6/forum_zp080227.shtml, February. 27, 2008.
5 "Premier Wen Jiabao's Press Conference Q&A at the 5th session of the Tenth National People's Congress", *People's Daily*, March 17, 2007.
6 Several articles from *People's Tribune* 2007–2012 have ongoing discussions on the Chinese model, which also include discussions on the Chinese democracy model.
7 Han Fuguo, "China's Space in Consociational Democracy", *Development of Deliberative Democracy*, Chen Shengyong and He Baogang (eds.). Beijing: Chinese Social Sciences Press, 2006, 128–129.
8 Huang Weiping and Chen Wen, "Realistic Choice of China's Democracy Development – on 'Competitive Democracy' and 'Deliberative Democracy'", *Political Science Review of Sun Yat-sen University*, Xiao Bin & Guo Zhonghua (eds.). Guangzhou: Sun Yat-sen University Press, 2005, 39–40.
9 Zhu Yunhan, "Reflections on Democracy and the Market: A Political Scientist's Deep Thought at the Beginning of the Twenty-first Century", *Thought*, 2006, 3.
10 Mao Zedong, *Selected Works of Mao Zedong*, Vol. 2. Beijing: People's Publishing House, 1991, 383.
11 Since the introduction of the reform and opening up policy, China's reform of the political system aims to fix the drawbacks of traditional model of socialist democracy, such as excessive concentration of power. Now these issues have been greatly improved.
12 Peng Zongchao, Ma Ben, and Xu Jiajun, "Cooperative-Harmonious Socialist Democracy: A Model of Chinese Democracy", *Comparative Economic and Social Systems*, 2010, 3.
13 Arend Lijphart, *Patterns of Democracy: Government Forms and Performance in Thirty-Six Countries*, New Haven, CT: Yale University Press, 2nd ed., 2012.
14 Arend Lijphart, "Consociational Democracy", *World Polities*, 1969, 21(2): 207–225.

15 Arend Lijphart, *Democracy in Plural Societies: A Comparative Exploration*. New Haven: Yale University Press, 1977.
16 Arend Lijphart, *Democracy: Patterns of Majoritarian and Consensus Government in Twenty-One Countries*. New Haven & London: Yale University Press, 1984.
17 Daniel A. Bell, *Beyond Liberal Democracy*. Princeton, NJ: Princeton University Press, August 13, 2006.
18 Fareed Zakaria, "The Rise of Illiberal Democracy", *Foreign Affairs*, 1997, 76(6): 22–43.
19 Fareed Zakaria, *The Future of Freedom: Illiberal Democracy at Home and Abroad*. New York: W.W. Norton, 2003.
20 Fareed Zakaria, "The Rise of Illiberal Democracy", *Foreign Affairs*, 1997, 76(6): 22–43.
21 Amy Chua (US), *World on Fire: How Exporting Free Market Democracy Breeds Ethnic Hatred and Global Instability*. Beijing: Encyclopedia of China Publishing House, 2005.
22 James Bohman and William Rehg (eds.), *Deliberative Democracy – Essays on Reason and Politics*. Cambridge, MA: MIT Press, 1997.
23 John S. Dryzek, *Deliberative Democracy and Beyond – Liberals, Critics, and Contestations*. Oxford: Oxford University Press, 2002.
24 James Berman, *Public Deliberation: Pluralism, Complexity and Democracy*. Cambridge, MA: MIT Press, reprint edition, 2000.
25 *Democracy as Public Deliberation – New Perspectives*, Maurizio Passerin d'Entrèves (ed.). Manchester: Manchester University Press, November 23, 2002.
26 *Development of Deliberative Democracy*, Chen Shengyong and He Baogang (eds.). Beijing: China Social Sciences Press, 2006.
27 See John Keane, *The Life and Death of Democracy*. New York and London: W.W. Norton & Company, 2009. John Keane, "Monitory Democracy and Media-saturated Societies", Griffith REVIEW Edition 24: Participation Society. 2009. Guo Zhonghua, "Monitory Democracy as the Trend of Democracy in the Contemporary Development – An Interview with Famous Scholar John Keane", *Social Science News*, April 7, 2011.
28 Du Weiming, "Cultural Implications of the Rise of Confucianism in East Asia", *Dialogue and Innovation*. Guilin: Guangxi Normal University Press, 2005, 159–181.
29 Liang Shuming, *The Substance of Chinese Culture*. Shanghai: Xuelin Press, 2000.
30 Tan Yuanping, *Chinese Political Thoughts – Confucianism and Democratization*. Taipei: Yang-Chih Book Co., Ltd., 2004.
31 He Xinquan, *Confucianism and Modern Democracy*. Beijing: China Social Sciences Press, 2001, 11.
32 Zhang Liwen, *Theory of Harmony and Cooperation – A Conception of the twenty-first Century Cultural Strategy*. Beijing: China Renmin University Press, 2006.
33 Xu Yatang, *People-oriented Governance*. Taipei: The Commercial Press, 2005.
34 Gao Fang, "Lenin on the Theory and Practice of Socialist Democracy", *Nanjing Journal of Social Sciences*, 1995, 1; Gao Fang, *Politics and Political System Reform*. Beijing: China Book Press, 2002; Gao Fang, *Voices of China's Political System Reform*. Chongqing: Chongqing Publishing House, 2006; Gao Fang, "Accelerating the Reform of the Political System to Improve the Chinese Model of Democracy", *Journal for Party and Administrative Cadres*, 2007, 10; Gao Fang, "Political Reform is Expected to Catch Up – To Effectively Implement the Concept of Socialist Democracy with Chinese Characteristics", *People's Tribune*, 2012, 33.
35 Li Tieying, "Some Issues of Democratic Theory", *Social Sciences in China*, 2001, 1. Also see Li Tieying, "Introduction", *On Democracy*. Beijing: China Social Sciences Press, 2001.
36 John Fuh-sheng Hsieh, "Democratizing China", *Journal of Asian and African Studies*, 2003, 38(4–5): 377–390.
37 Deng Xiaojun, *Integrated Logic of Confucian thought and Democratic Thinking*. Chengdu: Sichuan People's Press, 1995.

38 David Hall and Roger T. Ames, *The Democracy of the Dead: Dewey, Confucius, and the Hope for Democracy in China*. Chicago: Open Court, 1999.

39 Susan Ogden, *Inklings of Democracy in China*. Cambridge, MA: Harvard University Asia Center, 2002.

40 Ranjoo Seodu Herr, "Confucian Democracy and Equality", *Asian Philosophy*, 2010, 20(3): 261–282.

41 Jin Yaoji, *Dilemma and Development of the Chinese Democracy*. Taipei: China Times Publishing Co., 1984.

42 Yan Jirong, "Theoretical Construction of Chinese Democracy", *Comparative Economic and Social Systems*, 2010, 3.

43 Liu Xirui, "The Established Model of Democracy in China", *People's Tribune*, 2007, 4; Liu Xirui, "Integration: the Essence and Destination of Chinese Democracy", *People's Tribune*, 2009, 1; Liu Xirui, "Integrationism: Essentials of Chinese Democratic Model – On the Relations of the Chinese Democratic Model with the Western Representative System", see Huang Weihua and Wang Yongcheng (eds.), *Research Reports on the Politics of Contemporary China*. Beijing: Social Sciences Academic Press, 2010.

44 Chen Jiagang, "Introduction to Deliberative Democracy", *Marxist Theory and Reality*, 2004, 3.

45 Arend Lijphart, "Negotiation Democracy Versus Consensus Democracy: Parallel Conclusions and Recommendations", *European Journal of Political Research*, 2002, 41: 107–113.

46 Peter Warbasse, *Cooperative Democracy*. New York: Macmillan Company, 1923; Natylie Baldwin, *The Renaissance of Cooperative Democracy*. http://mtdiablopeaceandjusdce.blogspot.com/2005/11/renalssance-of-cooperative-democracy.html.

47 Rong Jingben and Cui Zhiyuan (eds.), *A Transformation from the Pressure System to a Democratic Cooperation system*. Beijing: Central Compilation and Translation Bureau Press, 1998.

48 Eric X. Li, "The Life of the Party: The Post-Democratic Future Begins in China", *Foreign Affairs*, 2013, 92(1).

49 He Zengke, *Political Reform in China*. Beijing: Central Compilation and Translation Press, 2004.

50 Such as Yang Chenggang, "Strategic Thinking of Deng Xiaoping's Political Reform", *Journal of Wuhan University of Technology (Social Science Edition)*, 2002, 5; Kang Xiaoguang, "Objectives and Strategies of China's Political Development in the Next 10 Years", *Strategy and Management*, 2003, 1; Xu Xianglin, "Goal-Setting and Strategy-Choosing of Political Reform Policy", *Journal of Social Sciences of Jilin University*, 2004, 6; Xin Xiangyang, "Jiang Zemin's Thoughts on Political Reform", *Contemporary World and Socialism*, 2007, 2.

51 Wang Zhengxu and Dragan Pavlicevic, "Citizens and Democracy: Shi Tianjian's Contribution to China Studies and Political Science", *Open Times*, 2011, 9; Shi Tianjian and Maya, "Demystify Democracy", *Open Times*, 2009, 6.

2 Historical analysis and comparison of democratic models

Democratic theory is not developed in a vacuum; democratic theories are not only a part of the history of philosophy, but also a part of political theories and history in general.[1] Theories on democratic models have different themes and forms in different stages of social development. Western liberal democracy and China's socialist democracy have different logics in development. This comparative study on the theoretical and practical development of these two democratic theories facilitates the understanding of their respective advantages and disadvantages, thereby to clarify the historical problems pertaining to democratic theory and practice in constructing a cooperative-harmonious democracy.

History of theories and institutions of liberal democracy

From the time of ancient Athens to the present day, Western democratic theory has developed and diversified, among which the major variants are classical democracy, liberal democracy, participatory democracy, and deliberative democracy. In fact, liberal democracy is still the predominant political system in Western countries. Though a self-contained ideology, both participatory and deliberative democracies are proposed and derived from the critical reviews on liberal democracy, and their institutional and practical structures don't make them the independent democratic regime models but a supplement to the liberal model of democracy.

Classical democracy

Speaking of the origin of democracy, ancient Athens is always mentioned. Of course, whether democracy originated in ancient Athens is controversial.[2] Since this is not an archaeological study of democratic theory, in order to avoid controversy, a reference to Pericles' words is made to support the legitimacy of Athens as the source of democracy: "Our democracy is never an imitation but a role model to others."[3] Classical democracy refers to democratic ideals and practice of ancient Athens and is considered as the enlightenment of human democracy.

The main content of classical democracy includes:

1　Humans by nature are a political animal. Participating in politics is not a means to other ends, but an end in itself. Because human nature is to participate in politics, only through free and fair participation in political life, can ethics be improved and human nature be fully realized.

2   Citizens are politically equal. No citizen will be excluded from political life for an external difference such as social rank or personal wealth. Everyone can enjoy equal citizenship and equal legislative and judicial responsibilities and actively participate in the process of self-governance.[4]

3   Citizens can directly participate in politics. Each citizen can set the policy of the city by participating in the general assembly and may hold public office by lottery. According to Aristotle, every one out of six citizens has the chance to hold public office; even without government position, every year there are more than forty general assemblies held to decide on major issues of the state. That is, classical democracy is a direct democracy; those who rule are also being ruled; the citizens directly exercise their power rather than delegate the power to others.

4   Public life has priority. Citizens are dedicated to the city and the state, and private life is considered a part of public affairs and the common good. A citizen of Athens will not put his housework over state affairs. Even those who are caught in business also have very clear political ideas. Only Athenians regard those who do not care about public affairs as not only harmless persons but also useless people.[5]

Here is only a brief summary of the content of classical democracy, which will be further expounded through the later discussion on the criticism of classical democracy from liberal democracy theories.[6]

Liberal democracy

In 322 BC, ancient Greek democratic practice ended with Macedonia's conquest. Democracy disappeared in the following two thousand years, during which the monarchy and the church-state dual system dominated the political world in the West. The highest principle of democracy – popular sovereignty – was almost entirely ignored. Some people even said people are thousand-face monsters, who have neither judgment nor rationality and that to expect useful advice or governance from them is tantamount to hope for intelligence from a madman.[7] Although during the first and second century BC, about the time of the Roman republic and the Renaissance, autonomous city-states in northern Italy saw some thoughts tackling the principles of democracy, they were either short-lived or not strong enough to change the deep-seated monarchy. This situation was not changed until the British Glorious Revolution, the American Revolution, and the French Revolution; democracy was gradually recovered afterward.[8] However, the resurgent democracy was very different from classical democracy in essence.

With the establishment of modern nation-states, classical democracy that once fitted a small city-state with a small population no longer met the needs of the modern nations with larger territory and population. Democracy in the modern Western world is "representative democracy" by Mill's term,[9] while the direct participatory democracy of the ancient Greeks gradually vanished. Since the essence of "representative democracy" lies in that the citizens entrust the governance power to others through elections, we can say that the core objective in modern Western democratic practice is to oppose the centralization of an authoritarian regime and to protect the individual's civil rights and freedom. It mainly manifests in expanding the voting power to everyone (taking on the form of universal suffrage, granting all citizens the right to vote) so that a representative government is formed, while power separation, party competition, and local autonomy are institutionalized. Theory is the summary and abstraction of practices. Generally speaking, liberal democracy prevailing in modern Western countries is distinguished from classical democracy with several highlighted democratic elements, such as citizens' political freedom (including the right to oppose the government), representative democracy, and political competition, to which many thinkers, such as Locke, Montesquieu, and Mill, made important contributions correspondingly. It is soundly supported that the theoretical foundation of Western liberal democracy draws on ideologies from various intellectuals.

With the development of representative democracy in political practice, in the 1920s and 1930s, Joseph Alois Schumpeter, among others, proposed that the theory of classical democracy is normative, which idealizes democracy from an imperative perspective. The theory is not able to provide a convincingly realistic analysis of how democracy works.[10] Therefore, Schumpeter tried to construct a democratic theory that could better explain the reality. Based on the actual operation of representative democracy in the Western countries, the theory of "liberal competitive democracy"[11] was gradually formulated, with Schumpeter as the representative thinker. This theory defines democracy as "the democratic method that is an institutional arrangement for arriving at political decisions in which individuals acquire the power to decide by means of a competitive struggle for the people's vote."[12] In the twentieth century, Schumpeter's democratic ideas could be viewed as an independent theory, as some scholars classify it separately.[13] However, we believe that Schumpeter's theory in fact is built on the former liberal democratic theory but emphasizes the roles of competitive elections and the elite; it is developed upon the actual practices of representative democracy, therefore, it should be regarded as a part of liberal democratic theory, even as one of the more prominent representative theories in the twentieth century. So, here we mainly discuss his liberal (competitive) theory of democracy.

Liberal democratic theorists' criticism of the classical theory of democracy

First, liberal democratic theorists question the concept of "common good" of classical theory of democracy. Schumpeter states that this notion is misleading not only because some people may need something different from the common welfare, but also because people have different interests, needs, and values in a modern society that sees economic differentials, political pluralism, and cultural diversity. Therefore the common good is bound to have a wide range of understanding and disagreement, and the common welfare could actually mean different things. These differences cannot possibly dissolve in an "all-encompassing common will." In addition, many deep-rooted differences of value and conflicts of interest are impossible to get resolved or reach consensus by rational discussions. Therefore, the common good that all people agree upon or attained through rational discussion is nonexistent. Even if the recognized common good exists, the means to achieve it may be very different. Furthermore, assuming that common good does exist, the assertion that it is the product of rationality only provides a convenient excuse to exclude different opinions and to welcome irrational disputes, and hence becomes a legitimate reason to justify exclusion. A concept like common good is absolutely incomparable to democratic theory.[14]

Second, classical democracy, from the perspective of liberal democracy, cannot guarantee satisfying "what people really want". In some circumstances, the decision made by a non-democratic institution is likely more acceptable than a "democratic decision" to people. Especially in the event of a deadlock, a non-democratic institution can take advantage of its special status to establish a policy which is hard to be attained democratically due to the disagreement among all related parties. The religious settlement forcefully engineered by Napoleon is Schumpeter's classic example to illustrate that a satisfactory policy can be formulated by dictatorial means. In the early nineteenth century, the most pressing political need in France was religious reconciliation, for which any possible result through democratic process was very likely to incite anger or endless conflicts. Napoleon was able to resolve the religious dispute in a decided and rational manner because those self-asserted groups could not reach an agreement through democratic process but were willing to accept the arrangement imposed by Napoleon. Schumpeter thinks that such an example is not an isolated one, "If results that prove in the long run satisfactory to the people at large are made the test of government for the people, then government by the people, as conceived by the classical doctrine of democracy, would often fail to meet it."[15]

The last critique of classical democracy from liberal democracy thinkers is the nature of the "will of the people" or the "general will". Schumpeter argues that the so-called will of the people is nothing but a metaphysical social concept, rarely with any independent or rational foundation. Using the evidences of crowd psychology and the effects of advertising in shaping consumers' preferences, he claims that individuals are generally fragile and foolish and easily changed by emotions and outside influences. Compared with personal affairs, national and international political issues seem more remote to the majority of the people. It is difficult for them to make a right judgment on a variety of competitive ideologies so they leave it in the hands of politicians. He thinks that people make no decisions, and questions concerning their fate are asked and solved for them by others. Thus, in political life, the will of the people is formulated rather than by human nature; the will of people in classical democracy is a product of the political process rather than a motive power. In this case, attempt at rational argument only spurs the animal spirits.[16]

Schumpeter concludes that, in order to avoid the worst political peril in modern times, people who are passionate about democracy must abandon their fictional assumptions: those propositions of "classical democracy theory" and the presumption that "the people" possess correct and rational views for all political issues. "The people" is only, and can only be "the producers of the government", and a mechanism to select "the decision maker". Therefore, democracy should be understood as a political approach, in which political leadership is selected by the people through regular elections. 'Competitive elitism' is the most practical, most effective, and most appropriate model of democracy.[17]

The main contents of liberal democracy

By reviewing the reasons of the rise of liberal democracy and its critique of classical democracy, we have a general understanding of the competitive model of liberal democracy. Following is a discussion on the main content of this democratic model.

LIBERAL DEMOCRACY IS A DESCRIPTIVE AND EMPIRICAL DEMOCRACY

Schumpeter holds a counter opinion toward the democratic theories since the classical age, and tries to separate the reflection on the nature of public life from what he sees is excessively speculative and arbitrarily normative. He believes that the classical theory of democracy is normative rather than descriptive. Whenever this theory is inadequate, it will resort to some kind of 'should be'. On certain key issues, the theory is either presented in an unsubstantial vacuum or conveyed as a reality. The result is the bafflement about the operation of democracy.[18] He tried to develop an evidence-based "realistic" model of democracy that is descriptive and aims to explain how democracy works so that democracy can be closer to reality. By the twentieth century, especially after World War II, some well-known political scientists, such as Lasswell, Sartori, and others, were influenced by behaviorism. Following Schumpeter's empirical research on democracy, they focused on the actual function of democracy by using practical methods to evidence the reconciliation between the elite and democracy, which is the only way to understand the political reality of "popular sovereignty", a "strange phenomenon" deviated from the theory of classical democracy.

LIBERAL DEMOCRACY IS A PROCEDURAL DEMOCRACY

Classical democratic theories encounter great difficulties in reality, because even those governments that could not be called "democratic" by definition are also able to fulfill or better meet the people's will and bring them happiness. The definition of liberal democracy is characterized by a strict democratic process, as "the democratic method is that institutional arrangement for arriving at political decisions in which individuals acquire the power to decide by means of a competitive struggle for the people's vote."[19] In this definition, democracy is not an end in itself, but a process, a way and a system to achieve political – legislative and executive – policies. In practice, those who successfully win the votes of the people hold the power of decision making.[20] The role of citizens in the process is only to choose leaders through elections. Democracy thus becomes a by-product of the competitive process of elite-selection. Sartori thinks liberal democracy has made a "minimum" procedural definition of democracy[21]; as in most cases, it is easy to identify and verify whether such procedures and methods exist or not. Therefore, this definition provides an effective criterion to identify a democratic or non-democratic political system.

LIBERAL DEMOCRACY IS ELECTORAL DEMOCRACY AND ELITE DEMOCRACY

Election is selection, originated from the word *seligere*, of which the original meaning is to select the better one from different competitors based on a set of criteria.[22] So the election itself means competition. Democracy through competitive elections is an institutional arrangement to choose the political elite. Weber believes that the importance of this democratic process is to establish an "elective dictatorship."[23] The right to rule given to the political elite is legitimated by the citizens' periodic elections. In this case, election is equal to democracy, and liberal democracy is thus also known as "electoral democracy."

Schumpeter agrees with Weber's view in that the concept of "popular sovereignty" of classical democracy is ambiguous, and is useless in reality.[24] Influenced by the theorists of crowd psychology, such as Le Bon,[25] Schumpeter argues that the ordinary people are cowardly, indifferent, depraved, and irrational "animals" who are emotional and vulnerable to outside influences, and he thereby deals a serious blow to the picture of man's nature which underlies the classical doctrine of democracy and democratic folklore about revolutions.[26] The typical citizen drops down to a lower level of mental performance as soon as he enters the political field. He argues and analyzes in a way that he would readily recognize as infantile within the sphere of his real interests. He becomes a primitive again. His thinking becomes associative and effective.[27] This situation will bring ominous consequences: the typical citizen would in political matters tend to yield to extra-rational or irrational prejudice and impulse.[28] Human nature in politics being what it is, some groups are able to fashion and, within very wide limits, even create the will of the people. In today's highly specialized and professional society, if we wish to face facts squarely, we must recognize that, in modern democracies of any type other than the Swiss, politics will unavoidably be a career.[29] Politicians so often fail to serve the interest of their class or of the groups with which they are personally connected. Politically speaking, the man is still in the nursery who has not absorbed, so as never to forget, the saying attributed to one of the most successful politicians that ever lived: "What businessmen do not understand is that exactly as they are dealing in oil so I am dealing in votes."[30] Thus, democracy is the rule of the political elite, which does not and cannot mean a true governance of the people; the people can only be the producers of a government, who only have to accept or refuse some type of elite who are to rule them.

The analysis above shows that under the impact of empiricism and behaviorism, Schumpeter, among other scholars, examines the drawbacks of classical democracy and suggests that the democracy in reality is different from what is depicted in classical democracy. He then proposed an alternative theory – democracy as competitive elitism. Democracy is described as a process with "election" as the essential operation and the core operator is the political elite, who acquire the power of decision making by means of a competitive struggle for the people's votes. The people actually are only a group of commoners, who are not able to participate in any political activity but to select the leader through election. Although this definition of democracy overturns the concept of "popular sovereignty" in classical democracy, it seems more in line with the function of democracy in the real world.

Political pluralism,[31] rising in the late 1960s and with Darfur as its representative theorist, is also a liberal democratic theory, which has made some criticism and modification to Schumpeter's elitist democratic theory. In its definition, democracy is a political system ruled neither by the majority nor by the elitist minority, but by multiple groups and elites. The interest groups have a huge impact on modern politics, and the power resources are distributed and diversified. Multiple governance and multiple political parties characterize modern democracy.

Participatory democracy

The nature of liberal democratic theory is to describe the characteristics of the Western political system with a realistic approach. The competition model of liberal democracy only resolves current practical issues of democracy. The paradigm to assess democracy is no longer the theory of classical democracy, but has been replaced by the "true democracy" in the West. Any model that deviates from this paradigm or the Western democratic practice is mistakenly regarded as empirically incorrect or undesirable.[32] Therefore, liberal democracy contains a set of criteria to determine whether a political system is "democratic" or not.[33] In this sense, the realistic and descriptive model of liberal democracy theory does not hold its initial argumentation but often slips from a descriptive explanation into a new normative democratic theory,[34] and eventually becomes another "democracy myth."[35] Rebounds occur when extremes are met – when liberal democracy had become the "legendary" democratic theory the people enshrined, a new theory was developed and emerged in the late 1960s. Participatory democracy – the broad participation of regular citizens – came to claim a place among the theories of democracy under the impetus of Carole Pateman, Macpherson, Barber, and Arendt and other scholars, whose critical discussions and reflections on the competitive model of liberal democracy serve the foundation for the rise of participatory democracy.

Participatory democracy theorists' critique of liberal democracy

LIBERAL DEMOCRACY OVERTURNS THE IDEAL OF CLASSICAL DEMOCRACY

Liberal democratic theory is an empiricist theory of democracy, focusing on the description of practical evidence. However, Sartori once quoted Boland Botticelli's words: Politics should be of empiricism as well as idealism, when both of which complement each other, it is true; while separated from each other, it is false.[36] In its critique of classical democracy, liberal democracy has abandoned the ideals and changed the fundamental formative meanings of democracy.[37] As totally based on the actual operation of the existing democratic countries, this theory makes a new mistake. Democracy is created and formulated through the interaction between the ideal and the reality, between the real driving force and the natural resistance. In other words, democracy is born in the tension between the value and the fact. What it is (the facts, the description) and what it should be (the values, the norms) are not on different tracks. On the contrary, they are always interfering and conflicting with each other. When the focus is placed on the "what it is", an improper application of realism will occur; when the focus is simply on "what it should be", democracy will fall in the trap of human perfectionism.[38] That is, if the normative perspective is the only concern, democracy will be like any other utopian idea: either an unreachable paradise or an actualized hell. On the contrary, if meeting the reality is the goal, democracy will become a worthless deception and thus lose driving force for development.[39]

Although the classical definition of democracy – rule of the people – does not help people to understand the actual operation of democracy, it is indispensable for normative purposes,[40] which is no less important than the descriptive discourse. The establishment of a democratic system is the product of the pressure of values. What democracy is and what democracy should be are inseparable theses. Democracy can only exist in the range between its ideals and its values permitted.[41] It can be said that even though the normative definition of democracy is incorrect from the descriptive perspective, it can serve as a constant and pressing reminder of what a democracy should be. Only by combining the normative and descriptive theories can democracy become a never-ending process of realizing the ideals. The experience accumulated from this process can be used not only to test the practicality of the ideal, but also to maintain the continuous improvement and development of democracy in history.[42] Participatory democratic theorists' criticism of liberal democracy is based on the aim to restore the norms of classical democracy.

THE "SYMPTOMS" OF LIBERAL DEMOCRACY IN PRACTICE

In the history of Western democracy, liberal democracy is the oldest and today's predominant form of operation. However, it is like a long-distance runner with a weak heart, who runs steadily in appearance but his internal strength is quickly depleted, and some "symptoms" start to show. This liberal democracy, supported by liberalism with multiparty competitive elections as a core function, ultimately becomes a "weak democracy" because of its inherent flaws.[43] Political equality and political participation are in opposite directions in a representative democracy. Arend Lijphart, president of the American Political Science Association, in his inaugural speech in 1996, remarked that the greatest dilemma of liberal democracy is the inequality of political participation, as those citizens with higher social and economic status tend to a have greater chance of participation, thus resulting in uneven political influence among the people.[44] The arbitrary nature of representative democracy and liberal democracy[45] limits the development of alternative democracies as well as hinders the pursuit of other "proper forms" of democracy; the complacent concept makes it difficult to examine the defects of liberal democracy. Political alienation of the populace is a striking signal for the liberal model, indicating the bankruptcy of the democracy. Competitive representative democracy undermines the political participation as well as the "citizenship". Barber points out that by the true principle of democracy, all citizens within any political system should govern all public matters themselves rather than delegate their power to other individuals, so as to be truly in line with the goal of "democracy". However, in order to adapt to a nation with greater population and extensive territory, the populace has to rely on the representatives to govern the country at the expense of the citizens' right to rule.[46] Routine election is the core design of a representative democracy, but its significance has been lost in the practice of the secret ballot, which is like "getting in line for the toilet": every individual of a group quietly waits in line for one's turn to walk into the concealed compartment, relieve oneself, pull down the lever of the voting machines, and quietly go home, giving way to the next person.[47]

Hannah Arendt, a famous political philosopher who advocates active participation of citizens, also criticizes liberal democracy. She believes that in terms of historical development, liberal democracy indeed opens a door to the political world for those who really want to and have the ability to participate in politics and end the autocratic regime. But today, democratic "participation" has become increasingly degraded and insufficient to meet the needs of the times. In fact, Arendt believes that liberal democracy is currently undergoing a major crisis for two reasons: (1) due to the rise of party politics, the ideal of people's direct participation has been further apart from liberal democracy; (2) due to the expansion of the bureaucratic system, the voice of the people has become increasingly weakened.[48]

LIBERAL DEMOCRACY DISREGARDS THE POSITIVE EFFECT OF PARTICIPATION

One of the theoretical assumptions of liberal democracy is that the average citizen is passive, indifferent, ignorant, and overly obedient to rulers; citizens' being generally apathetic to politics is the premise of a stable and efficient democratic operation. Active participation is not desirable.[49] However, for those theorists advocating participatory democracy, the biggest drawback of liberal democracy is the loss of participation, which is a significant part of classical democratic theory. The ultimate concern of classical democracy is the individuals' participation in the public decision-making process, through which people gain knowledge, understand their social responsibilities, and develop their potentials. As Mill puts it: "The most important point of excellence which any form of government can possess is to promote the virtue and intelligence of the people themselves. The first question in respect to any political institutions is how far they tend to foster in the members of the community the various desirable qualities, moral, intellectual, and active."[50] Participatory democracy theorists continue to emphasize the participation which is valued in classical democracy, and argue that the core issue of a competitive liberal democracy is no longer how to design a political system that encourages people to participate in political activities and to improve the moral development, but how to connect the real and effective participation of the people with a stable functioning power system.[51] Pateman questions the view that the increased participation of people whose inadequate knowledge and inability in politics will disrupt the stability of the democratic system. She believes that people learn by participation and practices and that their political efficacy can be strengthened in the process; participation reduces the sense of alienation toward power centers, develops civic interest in public affairs, and is proved to effectively eliminate individuals' non-democratic tendencies.[52] If people know there are opportunities to effectively participate in decision making, they will think that participation is valuable and will actively participate in the collective decision, which is believed to have binding effect. Conversely, if people continue to be marginalized in political life with a low level of representation, they may think that their views and preferences are rarely taken seriously or assessed or evaluated equally in a fair process compared with those of the others.[53] Participation nurtures participation; democracy nourishes democracy. Little experience in autonomy encourages the desire for more autonomy; a small amount of political action incites great desire for action.[54] Arendt, following the Aristotelian tradition, believes that people are born with an aptitude for politics; in order to realize this tendency, people should actively participate in politics. Political participation is not only a necessary means to protect their rights, but also a part of human nature, a practice and affirmation of being human. If the assumptions of competitive liberal democracy are valid, there is no difference between man and other animals, of which the purposes in life are but safety, comfort, food, and clothing with no more meaningful pursuit. In order to demonstrate the unique value of mankind, active participation must be strongly advocated.[55]

The main contents of participatory democracy

PARTICIPATORY DEMOCRACY IS A NORMATIVE DEMOCRATIC THEORY

Pateman believes that the recent competitive model of democracy is not fully democratic but merely describes the actual operation of the democratic political system. Democracy is not entirely empirical and should be morally desirable as well as embody moral values and principles. Based on the review of liberal democracy, theorists of participatory democracy have changed experience-oriented analysis of democratic theory since World War II and reaffirm the importance of participation in the democratic theoretical construct.[56] Any democracy without the participation of citizens can only be a "thin democracy." Therefore, from the normative perspective, participatory democracy is a democratic theory that values civic engagement. Although participatory democracy is a normative theory that criticizes the reality, it is not just unrealistically ideal but has a number of institutional designs to actualize people's direct involvement – for example, Arendt's Council System[57] and the three models proposed in Barber's Strong Democracy:

institutionalization of democratic discussion, decision making, and operation for a stronger democracy.[58] These systems, especially Barber's models of institutionalization, have great influence in the future design of the deliberate democratic system. If only from a practical point of view, participatory democracy appears to be a failure; however, if practical effect is not the sole criterion in evaluation, the significance of participatory democracy emerges. Good things in history are usually transient. However, they have lasting and critical impact in the future. For example, the wonderful classical period of the ancient Greeks was short-lived, but so far we still benefit greatly from it.[59] Moreover, the idea of participation advocated by participatory democracy has been passed on; the emerging deliberative democracy already continues to construct a new democratic model to complement the deficit of liberal democracy. In this sense, the normative theory of participatory democracy is not discriminated for being impractical; on the contrary, it facilitates the democratic progress, which, after all, depends on the driving force of norms and the pressure of values.

THE IMPLICATION AND EXTENT OF PARTICIPATION

Participatory democracy theorists believe that "electoral participation" is not a true participation, and the meaning of participation is personally involved, is voluntary participation. In other words, participation is not just "being a part of" (merely getting involved in something), and definitely not involuntarily "made into a part of".[60] This personal involvement means that the people directly and fully participate in policymaking. That is, people are directly involved in the proposal, agenda, discussion, and final decision of policies, instead of selecting representatives to make the decisions for them.

In terms of the extent of participation, Pateman believes that individuals cannot be separated from the institutions they are in; a representative system at a national level is necessary but is not sufficient for democracy. To maximize popular participation, democratic socialization or "social training" must be carried out in other areas; that is, the governing structure in all areas within society is to be democratized through a participatory process.[61] While participation in various areas is emphasized, Pateman believes that the most appropriate areas for people's direct involvement are those closed to their everyday lives, such as the workplace, the community, and local autonomy, which contain the affairs they are interested in and to their best understanding. Although there are two forms of participation, at the community and national levels, in his institutional designs, Barber agrees more with what Tocqueville advocates – every democratic revolution starts with local participation.[62] Without local participation, there will be no democracy. If people are not ready to participate at the local level, it is of no use for them to participate in national elections and government; it is at the local level that people learn how to manage themselves. The intelligence, morals, and character required by a political activity that is held only once in every few years are far away from the citizens' everyday experience, thus the citizens are not well prepared for this political activity. That is, individuals in a great country are often able to effectively participate in the grand social management, then the capability necessary for such participation must be trained and developed at the grassroots level.[63] Participation at the local level is not only to exercise the powers or to formulate policies, but also to gradually develop citizens' participating with morals, intelligence, and ability. Therefore, places close to people's lives, such as workplaces and local organizations, are the best fields of participation.

Participatory democracy and liberal democracy

Most scholars who advocate participatory democracy do not think elections or representative systems should be dropped. Even the "participation theorists" who cherish direct democratic ideals rarely make their theories fully consistent with direct democracy.[64] Pateman also disagrees with the view that liberal democracy should be abandoned and direct democracy be widely adopted to achieve completely equal and liberal management in all political, economic, and social spheres. In fact, Pateman believes that many core systems of liberal democracy – such as competitive political parties, political representatives, and regular elections – will be the indispensable elements of a participatory society. The competition among the political parties and interest groups in the field of public affairs can be the most practical way to promote the principles of participatory democracy.[65] Barber also states that direct democracy implies a form of government in that everyone is able to manage all public affairs at all times; we could not expect direct democracy to operate effectively in a big country that has hundreds of citizens. In this case, liberal democracy, as a new democratic form of government, replaces direct democracy. In a liberal democracy, the representatives selected by all citizens manage the public affairs full time and thus improve the efficiency of governance. However, Barber regards that liberal democracy gained efficiency at the expense of people's participation and citizenship. Therefore, he advocated a strong democracy to actively promote and implement the participation and citizenship under the premise of an effective liberal democracy.[66] In short, participatory democracy is to complement the inadequacy of liberal democracy rather than function as a radical replacement.

Deliberative democracy

The rise of deliberative democracy

In the 1990s, as more people believed that the "essence of democracy is deliberation rather than voting,"[67] the democratic theory that centers on "voting" was gradually being replaced by the democratic theory that focuses on "deliberation". The democracy upheld by the former is of fixed preferences and interests competing for ballots, while the focus of the latter is the process of open discussion, negotiation, and communication before voting and attentiveness to how to alter preference, reduce disagreement, and attain rational opinions. We can say that from the early nineteenth century to the twentieth century, democratization concerned the expansion of elections to make sure that every citizen had the right to vote; today, the focus of democratization is to expand the public sphere so that every citizen can voice his/her opinion. Voice instead of vote is a new way of empowerment.[68]

In fact, deliberation is not a new concept – relevant examples or expositions can be found in the ancient Greek city-state governments and Western classical political theories. As Elster puts it: deliberative democracy or the concept of collective decision making through free and fair deliberation among citizens is not an innovation, but a revival; this concept and its practice are as old as democracy itself, originating from Athens in the fifth century BC.[69] The ancient Athenian governor Pericles in his famous Funeral Oration states that everyone in this country is concerned about not only personal matters but also national affairs; even those who are always caught up with their own business can still make a good judgment on public affairs – that is our feature. We do not think that any individual who is not interested in politics minds only his own personal affairs; we just think this person does not have anything to do here. We Athenians make our own decisions; even if we did not initiate the proposal, we still have the ability to judge it. We do not think discussion would impede action, on the contrary, we believe that discussion is an indispensable prerequisite for any sensible action and that the worst thing is to rush to take action before appropriate public discussion.[70]

Aristotle does not like the ancient Athenian democracy but still considers "deliberation" valuable. The decisions reached through the regular citizens' discussion are more effective than those made by experts independently.[71] The modern and contemporary theorists, including Rousseau, Burke, Mill, and Dewey, have made varying degrees of contributions to the theory of deliberative democracy. The scholastic notion of "deliberative democracy" was coined by Joseph M. Bessette in his 1980 article "Deliberative Democracy: The Majority Principle in Republican Government". Afterward, Manin and Cohen's research furthered the theory of deliberative democracy.[72] By the late 1990s, deliberative democracy had become a famous school of democratic theory. At this time, the most prominent theorists, John Rawls and Habermas, all turned their focus to deliberative democracy while seeing themselves as deliberative democracy theorists in their major works[73]; their academic reputation greatly enhanced the importance of the theory.[74] It can be said that since ancient Athens, deliberation has always been a part of democracy; as the practice continued into the 1990s, deliberative democracy became an important democratic theory.

Origin and the major content of deliberative democracy theory

From the perspective of theoretical origin, deliberative democracy continues the critical review on competitive liberal democracy of the participatory democracy theorists.[75] Deliberative democracy theory, also based on the review of liberal democratic theory, recognizes again the positive effect of citizens' participation in public affairs. This theory holds that the political participation of citizens should not be limited to activities such as periodic voting and occasional protests or demonstrations; under the conditions of information transparency, the citizens should have open and adequate discussions on the public policies that would affect them according to certain procedures and free from unequal political power, and through public deliberation legitimize a decision and enhance the quality of democratic governance. So, what is the deliberative democracy theorists' criticism of liberal democracy? What are the notion, characteristics, and principles of deliberative democracy? This section is to interpret the major contents of deliberative democracy from these two aspects.

DELIBERATIVE DEMOCRACY THEORISTS' CRITIQUE OF LIBERAL DEMOCRACY

Critique of the argument that citizens have neither knowledge nor ability to participate in politics and policymaking   The competitive liberal democracy theorists, with Schumpeter as their representative scholar, believe that citizens are indifferent, sentimental, and gullible. In the complex industrialized and highly specialized society of today, citizens are constrained by their limited knowledge and ability to understand the policy issues; if these incompetent citizens participate in political decision making, the quality of the policy will be undoubtedly undermined. Therefore, the role of citizens in the democratic process is to select leaders through elections, and democracy can only become a by-product of the competitive struggles in selecting leaders.[76] On the contrary, the role of politicians is not to reflect the will of the citizens, but to shape the public will through competition, advertisements, and other political propaganda, because the will of the people does not exist and the citizens are capricious, weak, and hopeless fools.[77] Deliberative democracy theorists criticize this attitude toward the citizens in a competitive liberal democracy.

If the regular citizens, according to the theory of competitive liberal democracy, are really incapable of decision making and are weak and apathetic, then how can they wisely tell the ability of the political candidates who will be their decision maker during the election?[78] How capable and wise can the political leaders be if they are chosen by a group of mobs that have no knowledge, ability, or willpower? In a mature democracy, citizens mainly play two important roles: judges and participants. But the competitive elite democratic theory only stresses the role of judges, while ignoring the importance of participation.[79] In fact, national decision making requires not merely scientific knowledge by a strict definition; all major decisions, whether related to individuals or to government, require moral judgments, evaluations, and balancing between the conflicting purposes. With limited resources, every citizen should have a proper opportunity to understand the relationship between means and ends, his/her own interests, as well as the relationship among the expected consequences of policies, self-interest, and the interests of all others. This balance and understanding cannot be achieved just with specialized knowledge but requires the introduction of public participation and discussion.[80] In fact, the citizens' cold, passive characters are somehow developed in the absence of necessary understanding, information, and opportunities for participation. Therefore, to advance the current democratization, the most prominent barrier is the specialization of knowledge controlled by political powers, which prevents citizens from having the necessary expertise to form their own political opinions.[81] Citizens' lack of knowledge and ability could not then be used as an excuse to exclude their participation in decision making. Citizens are not born with knowledge and ability, and deliberative democracy through participation must help them acquire knowledge, improve ability, develop virtue and accountability, and ultimately enhance the quality of democracy.

Critique of simple majority rules   Election-based liberal democracy is often reduced to the elections, which is reduced to a ballot, which is further reduced to a majority decision. Variants of the majority rule have been a form of decision making that liberal democracy relies upon. It would be the best result if a political candidate or a policy wins the unanimous consent of all citizens, which still remains a myth of democracy, unless attained by force. The essence of the majority rule is a decision rule that makes choices by a quantitative comparison when unanimous consent among all citizens is impossible. Difference by one or two percentage points is sufficient to determine a shift in public policy or the career of a political figure. The quantitative battles in the democratic process might evoke excitement similar to the pleasure of watching a sports game, from the active participants, but behind the battle is a serious implication that cannot be found in sports games, since the results of the majority decision rule will have binding effect on the livelihood, behavior, and choices of each member in society. Thus the quantitative comparison as the ultimate decisive factor is worth reassessment.[82]

From the historical and realistic perspective, majority rule is not unambiguously accepted. Majority merely represents a quantity; yet, what right does a pure quantity have? Why does a greater number have a greater value? Here, quantitative change obviously won't produce qualitative change, since the ignorance of 10 million people does not add up to a little bit of knowledge. In fact, leaving aside the questioned majority rule, voting is the most criticized part in a quantitative comparison, because voters do not need to publicly justify their choices. A voting booth is a place where the voters' expression of personal preferences and desires is under protection. In the voting booth, even if a choice is made for selfish reasons (for example, a vote for party B is simply out of the fear that some personal benefits might be canceled if party A takes the office, or simply because candidate A is prettier than candidate B, etc.), the voter does not need to explain to others about the choice, whether it is a rational product based on considerations of public interest, or is for selfish reasons, or is simply a reflection of personal momentary emotions. This situation has been questioned by deliberative democracy theorists: the consequence of being private and secret is that voters have no obligation to justify their votes in public, therefore there is nothing to stop voters from voting entirely according to their own interests; they also don't need to consider what a good policy for the group is.[83] In this case, the legitimacy of most people's preferences and desires is based on the advantages of quantity, rather than on the validity or approximate accuracy deducted from a rational discussion. Thus, another question stemmed from majority rule decision mechanism in a democratic election is whether or not the choice most people agree upon is an option of a more comprehensive and public-interest-oriented consideration after rational examinations. A simple majority decision rule once caused a tragic consequence: the death of Socrates in 339 BC, which is an irony to the rationality of the majority's opinion. Even worse, this kind of irony has been repeatedly seen in modern democracies: that Hitler came to power in Germany was legitimized by a majority decision. This prompted the democratic theorists to face the serious problem of majority rule.[84]

The theory of deliberative democracy was created to criticize and solve the problems of majority rule. Deliberative democracy stresses the quality of selection and highlights the appeal of rationality (rational choice), trying to liberate democracy from Schumpeter's market analogy and to overturn the tyranny of majority rule in the democratic process. Deliberative democracy focuses more on the quality of participation and decision making, particularly on how to reach a decision that is rationally justified and consistent with public interest. To achieve this goal, a process of open discussion is needed. When the public deliberation on a proposal is institutionalized, it is impossible for citizens and politicians to try to convince others for private purpose or the interest of a small group.[85] Among the modern deliberative democracy supporters, no one believes a full and comprehensive deliberation requires everyone to successfully put personal view as a precondition for any collective decision making.[86] If consensus on some policies, especially on urgent issues, cannot be reached, people will turn to some form of majority rule, or even more authoritative means for decision making. Deliberative democracy theorists do not entirely negate majority rule but stress that majority rule, in which the majority is the only decisive factor, must coexist with public deliberation, in the hope of adding humanity and quality to quantitative comparison. Public deliberating and extensive discussions, on the one hand, can minimize the expression of self-interest and emotional impulses; on the other hand, deliberation facilitates mutual understanding among different values and preferences; even if no agreement is reached, the existing differences can be approached with an "enlarged mentality."[87] Thus the majority rule after public deliberation produces a quality decision, of which the legality and legitimacy have been greatly enhanced.[88]

Critique of the aggregated preferences of liberal democracy   Theorists of liberal democracy compare politics to the market, and the citizens to the voters. The political elite in the open market sell their products (platforms) and compete for votes. The result of aggregate-preferences competition is then determined by majority rule.[89] In particular, after World War II the coexistence of political competition and market competition made it a trend to study political phenomena through economic analysis, thus giving rise to *rational choice theory*. The rational choice theory pushes to an extreme the hypothesis of liberal democracy and blurs the boundary between the political and market sectors; citizens in the political sphere are rational and selfish with their own preferences; the purpose of selection is to maximize their own benefits; the democratic process is to choose qualified politicians or suitable policies by calculating the aggregation of individual preferences. In the process of the aggregate democracy, after a rational calculation, common people believe that their influence on the political process is very small, therefore they are less motivated to complete the obligations of an ideal citizen in a democratic system and become "rational ignorant", as Downs described.[90]

Aggregate democracy holds that personal preference is deemed unchanged; therefore, the aggregation of personal preferences can formulate a public policy. An aggregate democracy without public discussion is simply a majority rule of aggregated personal preferences. Totally relying on the aggregating process not only cannot improve the quality of democracy, but also produces arbitrary collective choices, which are not based on public interest and with no reasonable explanation for the need of public interest. In a mature democracy, citizens mainly play two different roles: arbiter and participant. Yet competitive liberal democracy stresses only a citizen's role as an arbiter, and ignores the role as a participant.[91] Apparently today's democratic system structurally limits citizens to a passive role of who chooses their decision maker from the competing politicians by means of ballots; corresponding to citizens' passive role, the democratic process is regarded as a process to select policies by calculating the aggregation of personal preferences. Competitive liberal democracy functions not to change everyone's preferences, but to prioritize the preferences of the entire society through a quantitative comparison. In contrast, deliberative democracy believes that personal preferences are not innate and fixed; personal preferences can be and should be altered in the process of rational and open discussion on public interests and through interacting with others. In a democratic society that genuinely encourages negotiation, the preference will be changed when the citizens are better informed of the policy as well as when they learn about others' preferences and discover other policy options that have not been previously taken into account.[92] Therefore, deliberative democracy emphasizes public deliberation through an open, fair, free, and equal discussion to modify personal preferences and values and to transform conflicting interests into common interests. In short, the theory of deliberative democracy is trying to face the problems of unreflective preferences, which are easily manipulated in the practice of competitive liberal democracy, and aims to develop the citizens' deliberation potential to achieve an unselfish mission centering on public concern and interests. This is the major difference between deliberative democracy and liberal democracy.

CONCEPT, CHARACTERISTICS, AND PRINCIPLES OF DELIBERATIVE DEMOCRACY

The concept of deliberative democracy   A concept generalizes the essence of things. We also hope to understand the nature of deliberative democracy through the conceptions of deliberative democracy. Unfortunately, just like any other theory, the theory of deliberative democracy has internal differences, as Phelan remarks;

any attempt to give a definition of deliberative democracy will fall into an argument about accurate understandings.[93] But, does this mean that the conceptions of deliberative democracy are not referential? In fact, it would be incredible if there is no difference in the understandings of deliberative democracy among so many studies. No matter what kind of interpretations, there should be a "common denominator" among the varying conceptions of deliberative democracy; otherwise the theory would become conceptually confused because of completely different opinions. Therefore, we cannot expect a uniform ideology but hopefully we can find the "common denominator" among the different conceptions of deliberative democracy.

Maeve Cooke believes, in the simplest terms, deliberative democracy refers to a democratic government that provides a basic platform for rational discussion about political life.[94]

Guevara Fernandez believes that deliberative democracy is a form of democratic governance with great potentials, which can respond effectively to the dialogue among multiple cultures, promote mutual understanding of different political discourses with particular emphasis on the responsibility for the public interests, and support public policies that value the interests and needs of all people.[95]

Gutmann and Thompson believe that deliberative democracy can be defined as a form of governance in which the free and equal citizens give reciprocally acceptable reasons through certain procedures to justify decisions.[96]

Jon Elster's definition is most easily understood. Deliberative democracy can be divided into two parts: deliberation and democracy. Democracy means that any collective decisions must be reached through the participation of all affected citizens or their representatives; deliberation means that the decision-making process is carried out through public discussion, in which the participating citizens or their representatives are expected to cherish the value of rationality and fairness.[97]

Of course, there are many definitions of deliberative democracy, and it is impossible to enumerate all of them. The common denominator derived from the conceptions of democratic deliberation mentioned above has two important aspects: first, civic participation, meaning citizens affected by the decision have the right to participate in public policymaking; second, public deliberation, meaning the democratic decision making should be based on public deliberating, and any support or disagreement of public policies should be discussed from the standpoint of promoting common good. These two aspects suggest a shift of focus from the power, knowledge, and wealth of a few elite to the power of ordinary citizens in a deliberative process.

The characteristics of deliberative democracy According to Gutmann and Thompson, deliberative democracy is characterized by the following four features:[98]

First, reason-giving. Deliberative democracy believes justification of the public decision making needs to be made by the citizens or their representatives; in a democratic country, citizens or their representatives must justify the reasons why they are for or against the public policies. The moral basis of the reason-giving process is the conception of democracy: citizens should not be merely regarded as the target of legislation or public policy or as the passive ruled, but should be considered as independent and active individuals who participate in governing society directly or indirectly through their representatives. In a deliberative democracy, an important way to participate is to give reasons as well as to respond to the reasons given by the others. The significance of giving reasons during policymaking as required by deliberative democracy is on the one hand, to obtain a public policy that can be justified, and on the other hand, to show the value of mutual respect. If a public policy is achieved only through the ballot without reason-giving, even though it is favored by the majority, this process not only violates the requirements of deliberative democracy but also shows no equal respect for the minority.

Second, the reasons given are accessible to all citizens. The reasons given in the public deliberation process should be accessible to all the audience or can be understood by everyone. Such a democratic form of reasoning fulfills accessibility in two senses: first, deliberation itself must be carried out in public; second, the content of the reasoning must be disclosed. If other citizens involved in the deliberation have no access or cannot understand the content of the reasons, the legitimacy of the public policy is in no way to be justified through deliberation. Though in the course of discussion, some proofs may be too specialized, it does not mean that the reasons given are something beyond everyone's understanding.

Third, a consensus obtained after deliberation leads to a binding collective decision. The purpose of a deliberating procedure is to generate a policy. Different from being in a talk show or symposium, the participants in the deliberation do not just debate for demonstration purposes or for truth itself; the goal of deliberation is to influence the government's decision making or have impact on future policymaking. Therefore, if a consensus can be achieved after deliberation, then, it should be a binding collective decision.

Fourth, the deliberation process is dynamic. The purpose of deliberation is to formulate a justifiable policy, of which the success is not guaranteed. Therefore the possibility of continued dialogues should be kept open. A public policy is likely to last for a long time, but in a sense is temporary, as it must be open to future challenge. Because in politics, like in many real-life situations, the procedures and results of decision making are not perfect; we cannot guarantee today's policy will be a correct one for tomorrow. In addition, since most public decisions in politics are not entirely agreed upon, there is a greater chance for those who disagree to accept the present decision if they know there is opportunity to amend it.

The principles of deliberative democracy In order to truly implement deliberative democracy, there are certain principles to follow in the process of public deliberation.

First, publicity. Publicity means that citizens and officials need to rationally and publicly justify their actions and decisions. A general rule of today's democracy is to express personal preferences and choices through secret ballots. In this process, an individual has no obligation to explain his or her motives or reasons for the decision, or to give any reason for personal preferences or choices, which leaves the opportunity for accepting bribes, voting for relatives, protecting personal interests, etc. Therefore, personal preferences or choices can be privately expressed. On the contrary, the belief of the deliberative democracy theory is that without the obligation to publicly explain personal choices, individuals are likely to pursue self-interests in the asylum of confidentiality; every individual should state publicly the reasons for his or her choices. The process of public deliberation forces individuals to exercise a special reflexivity on personal preferences or choices; when deliberating, an individual has to present good reasons to the participants in an open discussion, a process that will push participants to ponder what reason is good for all people involved. Therefore, participants will be forced to consider their choices from the standpoint of all relevant parties, whose approval is decisive to their appeals.[99]

Second, reciprocity. Reciprocity means that citizens can think rationally and reciprocally, when they express their requirements from each other's principles and positions; this is the mutual respect among the citizens who seek a fair term of cooperation. The assumed motive of deliberative democracy is a desire to justify to others, therefore, that reciprocity is an important principle in the course of its operation. Gutmann and Thompson hold reciprocity as the core principle of democracy, because the process of discussion and deliberation may not be able to attain a conclusion that everyone agrees on and moral disagreement still exists; in this case, although a final decision has to be made by resorting to the majority decision rule, the element of mutual respect in the principle of reciprocity at least secures some room for continuous meaningful dialogues in the future. In the face of conflicts, mutual respect helps not only maintain the presence of the community but also regulate the conflicts; mutual respect offers the possibility for different, more flexible solutions in the future.[100]

Third, accountability. Accountability means that during the deliberation, participants are accountable for their actions. In the process of deliberating, participants need to know their own preferences as well as understand the positions of others; they should also be aware of that any promotion of a policy of public interest must be supported by a consensus of all parties. Therefore, citizens who participate in deliberation are liable to justify their reasons and to convince the other participants in the process; they are responsible for responding to the arguments and reasons of the others; they are also accountable for modifying the proposals according to the reasoning and views raised during the deliberation in order to realize a mutually acceptable proposal.[101]

Fourth, equality. Equality means that all citizens affected by the collective decision making enjoy equal opportunities and have the right to express their ideas and interests, without being intimidated or dominated in the process of participation. Although the theory of deliberative democracy emphasizes the process of public deliberating, some people cannot equally and effectively participate in the process of rational discussion and have their argument effectively expressed due to their economic, political, and educational backgrounds. Therefore, deliberative democracy tries to avoid unequal deliberation. In addition to an equal democratic procedure, deliberative democracy emphasizes substantive equality, which ensures that everyone has equal opportunities, or equal political power, to show their political influence. That is, in the deliberating process, the best decision is produced based on the power of argument that could convince others to change their preferences and opinions rather than on the imbalance of the participants' political, economic, and educational resources. To ensure that everyone has an equal opportunity to negotiate and influence the others, a deliberative democratic system must encourage everyone to participate actively in the process of discussion so that individuals can develop the ability of reasoning in order to convince the others instead of being confined by the authority or other limited resources. The relationship between people of different views and positions must be free and not subject to one another, so the people have an equal opportunity to express their ideas and to convince the others.[102]

Fifth, inclusion. Because the theory of deliberative democracy emphasizes rational persuasion and argument, this model of democracy is more favorable for those who have the ability to reason and to argue than for those who are less articulate, more emotional, or of specific groups and communities, such as women or minorities whose communication conventions are different from the dominant one. If the deliberate democracy ignores different styles of communication (such as storytelling, narration of personal trauma, cultural customs to express anger, or other ways to evoke personal association), then the special situations of the presenters and the cultural implications of these expressions will also be ignored, which leads to substantive inequality. Sanders believes that some people are more persuasive than the others with better control of reasoning language, even though their ideas or claims are not true or valuable.[103] In the public domain, when participants do not share the same culture, reasoning approaches, or evaluation criteria with the mainstream, they may be regarded as irrational and be excluded from the deliberation. Especially for certain institutionally ignored issues which are voiced by the already disadvantaged groups, they should not be excluded due to incompatibility with a specific form of expression or the criterion of rationality. A deliberative democratic system should accommodate diverse and different voices. No one can dominate the deliberation process or force others to accept or reject an opinion. People can express their interests, needs, and positions but cannot be excluded because of lack of appropriate forms of expression and knowledge.[104] People can effectively use their cultural resources through communication and the deliberation process, encourage individuals or groups with different social status and cultural background to understand one another's differences and experiences, so that individuals or groups can reach beyond their narrow self-interests and chauvinism and develop a more comprehensive understanding of society.[105]

History of the theories and institutions of socialist democracy

The foundation of China's socialist democracy is the combination of theoretical characteristics of traditional socialist democracy and the practical experience of China. The ideology of traditional socialist democracy is mainly reflected in the discussions of Marx and Lenin. Perceiving that capitalist democracy is not real democracy, they understood the true essence of democracy and hoped to build a democratic model that was different from Western liberal democracy.

Traditional socialist democracy

Marx once said: What is democracy? It must have certain implications to justify its existence. Therefore, it is all about a true definition of democracy. If we can define democracy, then we can deal with it; if not, we are doomed.[106] Back then, Marx often discussed his ideas on proletarian democracy instead of socialist democracy.[107] However, his discussions on democracy and proletarian democracy are the foundation of the Marxist democratic ideology.

In his *Critique of Hegel's Philosophy of Right*, Marx states: In democracy the constitution itself appears only as one determination, and indeed as the self-determination of the people. In monarchy we have the people of the constitution, in democracy the constitution of the people. Democracy is the resolved mystery of all constitutions. Here the constitution not only in itself, according to essence, but according to existence and actuality is returned to its real ground, actual man, the actual people, and established as its own work. The constitution appears as what it is, the free product of men.[108] To Marx, people are the decisive factor of all political life of a state. A national constitution should be the ultimate representation of the will of the people. The key concept to a democratic system is that individuals and civil societies come before a state, not vice versa; people have the right to participate in and to control the politics of a state, a process where people can find their existence and development. It is because people make up society on which a nation is built. It is the fundamental and logical relationship between people, society, and nation. Among them, people are the deciding power, and society is a nation's foundation. In the real world, human beings are constantly changing, which inevitably leads to the fundamental or organizational change of society. Although these changes won't affect the "deciding or being decided" relation between the nation and society, they will change the actual power structure between them and thereby the logic and style of people's political life when they interact with the nation and society.[109]

In his critique of capitalist democracy, Marx argues that though bourgeois democracy represents a certain historical progress, in which, for example, the monarchy is replaced by a parliamentary system, the election system dismisses the hereditary system, and term-appointment abolishes the tenure system, this model of democracy is still hypocritical, which mainly manifests in class inequality. Bourgeois democracy is the dictatorship of a social class over another, bourgeois class only speaks highly of democracy, but never actually wants to be a democratic class; it recognizes the justice of principle, but such principle was never implemented in practice.[110] In order to achieve true democracy, we must rely on the dictatorship of the oppressed proletariat; the dictatorship of the proletariat is the democracy of the proletariat. In the proletarian regime, the greatest majority of the working class can really enjoy democracy and exercise the right to political participation freely and equally; it guarantees that most people enjoy democracy.

Marx witnessed and was inspired by the Paris Commune, a particular form of practice that is essentially different from the regime of the capitalist countries. In his *Civil War in France*, Marx spoke highly of some democratic measures of the Paris Commune, in which he found "real democracy" sprouting, and expounded in details the essence of the people's democratic regime. Government officials are elected by suffrage, get paid the same as any skilled worker, and is supervised by the people and can be removed from their position at any time. Therefore, the people's self-governance can be protected and realized. Commune – this is a society that reclaims the state regime, which is transformed from a ruling and oppressing power to a vital power of society itself; this is people repossessing the nation's regime; they formed their own power to replace the organized oppressing force; it is the people's political form to obtain social liberation, a political form that replaces the oppressing force used by the people's enemies; it has a very simple form, like all great things.[111] He also said: the existence of the Commune itself implies the end of monarchy, which, at least in Europe, is the sarcoma and indispensable coat of class rule, and commune lays a true foundation of democracy.[112] Engels also called the Paris Commune a new and truly democratic regime.[113]

To Marx, democracy is still a historical event, a developmental product of human society, and will vanish as the state withering away. In a true democracy, the political state disappears, which can be correct because in a democracy, the political state itself as a constitution is already not a cohesive whole entity.[114] Because in the realm of necessity it is essential to have democracy as a form of the state, while in the advanced stage of communism, as it has entered the realm of freedom, no major decision needs to be made and thus no need of any form of democracy.[115]

Yu Keping believes that Marx examines the problems of democracy as well as explores the general concepts, universal values, and common forms of democracy mainly from the perspective of class analysis. Marx's idea of democracy stemmed from Rousseau's popular sovereignty and holds that democracy is the sovereignty of the people. Marx acknowledges the universality of democracy. In his comparative analysis on democratic institutions of different nature, he also recognizes many common forms that people devise in realizing democratic values, such as the mechanism of representation, universal suffrage, social autonomy, public participation, people's supervision of power, clean government, and inexpensive government.[116]

Lenin inherited and developed Marx's democratic discourse and put it into practice. In Lenin's view, democracy is a form of a state, a type of a nation. Therefore, like any state, it signifies an organized and systematic force against people on the one hand; on the other hand, it represents formal recognition of equality among all citizens and their equal rights to decide the constitutions and to govern the state.[117] In addition, he believes that capitalist democracy is an incomplete, poor, and false democracy, only in the service of the rich and the minority.[118] The bourgeois democracy is different from proletarian democracy in that the former is focused on proclaiming various freedoms and rights, which, in fact most of the residents, who are the workers and peasants, do not have the slightest chance to fully enjoy. On the contrary, proletarian or Soviet democracy, instead of focusing on declaring the rights and freedoms of all people, focuses on making sure that those workers who have been oppressed and exploited by the capitalists can actually participate in the national administration. So the exploited workers can really enjoy the welfare of culture, civilization, and democracy.[119]

As the "Soviet system provides the maximum of democracy for workers and peasants, at the same time, it marks a break with bourgeois democracy and the rise of a new, epoch-making type of democracy, namely, proletarian democracy, or the dictatorship of the proletariat."[120] Strictly speaking, proletarian democracy and socialist democracy are different; the former, as the first stage of socialist democracy, places more emphasis on a democratic model in transition. Compared with capitalist democracy, socialist democracy is a new and advanced type of democracy, not only because it is the democracy of most people, but also the socialist democracy can be further developed into a form of true and full democracy, namely the "communist society." Following this logic, the more complete the democracy, the democracy as a form of state will disappear, from a political democracy advancing into a non-political democracy, which is the communist management of a classless society.

Lenin's ideas of democracy as discussed above cover four basic aspects: (1) democracy is a concept of political power. Democracy refers to a form of organized political power, a political superstructure in the overall social architecture. However, democracy is not the only form of a state, but the opposite one to the autocratic state. (2) The form of democracy reflects a combination of democracy and dictatorship. Democracy simply refers to the democracy of the ruling class, which provides the rulers a degree of equality that can be achieved in power distribution, while dictatorship indicates the situation of the ruled, that is, the degree and extent of oppression of the ruling class over the ruled. Democracy and dictatorship are two indivisible facets of state power, just like two sides of the same coin. Therefore, democracy always implies class democracy, or the democracy of the ruling class, and there will never be a transcendent class or pure democracy. (3) There are two major principles of democracy. One is "popular sovereignty", that is, "to recognize the equal right to decide the state constitutions and to govern the state." This means that the supreme power of the state or government comes from and ultimately belongs to the people, who have the right to participate in the direct governance of state and exercise the right to vote, to supervise, and to impeach national leaders. The other principle is "people's equal rights", that is, to "recognize that all citizens are equal." This means that based on the class analysis, all citizens have equal rights in politics, economy, culture, and education. Only by realizing the principles of popular sovereignty and people's equal rights can citizens therefore win societal freedom. (4) Democracy is a historical event, a developmental product of human society and an inevitable development stage of human history. Since the state is the product of private ownership and social class, it will dissolve as the private ownership and class disappear at a certain stage of development. Democracy, as a transitional form of the state, is created and developed as the social class and the state are formed; and it will vanish as the social class and the state disappear.[121]

Lenin's systematic analysis of democratic centralism is a valuable contribution to the development of Marxist democratic theory. The Russian Social Democratic Labour Party (R.S.D.L.P.) was initially an organization of some individual and completely independent groups, including local or national proletariat groups. These groups were characterized by organizational dispersion and independence. This caused great difficulties to establish a unified party organization. In 1898, the Social Democratic Labour Party was established in the first party congress participated in by Social-Democratic organizations throughout Russia. A provision pertaining to the party's local committees is (local committees) have the right to refuse the demand from the Central Committee if their reasons are presented. Therefore, after the first Congress, the Marxist circles did not establish a truly unified organization. Soon after the Congress was adjourned, the Central Committee was sabotaged, while the local party organizations were still active. In 1899, Lenin, in order to solve this problem, proposed to completely clear out the constraint of local dispersion, and the local activities of the Social Democratic Party must be completely free, but they also must establish a uniform and therefore a centralized party.[122] In 1904, Lenin in his "One Step Forward, Two Steps Back" proposed the revolutionary idea of party as the leading organization of the proletariat.[123] He thinks that centralism is to resolve all local and minor organizational issues with a set of principles and is the only and principal idea and should be adhered to throughout the entire party constitution. In 1905, the Third Congress of the Russian Social Democratic Labour Party proposed to clearly define the limits of centralism in every organization and to fight for strict centralism. In 1906, the Fourth Congress confirmed democratic centralism as the principle of the organization of the party for the first time. Democratic centralism was constitutionalized as a fundamental principle of the party's organization system.

Democratic centralism also stresses the principle of democracy, for example, the Constitution enacted in the 1906 and 1907 Congresses specifies that the representatives of the Congress are elected and the Central Committee is elected by the Congress. The Party is organized according to the principles of democracy. That is to say, all the Party affairs are governed equally either directly by all Party members or through representatives; also, all the executive members, leaders, governing bodies of the Party are elected and required to report to the Party members; they can also be removed, and all Party members should be allowed to and be able to independently express their views on the controversial issues related to the entire organization when electing Party representatives.[124] After the victory of the October Revolution, the Eighth Congress in 1919 granted the Charter of the Russian Communist Party (Bolshevik), which clearly states: the highest leading body of the Party is the General Assembly, council or congress, and the Party General Assembly, council, or congress elects the Party committees, which are their executive organs, directing the daily work of the local organizations. And this further solidified the democratic principles of the party.

From the discussions above, democratic centralism contains two major aspects: democracy and centralism. Democracy refers to the principles of democracy by which the organization of the party at all levels is established; centralism means the overall centralized operation among all organizations. Democracy and centralism are complementary rather than mutually exclusive or mutually opposing. However, situated in the special circumstances of seeing the power struggle between Mensheviks and the Bolsheviks within the party, and coming into power at the time of civil war, Lenin placed more emphasis on centralization. His democratic centralism is sometimes simplified as centralism, or the word "centralism" is underlined to indicate its importance in this term.[125]

Even as centralism is upheld, Lenin himself still values the principles of democracy; especially after the October Revolution, he demonstrated a democratic leading style. Lenin, as Chairman of the Council of People's Commissars, "when the majority of the People's Commissars voted for the resolution he disagreed with, would either accept or (if the issue has significant principles implication) submit it to the highest governing level, which is the All Russia Central Executive Committee or the Politburo."[126] Since Lenin led the socialist construction for only seven years before his premature death, democratic centralism was still far from the stage of institutionalization, normalization, and standardization. After Lenin's era, the Russian communist party leaders abused democratic centralism, which was turned into authoritarian and exclusionary tools in the service of individual interests. Thus the whole political system became increasingly conservative and highly centralized. Eventually Gorbachev completely abandoned democratic centralism, which meant the collapse of the fundamental principle of Soviet Communist Party and state organization and finally led to the dissolution of the Party and the Soviet Union.

In summary, the essence of traditional socialist democracy theory is shown in the following aspects:[127]

1   Democracy is a form of the state. In the development of human history, democracy is the conclusion of all forms of the state. Although since the state first appeared in human society, there have been different forms of political systems and institutions, only a democratic system is the most complete as well as the ultimate one. That is, at different stages of development, there will be different democratic classes and varied degrees of democracy. People are involved in all aspects of democracy and only through a true democracy can people gain complete liberation. Communist society is a consortium, in which the development of liberty for all is conditioned by the development of individual freedom.[128] Any operation of public administration needs neither executive order nor authority, but totally depends on people's highly moral self-discipline and behavioral consciousness. When democracy does not have soil to exist, it will wither away with the disappearance of the state.

2   Socialist democracy features are "people oriented". Socialist democracy is a model of democracy that the majority of working people can enjoy. This

is because democracy is about class rule and is a concrete matter; as a concept, the essence of democracy is "power of the people", and "the people governing." Yet, in a class society, democracy is related to a certain ruling class. In the history of human society, the form of "democracy" changes as the ruling class changes. Therefore, there is no "absolute democracy" or "pure democracy" in the world. In a class society, democracy is associated with a certain ruling class. Marxists never forget to ask the question: Which class is the democracy for?[129] In world history, the bourgeois democratic republic is a huge step forward, but capitalist democracy is an incomplete, poor, and false democracy, which only provides service for the ownership of private property. Proletarian democracy is a new democratic model that inherits, sublates, and transcends capitalist democracy; it is a higher level of democracy, in which the majority of the mass working people is the ruling class and enjoys extensive democratic rights as well as the true benefits of civilization and democracy.

3   The socialist democracy is a dictatorship tool against the enemy. This is because democracy is a form of the state, a superstructure and a form of government. Democracy and the state have an inseparable relationship. As a form of the state, democracy is always and necessarily linked to the class dictatorship, embodying the nature of a state – the dictatorship of a certain class. Similar to any state, it exerts organized and systematic forces against somebodies. A socialist democracy means that the people own the power of government. Although the socialist democracy is more advanced than the capitalist democracy, it still retains the basic function of a state's hostile repression over the opposing classes. It can be said that democracy is the foundation of dictatorship; only when the ruling class or the people achieve full democracy can the government obtain effective political support and the necessary political power to effectively implement the dictatorship of the ruling class. Dictatorship also ensures the actualization of the people's democracy; only the autocratic control of the ruled and opposing power can fortify the political order of the ruling class and the realization of people's democracy.

4   Socialist democracy is based on public ownership of the means of production. This is because democracy is certainly a reflection of a certain economic base; its nature is subject to the constraints of the economy. We can say that the nature of ownership determines the nature of democracy. In a class society, the ruling power of any class is built on specific ownership, the nature of which determines whether the democracy is for the majority or just for a few. Thus, democracy is not only written in the declaration on the Constitution, but also requires material support. The liberal capitalist democracy is established in a situation where a few people own the means of production; private ownership determines the model of liberal democracy, a democracy enjoyed by a few capitalists. Socialist democracy is established on the basis of public ownership, and the mass working class is the owner of the means of production. Only established on public ownership, the democracy is truly for the most people, a genuine democracy.

5   Democratic centralism is the fundamental principle of the operations of socialist non-communist parties and state power. In 1905, democratic centralism was formally proposed in the separate congress of the Russian Social Democratic Labour Party held by the Mensheviks, indicating the opposing theories of centralism and democracy began to move toward a unified democratic centralism, and serve as the organizational principle of the proletarian party. In March 1906, Lenin proposed in his "A Tactical Platform for the Unity Congress of the R.S.D.L.P." that "the principle of democratic centralism in the Party is now universally recognized." In April, the principle of democratic centralism that all Party organizations are set up according to the principle of democratic centralism was first written into the Organizational Rules of the Russian Social Democratic Labour Party passed by the fourth congress. Lenin said: We have reached consensus on the principle of democratic centralism, on protecting the rights of the minority or of any loyal opponents, on the autonomy of each Party organization; in recognition of that, all the Party representatives must be elected, be required to make progress report, could be removed, and so on. We believe that the effective compliance with and sincere and consistent practices of these organizational principles can ensure that the party divide does not occur, to ensure ideological struggle within the party can and should work with strict organizational unity, and be completely consistent with the decision of the congress that everyone agreed upon.[130] With the establishment of the countries of socialist democracy, democratic centralism has gradually become the organizational principle of the socialist state governance. The Soviet Union had democratic centralism explicitly written into the Constitution not until 1977, while China already had it written into the first Constitution as early as in 1954.

History of theories and practices of Chinese socialist democracy

The socialist democracy theory of Marxism is a significant and practical guide in the development of China's socialist democratic politics. Under the guidance of this theory, and based on the lessons learned from the Soviet model of socialist democracy, the Communist Party of China gradually develops the theory and model of socialist democracy with Chinese characteristics based on the innovative practices in the actual situation in China.

The theory and model of Chinese socialist democracy is originated from the exploration during the New-Democratic Revolution period, such as the Soviet Red political power during the revolution at the Jinggang Mountain, the three thirds system in the northern Shanxi revolutionary base during the Anti-Japanese War, and the democratic practices of the people's government in the liberated areas during the liberation war; these are the early practices of China's socialist democracy. Particularly Mao Zedong's works, such as "On New Democracy" (1940), "On Coalition Government" (1945), and "On the People's Democratic Dictatorship" (1949), are the classical theories of the Chinese Communist Party in exploring China's new democratic practice.

The theory and model of China's socialist democracy are also derived from the relevant explorations during the primary stage of socialist construction, a period after the founding of the People's Republic of China up until the beginning of reform and opening up. The construction of New China's democracy basically follows the design done before the founding of New China and mainly concerned the implementation of the CPC-led multiparty coalition government and the first session of the National People's Congress held in 1954 when China's first Constitution was promulgated. Mao Zedong in his 1956 "On the Ten Major Relationships" and 1957 "On the Correct Handling of Contradictions Among the People" expounded his ideas about the construction of socialist democracy.

In these two historical periods, Mao Zedong made the most valuable contribution to the theory and practice of socialism with Chinese characteristics. He created the theory of the people's democratic dictatorship, scientifically illustrated the notions of state and government, and put forth the idea that people's democratic dictatorship is our state system while the system of the people's congress is the governing system; he explained the united front theory, and the theory of multiparty cooperation and political consultation under the leadership of the Communist Party, etc.; he led the development of New China's first Constitution and the rational allocation of state power; in particular, he proposed to promote democratic centralism from the guiding principle within the Party organizations to the basic principle of national governance. He also proposed the theory of regional ethnic autonomy, advocated to correctly handle problems among the people by employing democratic methods, and promoted "letting a hundred flowers bloom and a hundred schools of thought contend" to facilitate the progress of science and culture. His theories are the theoretical and institutional foundation of socialist democracy with Chinese characteristics.[131]

After 1957, China's democratic construction went on a long detour; the expansion of "the Anti-Rightist Movement" and "the Great Cultural Revolution" caused huge damage to the practice of socialist democracy in China. Especially, the national Constitution lost its authority during the Cultural Revolution, and the system of the people's congress came to a halt for up to eight years; multiparty cooperation and regional ethnic autonomy also took a tremendous hit. Powers of the government, on the one hand, were highly concentrated in the hands of a few leaders, yet on the other hand, were abused by some commanders of various movements and the so-called great democracy in society. These are grave lessons to take.

The theory of socialist democracy with Chinese characteristics and the preliminary model of this democracy were established during the thirty years after reform and opening up. Given the profound lessons of the Cultural Revolution, the supreme authority and legal status of the Constitution was the first to be recovered, and then the Party and the governing system of the state underwent a lot of reforms. Especially, life tenure was abolished, the intergenerational leadership transfer was gradually completed, and the collective leadership was achieved; the multiparty cooperation and political consultation under the leadership of the CPC, regional ethnic autonomy, and community-level democracy witnessed continued reforms and improvements; and the principle of "one country, two systems" was established.

The second generation of collective leadership, with Deng Xiaoping at the core, inherited the ideologies pertaining to the construction of socialist democracy developed by Mao Zedong and the first generation of collective leadership. With the actual practice of reform and opening up, as well as socialist modernization, these leaders actively explored and established a theoretical framework of socialist democracy with Chinese characteristics, which mainly concerns the relationship between democracy and socialism. Deng Xiaoping specifically points out that democracy is the essential element of socialism; without democracy, there will be no socialism and modernization. He actively promoted several major reforms of the Party and the state political system during this period and highly emphasized the legalization and institutionalization of democracy.[132]

The third generation of collective leadership, with Jiang Zemin at the core, explored further the concept of China's socialist democracy with Chinese characteristics. This generation of leaders continued to adhere to Deng Xiaoping Theory. While systematically presenting the important thought of Three Represents, they actively extended the representation and governance foundation of the Communist Party and specified a political reform roadmap for the unity of the leadership of the Party, the position of the people as masters of the country, and law-based governance.

After the 16th CPC National Congress in 2002, the fourth generation of collective leadership, with Hu Jintao as the General Secretary, adhered to Deng Xiaoping Theory and the important thought of Three Represents; this generation of leaders clearly put forward the Scientific Outlook on Development, attached great importance to socialist political progress, continued to promote the political system reform, and emphasized the people's democracy as the brilliant banner the Party always upholds and intra-Party democracy as the life of the Party. Especially the 18th CPC National Congress, for the first time, explicitly proposed to develop socialist consultative democracy with every effort.

Therefore, four generations of Chinese senior leaders paid close attention to the construction of a socialist democracy, about which they have had many discussions and have made valuable contributions to. Taken together, the main contents of the theory and practice of socialist democracy with Chinese characteristics are as follows:

1 Chinese socialist democracy is a democracy featuring collectivism. "The democracy Chinese people need today can only be the socialist democracy, known as the people's democracy, rather than a democracy of bourgeois individualism."[133] That is, China's democratic model is actually a continuation of socialist or collectivist democracy advocated by Marx and Lenin; the basic unit of democracy, which is every social class of the people (such as the working class, the peasantry, the urban petty bourgeoisie, and handicraftsmen during the early years of New China) rather than individuals, is regarded as one of the driving forces of history. Any individual struggle for democracy is also for class liberation, which means that according to the thoughts of collectivism or socialism, democracy is not a right obtained from the individual's endeavor but a right granted by the groups of society.

2   Democratic centralism and the combination of legislative and executive pow-
     ers are the operational principles. To embody the democratic concept of
     collectivism, the basic principle for Chinese socialist democracy is that the
     democracy must be tied to centralism; the overall system relies on the prin-
     ciple of democratic centralism to ensure the implementation of this collectivist
     democracy. Mao Zedong believes: "The organizational principle of the new-
     democratic state should be democratic centralism, with the people's congresses
     determining the major policies and electing the governments at the various
     levels. It is at once democratic and centralized, that is, centralized on the
     basis of democracy and democratic under centralized guidance."[134]

   After the victory of the new-democratic revolution, the "Common Programme of
the Chinese People's Political Consultative Conference" and later the new Chinese
Constitution explicitly set down that "all state power belongs to the people", which
embodies the principle of the people's democratic dictatorship of the state system.
At the same time the "democratic centralism", the organizational principle of the
Party, was incorporated into the national constitutional system and became the
organizational principle of the government. "Democratic centralism" horizontally
regulates the relationship among the People's Congress, people's government, people's court and people's procuratorate, and the army. Different from the separation
of powers in the Western government system, the People's Congress exemplifies
the principle of the combination of legislative and executive powers, namely, the
People's Congress represents the collective will of the people and controls all state
powers, with the right to produce national administrative, judicial, procuratorial,
and military organs, to whom these political powers are respectively delegated, and
whose work is overseen by the Congress. In the vertical power structure, the centralized control and unitary system see state power generally concentrated on the upper
to national or central levels, while regional ethnic autonomy is only implemented
in a few ethnic minority areas, and the special administrative region autonomy is
only conducted in Hong Kong and Macao, and will be in Taiwan in the future. On
the relationship between the Party and government, the Communist Party of China
also plays the role as the core of leadership; therefore, the Party is the key operator
of "democratic centralism" in the country's governance.[135]

3   The multiparty cooperation and political consultation are realized under the
     leadership of the Communist Party of China (CPC). To establish and implement
     multiparty cooperation and political consultation under the CPC leadership is
     the choice of history. The prominent feature of this system is the leadership of
     the CPC and the multiparty cooperation. The CPC is the ruling party, while
     the non-communist parties are not opposition parties or out-parties but the
     participating parties that participate in national affairs governance. The CPC
     is the political leader of the non-communist parties, that is, to provide guidance
     on political principles, political directions, and major policies, while the non-
     communist parties enjoy full political freedom and organizational independence.
     Political consultation is an important part of the system of multiparty

cooperation and political consultation under the leadership of the CPC, of which the Chinese People's Political Consultative Conference (CPPCC) is the platform and an important portal to carry out socialist democracy.

The above discussions suggest that the socialist democracy model with Chinese characteristics has taken shape, which is different from Western liberal democracy but an innovative exploration of Chinese style based on the lessons from the past socialist democratic models, such as the ideas and practice of collaboration and coalition of political powers among the revolutionary or progressive classes (the three thirds system during the Anti-Japanese War and the coalition government in the early years of the People's Republic of China). This model clearly highlights the effect of the democratic centralism principle in the construction of Party and national organizations; it does not adapt the one-party system or a multiparty system but implements the system of multiparty cooperation and political consultation under the leadership of the Communist Party of China. The system of the People's Congress is not structured as a bicameral but a unicameral legislature. As a big nation, China does not employ the federal model but adopts a unitary system of government together with the regional ethnic autonomy system and the practice of "one country, two systems", and actively promotes the socialist consultative democracy. It is worth noting that the Chinese characteristics that mark this democratic model are that they intentionally or naturally reflect the Chinese cultural tradition, as previous leaders value the populace, the organic integration of various political elements of democracy, the three-thirds system, coalition government, multiparty cooperation, regional ethnic autonomy and one country with two systems, and the integration of the leadership of the Party, the position of the people as masters of the country, and the law-based governance of the country. In fact, all of the above have embodied the essence of the "harmony and cooperation" thought. Therefore, we can say that the socialist democracy with Chinese characteristics meets the basic requirements of the democratic ideas of classic Marxist writers, and by combining the actual practices in China, this model to some extent reflects the impact of its excellent historical and cultural traditions, revealing certain attributes of a cooperative-harmonious democracy. This model of democracy was influential during the revolutionary war and sometime after the founding of the People's Republic of China, with positive effects in reality: such as amassing collective power for grand endeavors in resource-limited conditions as well as maintaining social stability that provides a good political environment for economic development in a certain period in history.

However, with the development of history, the change of society and the people's increasing awareness of their rights, this model of democracy obviously shows its limitations. In reality, as the Communist Party of China plays the role as the core of leadership, although the institutions of democracy within the Party have seen significant progress, there is still room for improvement; the role and the participation capability of the non-communist parties need to be further enhanced and expanded; the system of the People's Congress is not yet fully effective in governmental organizations at all levels. Therefore, the biggest limitation of this democratic model is that the current institutional arrangements tend to be overly centralized; the state power is too concentrated in the government, the Party, the major Party leaders, and the high-level organizations and their leaders. The consequences of excessive concentration of power are often serious, such as the unclear division of responsibilities between Party and government leads to unnecessary conflicts among organizations; the corrupt behavior of the leading cadres, even the senior cadres, is increasingly severe and has negative impact on the credibility of the Party and government; some major public policies due to insufficient public participation and scientific studies may lead to major mistakes that can trigger public discontent and frequent occurrence of civil unrest.

Therefore, although a preliminary model of Chinese socialist democracy has been formed and its relevant theoretical and institutional frameworks have been greatly improved, they are still not completely free from the constraint of traditional socialist democracy due to the over-emphasized centralization in general. Although it bears some characteristics of the "harmony and cooperation" thought, there is still much room for continuous improvement in this model's institutionalization, cooperation, coordination, integration, and combination of democratic strength and elements. Particularly, the current theory of socialist democracy with Chinese characteristics is still in need of the refined and conceptualized authentic Chinese elements. Therefore, advancing the theoretical research and practical exploration simultaneously is much needed, which calls for great determination and a clear direction in building the future Chinese democratic model. A long-term strategic consideration and arrangement as well as a scientific and practical top-level design are also indispensable in order to continue to carry out an even more daring and ambitious political reform and advancement.

Comparison between liberal democracy and traditional socialist democracy

Liberal democracy is essentially a capitalist democracy; the old socialist democracy, with more emphasis on collective values and centralized operation, can be referred to as traditional socialist democracy (mainly the socialist democracy in China before reform and opening up). Scholars of both democratic theories have made extreme critiques of each other's theory from different perspectives. Theorists of traditional socialist democracy (the previous socialist democracy) argue that liberal democracy is a false and incomplete bourgeois democracy. Liberal democracy theorists criticize traditional socialist democracy for being a synonym of autocracy. Given the development and practice of both theories, these extreme evaluations are not quite right. The comparison of these two democratic models should follow this principle: comparing reality to reality, or ideas to ideas.[136] We cannot simply say that liberal democracy is false, or that traditional socialist democracy is synonymous with autocracy.

This is because the democratic ideals cannot define democratic reality, and the reality of democracy is not equivalent to the ideal of democracy. Since democracy in any society is not isolated or abstract but has been developed in certain historical, social, and cultural contexts, it is constrained by the economic, political, and social reality. In fact, from the historical point of view, both democratic systems share a common origin and a common goal, namely, to liberate the people from the oppression of the old system that was based on strict social identity and to establish a political society of popular sovereignty to reflect the political and social foundations of democracy.[137] In terms of democratic practice, democratic politics remains an unfinished business for both liberal democracy and socialist democracy.

The comparison between the two shows that in terms of values, liberal democracy pays more attention to individual freedom, highlighting the inviolability of individual rights, while traditional socialist democracy focuses more on collective welfare, underscoring the right of development. In terms of government control, liberal democracy advocates the people's direct election in a party competition system to produce the Congress members, or the state head, or the executive head, the separation of executive, legislative, and judicial powers, and a high degree of local autonomy; traditional socialist democracy advocates indirect election to produce middle and senior deputies to the National People's Congress (NPC) and leaders of government institutions, a system with multiparty cooperation under the CPC leadership, the combination of legislative and executive powers, and centralized authority with regional autonomy. In terms of the relationship between the people and the government, liberal democracy highlights the people's will and rights against the government; in traditional socialist democracy, the people are more subject to government authority and centralized leadership. In terms of game model, liberal democracy and traditional socialist democracy both reflect non-cooperative game that features a zero-sum, meaning that the stubborn bigotry and the over-pursuit of either individual or collective values and interests prevent a cooperative win-win situation. In terms of regulation, liberal democracy values the rule of law the most, and then moral self-discipline; in the actual operation of traditional socialist democracy, virtue is often the main requirement.

The above comparison suggests that the future model for Chinese democracy should be a cooperative-harmonious socialist model that is positioned amid liberal democracy and traditional socialist democracy, and promotes the collaboration and harmonious relationship among the individuals, organizations, or between the individuals and organizations, or organizations and the state. See Figure 2.1.

These comparative analyses suggest that the biggest drawback of the current democratic model is the excessive concentration of power. Instead of taking China's existing democratic forms as a fixed pattern and being content with the

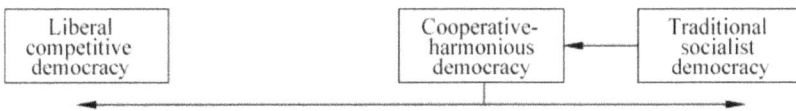

Figure 2.1 Democratic models classified by the degree of individual freedom versus organizational centralization

existing strength of democracy, we should truly recognize the gap in democratic practices and actively explore new models of democracy. We believe that in the process of democratization, the Chinese model of democracy needs to be freed from the restraint of excessive centralization and move toward a more democratic system that is focused on finding the right balance between centralization and democracy. The cooperative-harmonious model of democracy will be a possible alternative. A comparison of the features of liberal democracy, traditional socialist democracy, and cooperative-harmonious socialist democracy is shown in Table 2.1. In the following chapters, we will explore cooperative-harmonious

Table 2.1 Comparison of the characteristics of three different democratic models

Different models	Liberal competitive democracy	Traditional socialist democracy	Cooperative-harmonious democracy (harmony is the most valued; harmony yet diverse; cooperation and harmony)
Value basis	Individual – right of freedom	Groups – right of development	Harmonious correlation between individual liberty and collective interests
People and government	People have the right to rebel against the government	Authority of the government is protected	Cooperative coexistence (power from the people, people-oriented management; in service of the people, policy deliberation, trust, and cooperation)
Government and governance	Direct election Party competition Separation of powers Decentralization and/ or regional autonomy	Indirect election Multiparty cooperation under single-party leadership and combination of legislative and executive powers Centralized authority and local autonomy	Gradual implementation of direct and multi-candidate election Single-party leadership and full multiparty cooperation Combination of legislative and executive powers with necessary balance of power Centralization and modest local autonomy
Standard criterion	Rule of law – virtue	Rule of virtue- law based governance	Based on rule of law and virtue; law and virtue of equal importance

socialist democracy more in depth regarding its resources of traditional thought, the modern theoretical approaches, and the fundamental and practical issues in history and reality.

Notes

1 C. M. Sherover (ed.), *The Development of Democratic Idea*. New York: The New American Library Inc, 1974. Quoted from Zhang Minggui, *Theory of Democracy*. Taipei: Wu-Nan Book Inc., 2002, 41.

2 Some scholars believe that around 600 BC, the ancient Spartans already had legal regulations on civil assembly, while ancient Athens did not have it in law until 508 BC. Therefore, the ancient Spartans made an earlier contribution to democracy than the ancient Athens. See Simon Hornblower, "The Establishment and Development of Democracy in Ancient Greek", *Democracy: The Unfinished Journey*, John Dunn (ed.), & Lin Meng (trans.). Changchun: Jinlin People's Publish House, 2011, 1–20.

3 Thucydides (Greek), *History of the Peloponnesian War*, Xie Defeng (trans.). Beijing: The Commercial Press, 1960, 130.

4 Ancient Athenian citizenship is actually very restricted; only Athenian men were eligible for active citizenship, while slaves, women, and immigrants were not eligible. In the early years, only the nobles or property owners were the recognized citizens of a city-state. It was with the development of democracy that the middle and lower class of the populace were gradually awarded citizenship.

5 George Holland Sabine, *A History of Political Theory*, Hinsdale, IL: Dryden Press, 4th edition, 1973. Also see its Chinese version, Vol. 1, Sheng Kuiyang & Cui Miaoyin (trans.). Beijing: The Commercial Press, 1986, 34.

6 Reference to the Athenian democracy mainly from John Thorley (UK), *Athenian Democracy*, Wang Qiongshu (trans.). Shanghai: Shanghai Translation Publishing House, 2001. Lin Meng, "On the Classical and Modern Democracies – A Historical Perspective of the Study of Democracy", PhD. Diss., School of Government of Peking University, 2001.

7 Jennifer Tolbert Roberts, *Athens on Trial: The Antidemocratic Tradition in Western Thought*. Princeton, NJ: Princeton University Press, 1994. Quoted from Lin Meng, "On the Classical and Modern Democracies – A Historical Perspective of the Study of Democracy", PhD. Diss., School of Government of Peking University, 2001.

8 Jiang Yihua, *Ways to Freedom and Democracy*. Taipei: Linking Publishing Company, 2001, 27.

9 J. S. Mill (UK), *Considerations on Representative Government*, Wang Xun (trans.). Beijing: The Commercial Press, 1992.

10 In fact, Schumpeter's classical democracy includes the democracy of ancient Athens as well as the utilitarianism popular in the eighteenth century. The utilitarian idea of democracy still stresses common good and the will of the people, which are the same as the democracy of ancient Athens emphasizes. Therefore, some of Schumpeter's critique of the utilitarian democracy can be extended to the ancient Athenian democracy. Also supported by the research findings of behaviorism, elitism, and empiricism, other liberal democracy theorists through critical review of the democracy of ancient Athens obtained conclusions that endorse liberal democracy. That is, from the theoretical perspective, liberal democracy is developed from the criticism of ancient Athenian democracy.

11 In addition to Schumpeter, the well-known theorists of liberal competitive democracy are, among others, Lasswell, Sartori, and Dahl. The analysis here focusing on Schumpeter's theory is mainly because it is the oldest and influential theory of liberal competition democracy, which has impact on the later theorists.

12 Joseph Schumpeter (US), *Capitalism, Socialism and Democracy*, Wu Liangjian (trans.). Beijing: The Commercial Press, 2000, 395–396.

13 David Held (UK), *Models of Democracy*, Yan Jirong, Fang Xiangqin, Bai Pinghao & Qin Liyan (trans.). Beijing: Central Compilation and Translation Press, 1998.

14 Joseph Schumpeter (US), *Capitalism, Socialism and Democracy*, Wu Liangjian (trans.). Beijing: The Commercial Press, 2000, 370–378. David Held (UK), *Models of Democracy*, Yan Jirong, Fang Xiangqin, Bai Pinghao & Qin Liyan (trans.). Beijing: Central Compilation and Translation Press, 1998, 223–248.

15 Joseph Schumpeter (US), *Capitalism, Socialism and Democracy*, Wu Liangjian (trans.). Beijing: The Commercial Press, 2000, 378.

16 Joseph Schumpeter (US), *Capitalism, Socialism and Democracy*, Wu Liangjian (trans.). Beijing: The Commercial Press, 2000, 380–389.

17 David Held (UK), *Models of Democracy*, Yan Jirong, Fang Xiangqin, Bai Pinghao & Qin Liyan (trans.). Beijing: Central Compilation and Translation Press, 1998, 237.

18 Giovanni Sartori (US), *Theory of Democracy Revisited*, Feng Keli & Yan Kewen (trans.). Beijing: Oriental Press, 1998, 172.

19 Joseph Schumpeter, *Capitalism, Socialism and Democracy*, Wu Liangjian (trans.). Beijing: Commercial Press, 2000.

20 David Held (UK), *Models of Democracy*, Yan Jirong, Fang Xiangqin, Bai Pinghao & Qin Liyan (trans.). Beijing: Central Compilation and Translation Press, 1998, 225.

21 Giovanni Sartori (US), *Theory of Democracy Revisited*, Feng Keli & Yan Kewen (trans.). Beijing: Oriental Press, 1998, 171.

22 Giovanni Sartori (US), *Theory of Democracy Revisited*, Feng Keli & Yan Kewen (trans.). Beijing: Oriental Press, 1998, 186.

23 David Held (UK), *Models of Democracy*, Yan Jirong, Fang Xiangqin, Bai Pinghao & Qin Liyan (trans.). Beijing: Central Compilation and Translation Press, 1998, 217.

24 David Held (UK), *Models of Democracy*, Yan Jirong, Fang Xiangqin, Bai Pinghao & Qin Liyan (trans.). Beijing: Central Compilation and Translation Press, 1998, 227.

25 Le Bon believes that the people are incapable of reasoning, with no judgment of the critical spirit, irritable, and prone to exaggerate sentiments. Therefore, to mobilize the mass participation of the people will lead to a totalitarian movement. See Gustave Le Bon (France), *The Crowd – Study of the Popular Mind*, Feng Keli (trans). Beijing: Central Compilation and Translation Press, 2000. Serge Moscovici (France), *L'age des foules*, Xu Liemin (trans.). Nanjing: Jiangsu People's Publishing House, 2003.

26 Joseph Schumpeter (US), *Capitalism, Socialism and Democracy*, Wu Liangjian (trans.). Beijing: The Commercial Press, 2000, 379.

27 Joseph Schumpeter (US), *Capitalism, Socialism and Democracy*, Wu Liangjian (trans.). Beijing: The Commercial Press, 2000, 386.

28 Joseph Schumpeter (US), *Capitalism, Socialism and Democracy*, Wu Liangjian (trans.). Beijing: The Commercial Press, 2000, 386.

29 Joseph Schumpeter (US), *Capitalism, Socialism and Democracy*, Wu Liangjian (trans.). Beijing: The Commercial Press, 2000, 416.

30 Joseph Schumpeter (US), *Capitalism, Socialism and Democracy*, Wu Liangjian (trans.). Beijing: The Commercial Press, 2000, 416.

31 Robert A. Dahl (US), *Who Governs? Democracy and Power in an American City*, Fan Chunhui & Zhang Yu (trans.). Nanjing: Jiangsu People's Publishing House, 2001.

32 David Held (UK), *Models of Democracy*, Yan Jirong, Fang Xiangqin, Bai Pinghao & Qin Liyan (trans.). Beijing: Central Compilation and Translation Press, 1998, 266.

33 Carole Pateman (US), *Participation and Democratic Theory*, Chen Yao (trans.). Shanghai: Shanghai People's Publishing House, 2006, 14.

34 David Held (UK), *Models of Democracy*, Yan Jirong, Fang Xiangqin, Bai Pinghao & Qin Liyan (trans.). Beijing: Central Compilation and Translation Press, 1998, 266.

35 This new version of the "democratic myth" and standardized criteria are no longer the ideals of classical democracy that uphold "popular sovereignty", but an actual operation of the current system of the Western government, a method that "some individuals

acquire the power to decide by means of a competitive struggle for the people's vote". The value of classical democracy has vanished. The liberal competitive democracy itself emphasizes the foundation of experiences and the principle of neutral value, but in fact has become the form in which the Western democracies defend their current status.

36 Giovanni Sartori (US), *Theory of Democracy Revisited*, Feng Keli & Yan Kewen (trans.). Beijing: Oriental Press, 1998, 43.
37 Carole Pateman (US), *Participation and Democratic Theory*, Chen Yao (trans.). Shanghai: Shanghai People's Publishing House, 2006, 13.
38 Giovanni Sartori (US), *Theory of Democracy Revisited*, Feng Keli & Yan Kewen (trans.). Beijing: Oriental Press, 1998, 14.
39 Giovanni Sartori (US), *Theory of Democracy Revisited*, Feng Keli & Yan Kewen (trans.). Beijing: Oriental Press, 1998, 9.
40 Feng Keli, *Ulysses Tied Himself*. Nanjing: Jiangsu People's Publishing House, 2004, 110–125.
41 Giovanni Sartori (US), *Theory of Democracy Revisited*, Feng Keli & Yan Kewen (trans.). Beijing: Oriental Press, 1998, 8.
42 Feng Keli, *Ulysses Tied Himself*. Nanjing: Jiangsu People's Publishing House, 2004, 110–125.
43 Cited in Guo Qiuyong, *Three Contemporary Democratic Theories*. Taipei: Linking Publishing Company, 2001, 85; also see Benjamin Barber (US), *Strong Democracy*, Peng Bin & Wu Runzhou (trans.). Changchun: Jilin People's Publishing House, 2006, 115–144.
44 Arend Lijphart, "Unequal Participation: Democracy's Unresolved Dilemma", *The American Political Science Review*, 1997, 91(1): 1–14.
45 As a criterion to determine if a government form is a democratic system.
46 Cited in Guo Qiuyong, *Three Contemporary Democratic Theories*. Taipei: Linking Publishing Company, 2001, 86; also see Benjamin Barber (US), *Strong Democracy*, Peng Bin & Wu Runzhou (trans.). Changchun: Jilin People's Publishing House, 2006, Chapter 8–9.
47 Guo Qiuyong, *Three Contemporary Democratic Theories*. Beijing: New Star Press, 2006, 86.
48 Arendt believes that bureaucracy is autocracy without a dictator, the most ruthless form of government in the history of mankind and in a well-developed bureaucratic system, we can't find any person who can discuss, protest, or impose (the people) power. See Jiang Yihua, *Ways to Freedom and Democracy*. Taipei: Linking Publishing Company, 2001, 216–220.
49 Joseph Schumpeter (USA), *Capitalism, Socialism and Democracy*, Wu Liangjian (trans.). Beijing: The Commercial Press, 2000.
50 John Stuart Mill (UK), *Representative Government*, Wang Xuan (trans.). Beijing: The Commercial Press, 1997, 26. Peng Huai'en, *The Theory of Elitist Democracy*. Taipei: Cheng Chung Book Co., Ltd, 1983, 83.
51 Peng Huai'en, *The Theory of Elitist Democracy*. Taipei: Cheng Chung Book Co., Ltd, 1983, 83.
52 Carole Pateman (US), *Participation and Democratic Theory*, Chen Yao (trans.). Shanghai: Shanghai People's Publishing House, 2006, 97–104.
53 David Held (UK), *Models of Democracy*, Yan Jirong, Fang Xiangqin, Bai Pinghao & Qin Liyan (trans.). Beijing: Central Compilation and Translation Press, 1998, 337–338.
54 Guo Qiuyong, *Three Contemporary Democratic Theories*. Taipei: Linking Publishing Company, 2001, 119.
55 Jiang Yihua, *Ways to Freedom and Democracy*. Taipei: Linking Publishing Company, 2001, 217–219.
56 Carole Pateman (US), Preface to *Participation and Democratic Theory*, Chen Yao (trans.). Shanghai: Shanghai People's Publishing House, 2006, 8–12.

57 Jiang Yihua, *Ways to Freedom and Democracy*. Taipei: Linking Publishing Company, 2001, 220.
58 Benjamin Barber (US), *Strong Democracy*, Peng Bin & Wu Runzhou (trans.). Changchun: Jilin People's Publishing House, 2006, 311–344.
59 Jiang Yihua, *Ways to Freedom and Democracy*. Taipei: Linking Publishing Company, 2001, 225.
60 Giovanni Sartori (US), *Theory of Democracy Revisited*, Feng Keli & Yan Kewen (trans.). Beijing: Oriental Press, 1998, 127.
61 Carole Pateman (US), *Participation and Democratic Theory*, Chen Yao (trans.). Shanghai: Shanghai People's Publishing House, 2006, 39.
62 Benjamin Barber (US), *Strong Democracy*, Peng Bin & Wu Runzhou (trans.). Changchun: Jilin People's Publishing House, 2006, 306–312.
63 Carole Pateman (US), *Participation and Democratic Theory*, Chen Yao (trans.). Shanghai: Shanghai People's Publishing House, 2006, 29.
64 Giovanni Sartori (US), *Theory of Democracy Revisited*, Feng Keli & Yan Kewen (trans.). Beijing: Oriental Press, 1998, 172.
65 David Held (UK), *Models of Democracy*, Yan Jirong, Fang Xiangqin, Bai Pinghao & Qin Liyan (trans.). Beijing: Central Compilation and Translation Press, 1998, 338–339.
66 Benjamin Barber (US), Preface to *Strong Democracy* (1984 edition), Peng Bin & Wu Runzhou (trans.). Changchun: Jilin People's Publishing House, 2006, 1–7.
67 John S. Dryzek (Australia), *Deliberative Democracy and Beyond: Liberals, Critics, Contestations*. Ding Kaijie, Xu Zengyang, Xu Lili, Yan Jian, Wang Jin, Zhai Qijiang & Xu Huan (trans.). Beijing: Central Compilation and Translation Press, 2006, 1.
68 Chambers Simone, "Constitutional Referendums and Democratic Deliberation", *Referendum Democracy: Citizens, Elites, and Deliberation in Referendum Campaigns*, M. Mendelsohn & A. Parkin (eds.). New York: Palgrave, 2001, 231–255. Cited in Lin Guoming and Chen Dongsheng, *Referendum and Deliberative Democracy*. Taipei: Seminar of the Referendum Democracy in Taiwan, 2004.
69 Jon Elster, "Introduction", *Deliberative Democracy*, Jon Elster (ed.). Cambridge: Cambridge University Press, 1998, 1.
70 David Held (UK), *Models of Democracy*, Yan Jirong, Fang Xiangqin, Bai Pinghao & Qin Liyan (trans.). Beijing: Central Compilation and Translation Press, 1998, 19. George Holland Sabine (US), *A History of Political Theory*, Vol. 1, Sheng Kuiyang & Cui Miaoyin (trans.). Beijing: The Commercial Press, 1986, 34–40.
71 Amy Gutmann and DenisThompson, *Why Deliberative Democracy?* Princeton: Princeton University Press, 2004, 8.
72 Cohen's works is Deliberation and Democratic Legitimacy. See James Bohman and William Rehg (US) (eds.), *Deliberative Democracy: Essays on Reason and Politics*, Chen Jiagang, Lin Li, Yu Hongqiang, Zhou Yanhui, Hao Wenjie, Xu Xingjian, Wang Wenzi, Chen Zhigang, Xu Huan & Zhang Caimei (trans.) Beijing: Central Compilation and Translation Press, 2006, 50–67.
73 Rawls (US), *Political Liberalism*, Wan Junren (trans.). Nanjing: Yilin Press, 2000. Habermas (Germany), *Between Facts and Norms-Contributions to a Discourse Theory of Law and Democracy*, Tong Shijun (trans.). Beijing: SDX Joint Publishing Company, 2003.
74 John S. Dryzek (Australia), *Deliberative Democracy and beyond: Liberals, Critics, Contestations*, Ding Kaijie (trans.). Beijing: Central Compilation and Translation Press, 2006, 2.
75 Deliberative democracy and participatory democracy share the same background, as they both originated from the criticism of liberal competitive democracy. In terms of their relationship, some consider that deliberative democracy is a kind of participatory democracy; while some think that deliberative democracy and participatory democracy are two different forms of democracy. We believe that deliberative democracy can be

regarded as a democratic form under the participatory democratic paradigm; because deliberative democracy has two main aspects: (1) emphasizing the participation, namely all citizens affected by the public policy have the right to participate in decision making; (2) emphasizing deliberation, namely public policy should be formulated based on public deliberation; any supporting or opposing opinion toward the public policy should provide acceptable reasons. In terms of their nature, participation is still the key component of deliberative democracy, but participatory democracy takes one step further by proposing a specific way to participate: through public deliberation. It can be said that deliberative democracy is the development and deepening of participatory democracy; the means of participation is also to achieve participation. The essence of deliberative democracy is still participatory democracy, so it can be included in the category of participatory democracy.

76 Giovanni Sartori (US), *Theory of Democracy Revisited*, Feng Keli & Yan Kewen (trans.). Beijing: Oriental Press, 1998, 171.

77 Wang Xingfu, *The Path to the Democratic Discourse – A Dialogue with Habermas*. Chengdu: Sichuan People's Publishing House, 2002, 119.

78 David Held (UK), *Models of Democracy*, Yan Jirong, Fang Xiangqin, Bai Pinghao & Qin Liyan (trans.). Beijing: Central Compilation and Translation Press, 1998, 244.

79 Ronald Dworkin (US), *Sovereign Virtue: The Theory and Practice of Equality*, Feng Keli (trans.). Nanjing: Jiangsu People's Publishing House, 2003, 414.

80 Robert Dahl (US), *On Democracy*, Li Baiguang & Lin Meng (trans.). Beijing: The Commercial Press, 1999, 79.

81 Habermas (Germany), *Between Facts and Norms-Contributions to a Discourse Theory of Law and Democracy*, Tong Shijun (trans.). Beijing: SDX Joint Publishing Company, 2003, 392–393.

82 Xu Guoxian, "Deliberative Democracy and Democratic Imagination", *Theories of Political Science*, 2000, 13: 62.

83 James D. Fearon (US), "Deliberation as Discussion", *Deliberative Democracy*, Chen Jiagang (ed.), & Wang Wenyu (trans.). Shanghai: Shanghai Joint Publishing Company, 2004, 10.

84 Xu Guoxian, "Deliberative Democracy and Democratic Imagination", *Theories of Political Science*, 2000, 13: 64.

85 Xu Guoxian, "Deliberative Democracy and Democratic Imagination", *Theories of Political Science*, 2000, 13: 78.

86 John Ferejohn, "Instituting Deliberative Democracy", *Deliberative Democracy*, Chen Jiagang (ed.), & Li Jing (trans.). Shanghai: Shanghai Joint Publishing Company, 2004, 192.

87 "Enlarged mentality" is Ahrendt's English translation of a view found in Kant's *Critique of Judgment*. Kant believes that if a man puts aside subjective opinion and personal interest to reflect on his own judgment from the standpoint of the others, it is the "expansion of the mind" or the "expansion of thinking mode". See Kant, *Critique of Judgment*, Deng Xiaomang (trans.). Beijing: People's Publishing House, 2002. Hannah Arendt, *Lectures on Kant's Political Philosophy*. Chicago: University of Chicago Press, 1989.

88 Xu Guoxian, "Deliberative Democracy and Democratic Imagination", *Theories of Political Science*, 2000, 13: 78.

89 Long before the formation of rational choice theory, Schumpeter had approached democracy theory with economics analysis by comparing politics to the market. Therefore, the renowned economists Paul Samuelson and William Nordhaus in their famous *Economics* (sixteenth edition) argue that Schumpeter created the rational choice theory in his *Capitalism, Socialism and Democracy*. Downs, the famous theorist of rational choice, also believes that Schumpeter's profound analysis of democracy is their source of inspiration. (See Green and Shapiro (US), *Pathologies of Rational Choice Theory*, Xu Xianglin & Yuan Ruijun (trans.). Guilin: Guangxi Normal University Press,

2004, 2. Fang Fuqian, *Public Choice Theory – Economics of Politics*. Beijing: China Renmin University Press, 2000, 1–4) These evidence that although Schumpeter did not explicitly state his democratic ideas as rational choice theory, his theory embodies the characteristics of aggregate democracy. It is just because the rational choice theory was not yet formed back then, there is no new generalization for his theory of democracy.

90 Anthony Downs (US), *An Economic Theory of Democracy*, Yao Yang & Hao Yuqing (trans.). Shanghai: Shanghai People's Publishing House, 2005.

91 Ronald Dworkin (US), *Sovereign Virtue: The Theory and Practice of Equality*, Feng Keli (trans.), Nanjing: Jiangsu People's Publishing House, 2003, 414.

92 Lisle Carter, Jr. (US), "Can Democracy Save Us?", *Deliberative Democracy*, Chen Jiagang (ed.). Shanghai: Shanghai Joint Publishing Company, 2004, 289.

93 James D. Fearon (US), "Deliberation as Discussion", *Deliberative Democracy*, Chen Jiagang (ed.), & Wang Wenyu (trans.). Shanghai: Shanghai Joint Publishing Company, 2004, 1.

94 Maeve Cooke (Ireland), "Five Arguments for Deliberative Democracy", *Deliberative Democracy*, Chen Jiagang (ed.), & Wang Wenyu (trans.). Shanghai: Shanghai Joint Publishing Company, 2004, 43.

95 Chen Jiagang, "Deliberative Democracy: Revival and Transcendence of the Democratic Paradigm", *Deliberative Democracy*, Chen Jiagang (ed.). Shanghai: Shanghai Joint Publishing Company, 2004, 2.

96 Amy Gutmann and Dennis Thompson, *Why Deliberative Democracy?* Princeton: Princeton University Press, 2004, 7.

97 Jon Elster, "Introduction", *Deliberative Democracy*, Jon Elster (ed.). Cambridge: Cambridge University Press,1998, 8.

98 Amy Gutmann and Dennis Thompson, *Why Deliberative Democracy?* Princeton: Princeton University Press, 2004, 3–7. Lin Huowang, "Deliberative Democracy and Citizens", *NTU Philosophy Review*, 2005, 29: 99–114. Amy Gutmann and Dennis Thompson (US), "Why Deliberative Democracy?", *Deliberative Democracy*, Tan Huosheng (ed.), & Tan Huosheng (trans.). Nanjing: Jiangsu People's Publishing House, 2007, 4–7.

99 Seyla Benhabib, "Toward a Deliberative Model of Democracy Legitimacy", *Democracy and Difference*, S. Benhabib (ed.). Princeton: Princeton University Press, 1996. Cited in Xu Guoxian, "Deliberative Democracy and Democratic Imagination", *Theories of Political Science*, 2000, 13: 68.

100 Amy Gutmann and Dennis Thompson, *Why Deliberative Democracy?* Princeton: Princeton University Press, 2004, 80.

101 Matthew Festenstein (UK), "Deliberation, Citizenship and Identity", *Democracy as Public Deliberation: New Perspectives*, Maurizio Passerin d'Entrèves (ed.), & Wang Yingjin, Yuan Lin, Liu Xianglin, Lin Yunjuan, Wang Wenyu & Wang Yongbing (trans.). Beijing: Central Compilation and Translation Press, 2006, 43–48. Chen Jiagang, "Deliberative Democracy: Concepts, Elements and Values", *Journal of Tianjin Municipal Party School*, 2005, 3: 56.

102 Jack Knight and James Johnson, "Aggregation and Deliberation: On the Possibility of Democratic Legitimacy", *Political Theory*, 1994, 22(2): 277–296. Cited in Chen Junhong, "NIMBY Syndrome, Technocracy and Democratic Deliberation", *Journal of Soochow University*, 1999, 10: 120–122.

103 Lynn M. Sanders, "Against Deliberation", *Political Theory*, 1997, 25(3): 349.

104 Some scholars question this inclusiveness: "deliberation is a means to achieve political decisions with a unique advantage its competitors wants. However, if all the means of political interaction become deliberative, then the uniqueness may not exist." See David Miller (US), "Is Deliberative Democracy Unfair to Disadvantaged Groups?", *Democracy as Public Deliberation: New Perspectives*, Maurizio Passerin d'Entrèves (ed.), & Wang Yingjin, Yuan Lin, Liu Xianglin, Lin Yunjuan, Wang Wenyu & Wang Yongbing (trans.). Beijing: Central Compilation and Translation Press, 2006, 146.

105 Chen Junhong, "NIMBY Syndrome, Technocracy and Democratic Deliberation", *Journal of Soochow University*, 1999, 10: 122.
106 Central Compilation and Translation Bureau (ed.), *Completed Works of Marx and Engels*, Vol. 7. Beijing: People's Publishing House, 1995, 304.
107 Li Tieying, *On Democracy*. Beijing: China Social Sciences Press, 2001, 68.
108 *Completed Works of Marx and Engels*, Vol. 3. Beijing: People's Publishing House, 1995, 39–40.
109 Lin Shangli, "Constructing Democratic Political Logic – Based on Marx's Theory of Democracy", *Academics*, 2011, 5.
110 Central Compilation and Translation Bureau (ed.), *Completed Works of Marx and Engels*, Vol. 7. Beijing: People's Publishing House, 1995, 589.
111 *Selected Works of Marx and Engels*, Vol. 3. Beijing: People's Publishing House, 1995, 95.
112 *Selected Works of Marx and Engels*, Vol. 3. Beijing: People's Publishing House, 1995, 58.
113 *Selected Works of Marx and Engels*, Vol. 3. Beijing: People's Publishing House, 1995, 13.
114 *Completed Works of Marx and Engels*, Vol. 3. Beijing: People's Publishing House, 1995, 41.
115 Takis Fotopoulos (Greek), *The Multidimensional Crisis and Inclusive Democracy*, Li Hong (trans.). Jinan: Shandong University Press, 2012.
116 Yu Keping, "Marx on the General Concept, Universal Values and Common Form of Democracy", *Marxism and Reality*, 2007, 3.
117 Central Compilation and Translation Bureau (ed.), *Selected Works of Lenin*, Vol. 3. Beijing: People's Publishing House, 1995, 201.
118 Central Compilation and Translation Bureau (ed.), *Selected Works of Lenin*, Vol. 3. Beijing: People's Publishing House, 1995, 191.
119 Central Compilation and Translation Bureau (ed.), *Selected Works of Lenin*, Vol. 3. Beijing: People's Publishing House, 1995, 724.
120 Central Compilation and Translation Bureau (ed.), *Selected Works of Lenin*, Vol. 42. Beijing: People's Publishing House, 1987, 172.
121 Nie Yunlin, "Is Lenin's Concept of Democracy not Comprehensive?", *Chinese Forum*, 1982, 6.
122 *Complete Works of Lenin*, Vol. 4. Beijing: People's Publishing House, 1984, 167.
123 *Complete Works of Lenin*, Vol. 8. Beijing: People's Publishing House, 1986, 236.
124 *Complete Works of Lenin*, Vol. 14. Beijing: People's Publishing House, 1987, 249.
125 Researches on democratic centralism see Wang Tongchang and Chen Chen, "Review of Recent Researches on Democratic Centralism", *Lingnan Journal*, 2011, 1.
126 Ye Weiping, *Western Lenin Studies*. Beijing: China Renmin University Press, 1991.
127 Wang Huning (ed.), *Logic of Politics-Principles of Marxist Political Science*. Shanghai: Shanghai People's Publishing House, 1998.
128 *Selected Works of Marx and Engels*, Vol. 1. Beijing: People's Publishing House, 1995, 294.
129 *Selected Works of Lenin*, Vol. 3. Beijing: People's Publishing House, 1995, 593.
130 *Complete Works of Lenin*, Vol. 12. Beijing: People's Publishing House, 1987, 362.
131 Li Tieying, "Several Issues on the Theories of Democracy", *Social Sciences in China*, 2001, 1.
132 Li Tieying, "Several Issues on the Theories of Democracy", *Social Sciences in China*, 2001, 1.
133 *Selected Works of Deng Xiaoping*, Vol. 2. Beijing: People's Publishing House, 1995, 175.
134 *Selected Works of Mao Zedong*, Vol. 3. Beijing: People's Publishing House, 1991, 1057.
135 Pu Xingzu (ed.), *Political System of the People's Republic of China*. Shanghai: Shanghai People's Publishing House, 1999, 608.
136 Giovanni Sartori (US), *Theory of Democracy Revisited*, Feng Keli & Yan Kewen (trans.). Beijing: Oriental Press, 1998.
137 Katou Takashi (Japan), *Politics and People*, Tang Shiqi (trans.). Beijing: Peking University Press, 2003.

3 Chinese traditional thought and cooperative-harmonious democracy

Cooperative-harmonious (*he-he*) democracy is essentially about he_1 (合) and he_2 (和). He_1 denotes cooperation, integration and fusion, and he_2 harmony, reconciliation and peace. The purpose of cooperative-harmonious democracy is to integrate benefits, resolve conflicts, dissolve confrontation, and create a socialistic democratic political landscape characterized by win-win cooperation, rapport and solidarity, and harmonious governance. The model of cooperative-harmonious democracy is, first of all, rooted in Chinese political reality. It gives adequate consideration to the merits of Chinese traditional "people-oriented" and "harmony and cooperation" thought, incorporates the experience and lessons related to democratic politics in other countries, and represents an innovation of institutional design from the perspective of the modern cooperative game theory.

Definition of cooperative-harmonious democracy

On the basis of drawing upon different democratic models, China should seek in the future a cooperative, harmonious model of democracy, an intermediate form between liberal democracy and traditional socialist democracy, which conduces to the mutual cooperation and harmonious co-progressiveness between and among individuals, organizations, and the state. Such a model does not entirely rule out competition; nor is it likely to avert conflict. Instead, it promotes cooperation to seek harmony so that all parties concerned can communicate and negotiate thoroughly, thus form mutual trust and common ground, and on this basis resolve conflicts of interest and differences in opinions. Cooperative-harmonious democracy is built, more than anything else, on Chinese collective values, traditional people-oriented and "harmony and cooperation" thought, and the socialist core values such as social justice; however, it does not rule out individualistic values but tries to seek a balance between collective and individual interests, then transcend the existing traditional socialist model of democracy, and through open, full communication, negotiation, and cooperation on equal terms, ultimately attain the harmonious development of political democracy and society in the truest sense.

On the one hand, cooperative-harmonious democracy transcends the thinking that the constants and game are in a purely competitive relationship in the perspective of individual rationality and proposes cooperation and a win-win relationship

on the basis of giving play to each other's advantages; on the other hand, it transcends the extreme utilitarianism of individuals and asserts that common interests
should be safeguarded and common values maintained while respecting individual
independence. Therefore, though cooperative-harmonious democracy and deliberative democracy are similar in that both pursue cooperation, the former embodies
the wish to throw doubts on liberal democracy in terms of philosophical thinking and values; on the basis of making up the deficiencies of traditional socialist
democracy, it breaks the stereotype that liberal democracy and traditional socialist democracy are antithetical to each other and advocates a model of democracy
characterized by the win-win cooperation and harmonious co-governance between
the individual, the collective, and all the other political forces.

Value of Chinese traditional thought

People-oriented thought: the direct origin of cooperative-harmonious democracy

Definition of people-oriented thought

People-oriented thought can be said to have a long history in China, lasting from
the Shang and Zhou dynasties all the way to the Ming and Qing dynasties. Though
it experienced ups and downs, it has never been interrupted. As one of the most
important sources of traditional Chinese culture, it mainly contains the following
four aspects: the people are the foundation of the state; popular opinion should be
observed and respected; the people's livelihood should be cared for; and the people
have the right of rebellion and revolution.[1]

1   The people are the foundation of the state. The people are fundamental to
    the state. Without the people, the state does not exist, not to mention state
    leaders. "The people are the foundation of the state; if the foundation is
    solid, the state is peaceful."[2] Mencius, the epitome of Chinese people-oriented
    thought in ancient times, asserted that "the common people are the most
    valuable; next is the state; the ruler is insignificant[3]; and he wrote, "Jie and
    Zhou lost the dominion over the land because they lost their people; they
    lost their people because they lost their support. The way to obtain the
    dominion over the state is: win over the people by winning their hearts."[4]
    Based on this view, it can be inferred that the state is collectively owned
    by the people. For instance, "When the Great Way (*da-dao*) is practiced,
    the state is jointly owned (by and for the people)."[5] "The state does not
    belong to one man, but to all the people"[6] – it is a principle of people-
    oriented thought that the people are fundamental to the state.

In the Ming and Qing dynasties, Chinese people-oriented thought culminated in
influence, with scholars like Huang Zongxi, Wang Fuzhi, and Gu Yanwu as representatives. Prior to Huang Zongxi, Chinese people-oriented thought stressed the

importance of the people from the standpoint of the feudal ruling class. Huang Zongxi targets his criticism at the supreme feudal ruler, exposing the crimes committed by the monarch who saw the land under Heaven as his private property. He argued that the monarch was nothing but an "autocrat" – "Now, the people under Heaven despise their monarch. They see him as enemy and name him autocrat. He surely deserves it."[7] He also condemns the autocratic monarch as "traitor to the people". Huang Zongxi advocates the overthrow of family-governing architecture and the establishment of public-ruling architecture. It can be seen that Huang is challenging the absolute monarchy and shows the germ of modern democratic thoughts.

2   Popular opinion should be observed and respected. The people are the foundation of the state. Following this logic, state rulers should observe popular opinion – "Heaven will certainly fulfill the people's wishes." Thus, "if a man is happy about what the people are happy about, then the people are happy about what he is happy about; if he is concerned about the people's concerns, then the people are concerned about his concerns. I have not seen a man who shares the weal and woe of the people under Heaven and has not become the monarch."[8] "If he lets the people under Heaven happy, they will reward him with happiness; if he causes them woe, their woes will be extended to him."[9] The rulers should voluntarily consider working "for the people" and observe and respect popular opinion. Only in this way can they win the people's support.

3   The people's livelihood should be cared for. The fundamental importance attached to the people and the attention paid to popular opinion should be materialized by the care for the people's livelihood. If the people live in destitution, the state will eventually cease to be a state. "The state is like the human body. The monarch is like the head, ministers are like legs and arms, and the people hands and feet. If the people feel troubled, the upper classes should not pursue pleasure; if the people are hungry, they should not have gourmet meals; if the people are cold, they should not dress adequately. It is against etiquette to be barefooted and wear the crown with tassels. Hence, if the feet feel cold, the heart feels bitter and if the people are poor, the state is harmed."[10] "If the monarch treats his people in the Ideal Way, the people will support him with the Best Things. If he grants his grace, they work harder. Such a virtuous cycle of payment and reward always stands and complies with principle."[11]

4   The people have the right of rebellion and revolution. If the ruler of a state does not watch popular opinion or care for the people's livelihood, then the people have the right to overthrow the tyrannical rule and carry out a revolution. As the *Book of Changes* writes, "The revolutions launched respectively by King Tang of Shang dynasty and King Wu of Zhou dynasty are in line with Heaven's and the people's will!"

After the Opium Wars, people-oriented thought evolved into different schools. Under the influence of Western culture, Kang Youwei set forth his theory that the monarch and people are consubstantial; Tan Sitong believes that the monarch is the least important and the people are the most important; and Yan Fu holds that the people should be the true master. All of them attach fundamental importance to the people under the premise of maintaining monarchy. In contrast, Sun Yat-sen advocates democratic republicanism, which is a new type of people-oriented thought based on the democratic republic system.

A comparison between people-oriented thought and democracy

Western democracy originated from the mode of governance adopted by ancient Greek city-states. Initially the word democracy meant "people's governance". During that time, in Athens, all citizens were directly engaged in public affairs of their city-state. Later, as the nation-state came into being and expanded in territory, direct democracy evolved into representative democracy. After comparing people-oriented thought and Western democracy, Liang Qichao said, "The governance advocated by Abraham Lincoln of the United States can be summarized by three prepositional phrases: 'of the people', 'by the people' and 'for the people'. Chinese theories have expounded the meanings of 'of' and 'for' but the exposition of 'by' is seldom heard. In other words, the state is of the people as a whole and for the people's common interests, hence there is governance. The Chinese of earlier times had seen this clearly and believed in it firmly. However, as for the assertion that all governance should be implemented *by* the people, they have not investigated its methodology or even acknowledged the theory. They merely say that the people are the foundation of the state and should be cared for; however, the power to practice governance falls beyond the reach of the people. How much effect can this populism excluding franchise have? Isn't this the greatest weakness of Chinese theories on governance?"[12]

Xiao Gongquan also wrote, "Since the pre-Qin times, there have been plenty of political commentators who uphold the idea that 'the people are the foundation of the state'; however, in modern terms, they generally only know that the state should be 'for the people' and 'of the people', but are unaware that it should be implemented 'by the people'. Moreover, Mencius and his followers hold that 'the man who wins the support of common people becomes the monarch' and expound the essence of 'government of the people' through their belief that the 'autocrat' deserves to be overthrown or killed. However, now that they have no theory relevant to 'government by the people', they lack the methodology for application. During the past two millennia, their theory has been reduced to empty talk in principle. Besides, those posterior to Mencius mostly uphold only 'government for the people'. They do not know about 'government of the people', not to mention 'government by the people'. Though the people are the purpose of government, the monarch is eternally the major agent of government. The thinkers have failed to accomplish their people-oriented ideals. Autocracy has been an undeniable fact. Therefore, ancient people-oriented thoughts are immature thoughts on civil rights; there is a considerable distance between them and modern concepts of democratic governance."[13]

That is to say, if democracy is defined as 'government of the people, by the people, and for the people', then in terms of practice, Western democracy focuses on 'government by the people' and Westerners believe that true democracy means the people can manage their own affairs. However, in a political system built on representative democracy, the people cannot run every affair. Now that the people cannot be directly engaged in governance, the electoral system which elects representatives becomes an inevitable choice. That is, they elect and entrust representatives to govern the state on their behalf. However, the people have the final right to change their representatives. This is 'government by the people'. Though ancient Chinese people-oriented thought stresses the fundamental importance of the people, they came into being under the rule of the monarch. The monarch had the power to govern. And this is "governance by the monarch". Constrained by traditional people-oriented thought, the monarch who governed should, in the same way, care for the people's welfare; "he should like what the people like and dislike what the people dislike".[14] His administrative measures attached more importance to "government for the people"; people-oriented thought could be elevated to "benevolent governance". However, in so doing, he deprived the people of the right to participate in public affairs and governance. Therefore, "Mencius' assertion that the people are of the greatest importance is different from the concept of civil rights in modern times. They should not be confused. In brief, the thought of civil rights is certain to entail government for the people, of the people, and by the people. Hence, the people are not only the target of government and the principal part of the state, but also have the right to participate in state affairs of their own will. By this measure, Mencius allegedly attaches the greatest importance to the people's advocates, in essence, 'government for the people' for the purpose of 'government of the people'; neither the principle nor institution of 'government by the people' is heard of."[15]

Modern value of people-oriented thought and its transformation

People-oriented thought is different from the concept of democracy. However, stressing that "the state does not belong to one man, but to all the people"[16] partly reflects the view that state power originates from the people. It can be said that though traditional Chinese people-oriented thought does not set store by government by the people, it stresses government of the people to some extent and attaches more importance to government for the people. This is consistent with some ideas of democracy at least in terms of practice. However, ancient Chinese people-oriented thought is, after all, a theory rather than an institutional arrangement. Therefore, it must work together with the rule of virtue. The people had to pray for a sage monarch and worthy ministers before people-oriented thought could be implemented. When the rule of virtue and people-oriented thought were coupled, there was certainly enlightened politics; when the rule of virtue and people-oriented thought did not come together, enlightened politics would definitely be absent. This was the source of the tragic recurrent cycle of peace and chaos haunting China over the past thousands of years. To cut loose the knot, the ancient people-oriented thought must be pushed further forward so that it could be materialized in the institutional design. That is, it must incorporate the Western concept of government by the people.[17]

The existing socialist democracy in China not only owes its origin to the basic theory of Marxism, but also has inherited traditional Chinese people-oriented thought. Therefore, in terms of government for the people, it is more in line with democracy. For instance, the concept of "wield power for the people, establish the emotional bond with the people and pursue benefits for the people" and many other views have all reflected this point. It can be said that liberal democracy and traditional socialist democracy are not significantly different in terms of government of the people. Both identify themselves with the concept of popular sovereignty. Of course, their understandings of "the people" are different. Whereas "the people" in the framework of the former refers to the people in a general sense, the latter, as stressed, refers to the ruling classes or classes that may contribute to the progress of history. Moreover, the two types of democracy are also different conceptually. Liberal democracy puts more emphasis upon the authorization of the people via election and a certain degree of government by the people but neglects the pursuit of government for the people; traditional Chinese socialist democracy is more concerned with the historical authorization of the people and a certain degree of government by the people, and attaches more importance to government for the people. The primary purpose of cooperative-harmonious democracy is to combine the two types. Government for the people remains the direct origin of cooperative-harmonious democracy; we cannot discard it and only pursue government of the people and by the people in form. The crux of the issue is: can cooperative-harmonious democracy find the best balance between government for the people and by the people? Whether we can resolve this issue depends on whether we can continue to explore the resources of Chinese culture and innovate in the design of a democratic system.

"Harmony and cooperation" thought: a traditional guide to cooperative-harmonious democracy

Meaning of "harmony and cooperation" thought

In such ancient books as *The Book of Documents*, *The Book of Changes* and *The Discourses of the State*, "harmony" is first discussed. "He (Yao the Great) gave play to Great Virtue and established close ties among the Nine Ethnic Groups. After the Nine Ethnic Groups were in harmony, he formed a clear picture of the affairs in the 100 Clans. After they were made clear, he meditated peace between the 10,000 States. So the people communicated changes and were on friendly terms."[18] "The Way of Heaven always changes. Everything has their nature or destiny. Then harmony is formed. This is auspicious."[19] "From Harmony different things are born. If they are the same, harmony will not continue. Combine many different things together and attain an equilibrium – this is called harmony. Harmony enables everything to thrive and grow. If the same things are gathered together, they will lose out."[20] On the basis of Chinese harmony culture in earlier times, Confucius founded a school of philosophy with harmony as a cardinal value, which was continued and developed by Mencius and Xunzi. If we investigate Confucian texts, we may find a recurrent key word – "harmony."[21]

It can be said that, as far as core values are concerned, "the cardinal spirit of Chinese culture lies in harmony and moderateness."[22] Under the principle of "all-embracing harmony", the relations between Heaven and man, between people, and between people and things are mutually conducive and beneficial so that they can all be natural and harmonious. Confucius, who grasped the principle stresses "the Middle" and harmony and set them into the Chinese's psychology architecture.[23] Confucius says, "Harmony is precious."[24] Mencius writes, "Opportunities of time vouchsafed by Heaven are not equal to advantages of situation afforded by the Earth, and advantages of situation afforded by the Earth are not equal to the union arising from the accord of Men."[25] Thus, harmony can be said to be the highest state of politics and a basic manifestation of peace and prosperity. The core value of traditional Chinese culture is harmony: between human and Heaven, between people, and between human and Earth.

As for the premises for "harmony and cooperation" thought, in traditional Chinese culture, the pursuit of harmony is not without principle or unconditional. The first priority is harmony without uniformity. Uniformity means that everything is the same. Uniform things are not enduring. "If they are the same, harmony will not continue." "If the same things are gathered together, they will lose out."[26] Thus, difference or diversity has been a premise for harmony in traditional Chinese culture. Difference means conflict. Harmony means "there are both conflict and fusion. Without conflict, there will be no fusion; without fusion, no conflict."[27] The purpose is to let the conflicting parties coexist and benefit each other while retaining each other's independence. Therefore, harmony in traditional Chinese culture allows difference and demands harmony so that, by complementing each other, things can attain the state of contradictory unity, or the state of harmony.

On the operational level, harmony means that different things should be combined together and harmonized. That is, things are blended and complement others' weaknesses with their strengths so as to achieve the best result.[28] When the concept of harmony is applied to social relations, it entails requirements on communication, consultation, mutual trust, consensus, cooperation, etc.

Besides, Prof. Zhang Liwen wrote a book titled *Theory of Harmony and Cooperation* to expound traditional Chinese "harmony and cooperation" thought. Here in our discussion about democracy we adopt the term cooperative-harmonious rather than harmonious-cooperative. What we are stressing is that we wish to attain harmony via cooperation. So "cooperation" is placed before harmony.

Modern value and significance of "harmony and cooperation" thought

Culture is the soil of institution. On the one hand, Chinese democratic politics must draw nutrients from indigenous traditional harmony culture; on the other hand, traditional Chinese harmony culture can only gain a new lease on life in politics in the body of a democratic system. Otherwise, it will be imprisoned in the realm of values. Only by combining these two aspects can we create a Chinese model of democracy.

As a matter of fact, some Western scholars have also pondered the possibility of marriage between Chinese harmony culture and democracy. Prof. Suzanne Ogden of Harvard University believes that under the influence of the harmony culture, in ancient times, the Chinese people had valued negotiation and consultation as a way to achieve consensus on certain issues. Therefore, the Chinese have a different understanding of democracy from Westerners; they attach more importance to equality and deliberation and see deliberation as a way to achieve consensus. Thus deliberation has played a significant role in the development of Chinese democratic politics and served as an important cornerstone in building Chinese democracy, because as a way to achieve consensus, the emphasis on deliberation in the Chinese political system is an important weapon for the development of democratic politics. In China, "harmony" is a treasure of its traditional political thoughts, as well as an important target of the Chinese political system in achieving consensuses and maintaining order.[29] China lays more emphasis on deliberation and harmony. Chinese harmony culture influences China's choice of model of democracy, and China will not follow the path of liberal democracy in the course of democratization. Perhaps someday in the future, the mode of democracy with Chinese characteristics will be more influential than Western liberal democracy.[30] It can thus be said that traditional Chinese culture with harmony as its core concept provides good ideological sources and cultural background for the establishment of cooperative-harmonious democracy.

David Hall and Roger Thomas Ames also believe that China will certainly realize a certain form of democracy, but not necessary modeled on liberal democracy. They think that China's future model of democracy will definitely bear the marks of traditional Chinese culture and assert that "saying no to traditional Chinese culture is saying no to the best hope of Chinese democracy". In their opinion, China has been and will always be a communitarian society; the realization of democracy for the Chinese calls for a form of democracy suiting this type of society, which runs counter to the predominant model of liberal democracy in the Western countries. Therefore, we can also say that the core traditions of the model of liberal democracy do not suit the actual situation of China. Traditional Confucianism contains some elements of democracy that can be transformed into a model of democracy suitable for communitarian society; they can be used to construct a vigorous, orderly model of democracy permeated with humanity. It can not only fit with the consciousness of traditional Chinese communitarian society, but also avoid the maladies of liberal democracy built on individual rights.[31] The challenges China will face in future in democratization are how to clearly enunciate the communalist model of democracy and whether this model can be consistent with the deepest-seated values of traditional Chinese society, particularly with traditional Chinese harmony culture. This has, no doubt, provided possibilities and inspirations for the construction of Chinese cooperative-harmonious democracy.

Limitations of Chinese traditional thought

Of course, traditional Chinese culture has its limitations that cannot be ignored. A widespread view is that no modern system of democracy has been conceived in traditional Chinese ideology. Our traditional culture pursues and values "harmony and cooperation" philosophy, emphasizing harmony. However, in *The Twenty-Four Histories* we can see many fierce struggles. In the political sphere, the harmony culture means the quest of harmony of the social and political order. Benevolent governance and rule by virtue were demanded to ensure its realization. However, in ancient Chinese society, sage monarchs were rare and "benevolent governance" was hard to come by. Therefore, in the ancient times of autocratic monarchy, though emphasis was laid upon the importance of harmony in the cultural sphere, ruthless struggle had filled the political world. In this lies an obvious paradox. In other words, the traditional Chinese philosophy of harmony indeed has considerable limitations.

This is mainly because, in the ancient Chinese autocratic system, there was a concept of a zero-sum game and a winner-take-all rule. That is, the supreme power was unitary and could not be divided; the marginal utility value of power was always growing. The greater power one had, the more power he could get. This value conception of power and the cruel form of struggle have been the tradition from the ancient Chinese history of autocracy that has been the most far-reaching and most harmful; they are also the great barrier to the progress of the Chinese political system.[32] Therefore, thought harmony, as the soul of traditional Chinese political theories, reflects political ideals; it has, to a great extent, a utopian nature and inherent flaws in terms of governance strategies and design of ideal politics.[33]

Contemporary Chinese democratic politics must overcome the limitations of traditional Chinese thought in the course of its development, discard the winner-take-all concept, break the stereotype that power can be unchecked, and build the mechanism for democratic participation, deliberation, negotiation, and compromise. Only in this way can China ensure that the concept of harmony will be truly applied in political practice. Therefore, in the development of Chinese democratic politics, the critical question that demands the great mental exertion to resolve is how to stress the concept of harmony and build the principle and mechanism for effectively resolving political conflict and struggle, promote power sharing, checking, and cooperation, thereby advancing the harmonious, stable, and orderly development of society.

Summary

Even though democracy is among the universal values, the democratic system is subject to the influence of national traditional culture when constructed in different states. If a state's historical and cultural traditions are disregarded, it will be hard for its reform of the democratic system to achieve the desired effect. Similarly, traditional Chinese culture is valuable in that it provides the foundation for the development of Chinese democratic politics, which cannot be built in the vacuum of Chinese traditions. Of course we should not reject democracy, but should understand that democracy is a product in the Western historical context. Thus it has a series of values rooted in its traditional culture. China has its own system of cultural values. Therefore, it has a bearing on the development of Chinese democratic politics by exploring the question of how to innovate democracy, particularly some democratic systems, and integrate it into the system of traditional Chinese culture (i.e., people oriented and Harmony), and draw nutrition from it.

Notes

1 Zhou Daoji, "Analysis and Review of Chinese People-Oriented Thought", *Selected Reportage IV*, Institute of the Three Principles of the People, Academia Sinica, 1985.
2 The Songs of the Five Sons, History of Xia, *The Book of Documents*, see Ruan Yuan (Qing Dynasty), *Thirteen Classics Explanatory Notes and Commentaries* (photostat copy), Beijing: The Chinese Publishing House, 1980, 156.
3 Mencius and his followers, "Jin Xin (part II), Mencius", see Ruan Yuan (Qing Dynasty), *Thirteen Classics Explanatory Notes and Commentaries* (photostat copy), Beijing: The Chinese Publishing House, 1980, 2774.
4 Mencius and his followers, "Li Lou (part I), Mencius", see Ruan Yuan (Qing Dynasty), *Thirteen Classics Explanatory Notes and Commentaries* (photostat copy), Beijing: The Chinese Publishing House, 1980, 2721.
5 Dai Sheng, "Li Yun, *The Book of Rites"*, see Ruan Yuan (Qing Dynasty), *Thirteen Classics Explanatory Notes and Commentaries* (photostat copy), Beijing: The Chinese Publishing House, 1980, 1414.
6 Lü Buwei, *"Valuing Justice, First Lunar Month of Spring"*, see Lü Buwei, The Annals of Lü Buwei (photostat copy), Shanghai: Shanghai Chinese Classics Publishing House, 1989, 14.
7 Huang Zongxi, "On the Monarch", see Huang Zongxi, Waiting for the Dawn, Beijing: The Chinese Publishing House, 1985, 2.
8 Mencius and his followers, "King Hui of Liang II, Mencius", see Ruan Yuan (Qing Dynasty), *Thirteen Classics Explanatory Notes and Commentaries* (photostat copy), Beijing: The Chinese Publishing House, 1980, 2675.
9 Xun Yue, "Miscellanies (part I)", see Xun Yue, On Lessons, Shanghai: Shanghai Chinese Classics Publishing House, 1990, 23-30.
10 Xun Yue, "Zheng Ti", see Xun Yue, On Lessons, Shanghai: Shanghai Chinese Classics Publishing House, 1990, 8.
11 *Ibid.*
12 Liang Qichao, *History of Pre-Qin Thoughts on Politics.* Shanghai: Oriental Publishing House, 1996, 5.
13 Xiao Gongquan, *A Chinese History of Political Thoughts.* Shenyang: Liaoning Education Press, 1998, 865.
14 Dai Sheng, "Great Learning, The Book of Rites", see Ruan Yuan (Qing Dynasty), *Thirteen Classics Explanatory Notes and Commentaries* (photostat copy), Beijing: The Chinese Publishing House, 1980, 1675.
15 Xiao Gongquan, *A Chinese History of Political Thoughts.* Shenyang: Liaoning Education Press, 1998, 87.
16 Valuing Justice, First Lunar Month of Spring (part I), *The Annals of Lü Buwei.*
17 Jin Yaoji, *A History of Chinese People-Oriented Thought.* Beijing: Law Press, 2008, 21–22.
18 The Chapter on Yao, The Book on Yu Xia, *The Book of Documents.*
19 Ji Chang, "Qian Tuan (Heaven), The Book of Changes", see Ruan Yuan (Qing Dynasty), *Thirteen Classics Explanatory Notes and Commentaries* (photostat copy), Beijing: The Chinese Publishing House, 1980, 14.

20 Zuo Qiuming, "Discourse of Zheng", see Zuo Qiuming, The Discourses of the State, Shang Xuefeng & Xia Dekao (trans.), Beijing: The Chinese Publishing House, 2007.

21 Gan Chunsong, *Confucianism Institutionalized*. Shanghai: Shanghai People's Publishing House, 2006, 22.

22 Liang Shuming, *Eastern and Western Culture and Their Philosophy*. Beijing: Commercial Press, 2004.

23 Tan Yuanping, *Chinese Political Thoughts: Confucianism and Democratization*. Taipei: Yang-Chih Book Co., Ltd., 2004.

24 Confucius and his followers, "Xue Er, The Analects of Confucius", see Ruan Yuan (Qing Dynasty), *Thirteen Classics Explanatory Notes and Commentaries* (photostat copy), Beijing: The Chinese Publishing House, 1980, 2458.

25 Mencius and his followers, "Gongsun Chou, *Mencius*", see Ruan Yuan (Qing Dynasty), *Thirteen Classics Explanatory Notes and Commentaries* (photostat copy), Beijing: The Chinese Publishing House, 1980, 2693.

26 Liu Zehua, *A History of Chinese Political Thoughts (Pre-Qin Times)*. Hangzhou: Zhejiang University Press, 1996, 45.

27 Zhang Liwen, *Theory of Cooperation and Harmony: A Conception of the Twenty-first Century Cultural Strategy*. Beijing: China Renmin University Press, 2006, 10.

28 Liu Zehua, *A History of Chinese Political Thoughts (Pre-Qin Times)*. Hangzhou: Zhejiang University Press, 1996, 45.

29 Suzanne Ogden, *Inklings of Democracy in China*. Cambridge: Harvard University Press, 2002, 257.

30 Suzanne Ogden, *Inklings of Democracy in China*. Cambridge: Harvard University Press, 2002.

31 David Hall and Roger Thomas Ames, *The Democracy of the Dead: Dewey, Confucius, and the Hope for Democracy in China*. Nanjing: Jiangsu People's Press, 2004.

32 Tang Tsou, *Twentieth Century Chinese Politics: From the Perspectives of Macro-history and Micromechanism Analysis*. Hong Kong: Oxford University Press, 1994, 204–265.

33 Pi Weibing, *The Pursuit in Political Ethics as Reflected in "Harmony Is Precious" – A Study of Pre-Qin Confucian Political Ethics in the Context of "Harmony"*. Shanghai: Shanghai Joint Publishing Company, 2007, 206.

4 Cooperative game theory and cooperative-harmonious democracy[1]

The model of cooperative-harmonious democracy is essentially about cooperation and harmony. Its purpose is to combine individual demands into collective interests by means of cooperation and reconciliation and attain a situation of democratic politics characterized by win-win cooperation, rapport and solidarity, and harmonious governance. "Harmony and cooperation" thought and cooperative game theory are intrinsically homogeneous. Therefore, modern cooperative game theory can serve as a powerful tool for analyzing and understanding the basic concepts of cooperative-harmonious democracy, the approach to building cooperative-harmonious democracy, possible system architecture, etc.

Basic idea and concept of a cooperative game

Basic idea of a cooperative game

Game theory has become a critical or even indispensable analytical tool for social scientists. As a matter of fact, so far, widely applied and discussed is one of the two branches of game theory, i.e., non-cooperative game theory, which presumes that participants cannot form an effective agreement or act in a coordinated fashion. Each participant, according to the information he or she has acquired, acts alone in pursuit of maximal self-interest. The other branch of game theory, parallel to the non-cooperative branch, is cooperative game theory, which believes that participants can reach agreement through negotiation and thus can act in a coordinated way to achieve the optimal outcome. Therefore, the major difference between cooperative and non-cooperative game theories lies in whether the participants can reach a binding agreement and act together. If they can, it is cooperative game, if they cannot, non-cooperative game. From the philosophical perspective, cooperative and non-cooperative games are different in terms of philosophical basis. Whereas non-cooperative game stresses individual rationality and researches what outcome individual rationality may bring about, cooperative game emphasizes collective rationality and discusses how to realize collective rationality and work out proper distribution schemes.

Cooperative game theory has formed a complete system. Its fundamental concepts include coalition and coalition value, the set of distributions, and the concepts of solution (core, Shapley value), etc. Here, we will introduce them briefly.

Basic concepts of cooperative game

Coalition and coalition value

The coalition refers to a collection of all or some participants who can act in a specific fashion according to an agreement they have reached. If *I* stands for the set of all the game participants, all or some of the participants are likely to form a coalition – let it be *S*. For every coalition, there exists a total attainable value, which is referred to as the value of coalition in cooperative game theory.[2] We can use V(•) to refer to the value of a certain coalition. Then V(•) is a function from the coalition set to the domain. If V(S) refers to the total value that Coalition S can achieve in the game, then V(I) refers to the total value achievable by the coalition formed by all the participants. We call the coalition of all the participants the Great Coalition and a coalition formed by some participants Partial Coalition.

Set of distributions and Side payment system

The value of a coalition determines the total value a coalition can achieve. How to distribute the total value among the participants is a very important question. If the distribution is not fair, the coalition will face the risk of ill organization or disintegration. All feasible distribution schemes form the set of distributions. Cooperative game theory believes that such distribution schemes have at least two features: first, individual rationality. That is to say, every participant can get more than if he is out of the coalition; second, collective rationality. That is, for a coalition, the total of all participants' individual gains cannot be less than the value of the coalition. In other words, the total value the coalition achieves must all be distributed. Otherwise, it will not be accepted by the group.

The range of the set of feasible distribution schemes is related to the cost of side payment. Side payment refers to the value transfer between individuals. If the cost of side payment is zero, distributions can be adjusted among individual participants without any cost. A distribution scheme is feasible as long as it fulfills the conditions of individual and collective rationality. Given the circumstances of a coalition, that is, if its achievable total value is set, the range of feasible schemes of distributions among its members is determined by the cost of side payment. The lower the cost, the greater the range. The higher the cost, the smaller the range.

Solution of game (core and Shapley value)

The set of distributions of a game may comprise many schemes. Which of them are the best or the likeliest to be realized? The distribution schemes that can be seen as the most feasible are referred to as the solutions of cooperative game. Obviously, which distribution schemes are identified as the solution has some bearing on the standards for "the most feasible". Therefore, there are some different concepts of solutions in the framework of cooperative game, including core, nucleolus, kernel, Shapley value, etc. Here only the concept of core – the most basic concept of solution – will be discussed.

The core can be thus defined: it is a set of distribution schemes, for each of which no group can reduce any member's individual gains and increase any other's by forming a new coalition. It is evident that the distribution schemes in the core can be accepted by any coalition, because no coalition can set forth a scheme more advantageous to itself. Furthermore, if the currently adopted distribution scheme is in the core, no new coalition will be formed; otherwise, the distribution scheme and the coalition that adopts it are unstable and a new coalition is bound to emerge, because participants can improve their situations by forming it.

Understanding democracy from the perspective of cooperative game

Democracy as the mechanism for social cooperation

In human society, the demand for collective coordination and joint action is certain to arise in production and communication. To realize collective coordination and joint action, there must be institutional arrangements of a certain form. Democracy is a type of institutional arrangement. Through some specific rules, programs, or means, it processes individuals' wills into collective will. Therefore, we can think of democracy as an institutional arrangement made to achieve social cooperation.

As an institutional arrangement of collective choice, democracy has basic functions at two levels: first, now that democracy is intended to realize some collective will, there exists the question of how to make the collective will realized better reflect the people's will. This question often manifests itself in how to make public authority better serve the people. We can refer to the function in this aspect as fulfilling collective rationality. In this lies the essence of democracy. Secondly, when different preferences exist within the people, how can different personal preferences be combined into unified collective will? Because the commonest form of democracy is to let the majority make the decision, we can thus call it "majority rule". In this the meaning of the democratic process lies. If we see democracy as an institutional arrangement to bring about collective cooperation, then because cooperative game is concerned with the formation of the all-encompassing coalition, it is evident that from the perspective of cooperative game, the former function of democracy is more important and key to assessing the quality of democracy. Moreover, the latter function should serve the first function, because the opinion of the majority represents the collective opinion and the minority is subordinate to the majority. This is nothing but the way to form the coalition and to fulfill collective rationality. Therefore, when we discuss democracy, we should look at substantive democracy, or the fulfillment of collective rationality; procedural democracy, or how to fulfill collective rationality, should be at the service of substantive democracy.

If we look on democracy as a means to collective cooperation, then the cooperative surplus underlies whether democracy can run stably. The cooperative surplus means that the total value that different interest groups can achieve via a certain means of cooperation is greater than the sum of the values they can achieve separately. In terms of cooperative game, if the set of all participants I is divided into two parts S_1 and S_2 then $V(I) \geq V(S_1) + V(S_2)$. Otherwise, the cooperation of the coalition will be groundless. $V(I) - [V(S_1) + V(S_2)]$ is the extra part S_1 and S_2 can gain from their cooperation, i.e., cooperative surplus. If the means to the cooperation across the great coalition is the institutional form of a type of democracy, then the interest groups concerned can achieve a cooperative surplus through this form of democracy. Everyone will support and actively participate in the construction and operation of this form. Otherwise, some interest groups will resist it, which will make it difficult for the democracy to operate.

Besides, whether democracy can operate healthily is also closely related to how it compares with alternative forms of expressing collective will. The above-mentioned values of partial coalitions, $V(S_1)$ and $V(S_2)$, embody the concept of the opportunity cost. That is, they depend on the returns S_1 and S_2 can achieve outside the democratic system if they enforce their respective collective wills by other means. The values are, of course, influenced by such factors as other (exogenous) social systems and the interest groups' other resource advantages. For example, if some interest group takes possession of more violence resources (say, military strengths) and the social and legal environment makes it possible to resort to violent means, the interest group is likely to resolve conflicts through violence. Other alternative means of expressing collective will may possibly include lobbying, bribery, street movements, etc. The more cooperative surplus the groups can get in the democratic system, the less effective the alternative means become and the more likely the democratic mechanism is to become the main channel for the expression of collective will. Otherwise, it is more likely to be replaced by other alternative means.

Side payment system and social compensation system

As an institutional arrangement made to achieve social cooperation, democracy may not benefit all the groups in the same way. There are often winners and losers. The compensational institutional arrangement targeting losers is called the social compensation mechanism. From the perspective of cooperative game, the mechanism is equivalent to the side payment system.

The social compensation mechanism can effectively improve the fulfillment of collective rationality fulfilled during the democratic process. Imagine a society consisting of three persons. Now there are two types of institutional arrangements A and B. Under system A, the total social value that can be achieved is 8 and the personal gains for the three persons are respectively (6, 1, 1); under system B, the total social value that can be achieved is 5 and the personal gains for the three persons are respectively (1, 2, 2). By the majority-rule principle, obviously scheme B rather than system A will be selected. However, under the circumstance that there exists costless side payment, according to the principle of cooperative game, scheme A will be selected by the coalition of the three persons, because while the total value remains unchanged, scheme A can be modified into a better distribution scheme Pareto-dominating scheme B, i.e., (2, 3, 3), via side payment. It can be seen that side payment can effectively improve the fulfillment of collective rationality. If side payment is not costless, this argument stands all the same. Suppose the total value of all the alternative schemes is V(S) and the cost of side payment is C(S) – then all the schemes whose total value is less than Max{V(S)–C(S)} are not likely to exist in the core. Thus the lower the cost of side payment is, the more likely collective rationality is effectively fulfilled. Therefore, an efficient social compensation mechanism makes it more likely for the optimal collective scheme to appear in the core of cooperative game and for the best scheme to be adopted via a democratic process.

In real society, the effectiveness of the social compensation mechanism tends to depend on the negotiation and coordination mechanism among different interest groups. Therefore, the more easily the groups can negotiate and the lower the cost is for them to trade interests, the more likely collective rationality can be fulfilled via a democratic process and the more effectively democracy can operate. In real society, the costs for extensive negotiation and bargaining are often so high that the mechanism for direct negotiation between the parties concerned can hardly be depended on to achieve effective side payment. However, when direct negotiation is in difficulty, the organization is a mechanism that can effectively achieve side payment.

The organization can build a cross-subject and cross-time transfer payment mechanism by combining different subjects together. If a side payment contract cannot be reached through direct negotiation, the organization can make a promise, which works effectively, that in order to fulfill collective rationality, the group whose interests are harmed on this subject will be complemented on another subject later on. In the case of the above-stated example, if there will be two more subjects besides the subject in question, the alternative distribution schemes A and B are respectively (1, 6, 1) and (2, 1, 2), (1, 1, 6) and (2, 2, 1), in the absence of side payment, by the majority-rule principle, scheme B will be selected on all the three subjects. In this way, the total gains of the three persons are (5, 5, 5). However, if there exists an organization which can effectively coordinate their choices, scheme A will be opted for every time so that their total gains will be (8, 8, 8). Obviously, the organization's coordination can effectively improve collective rationality. In the meantime, the organization can serve as a platform, through which trust can be built among insiders or interest groups so that they may have direct negotiation, which creates conditions for reaching transfer payment contracts. Thus by lowering the cost of reaching and implementing side payment contracts, collective rationality can be improved.

Anticipation of enduring equal opportunities for success and the stability of the democratic system

The key to whether a democratic system can operate in a stable and orderly fashion lies in whether all the interest groups have relatively equal anticipation of success when they picture the future. For instance, suppose there is now a voting game involving three persons. To simplify the scenario, let's say a cake, of which the value is 1, is going to be divided by three persons. Two of them may take the cake by their consent. Evidently, as far as a distribution is concerned, there is always one of them who will become the loser that gets nothing. If for various reasons he anticipates a higher chance of failure, he will have the motive to deviate from the track of the democratic system. On many decision-making occasions involving the anticipation of the future, if some interest group is always in the failed coalition, in most cases, the group would like to give up the opportunity to claim the interests within the framework of the democratic system and resort to means outside the system, or even to actions that give rise to conflicts or violence. Conversely, if all the interest groups have relatively equal opportunities to succeed in the future, even if some group ends up a losing side in one single decision-making session, it will accept it and stick to the channels within the system, because opting for cooperation rather than conflict and waiting for the future to come remain a better choice. This is consistent with the concept of cross-cutting cleavages set forth by scholars on pluralist democracy (who believe that though there exist conflicts over a certain aspect between social groups, they have consensus on another aspect, and thus there will not be serious conflict, but even cooperation between them).

From a long-term, dynamic perspective, equal anticipation of success is crucial to the sustainability of a democratic system. A specific democratic system should not be an institutional arrangement based on a time or an event, but should be long-standing and conducive to the state's enduring stability. Furthermore, when a specific system is selected, there might be a dynamic inconsistency before and after an event. All social interest groups choose a specific institutional arrangement before an event on the basis of their average anticipation of the circumstances they will face in the future; once the system is selected, various random events may occur and they may even be confronted with the impact of various crises. When these random events or crises occur, the actual situations of all the interest groups may be very different from what they initially expected. In terms of cooperative game, even though the distribution scheme brought about by the great coalition realized via democracy is expected to fall within the core, a certain event may cause the actual distribution to be outside the core. This, more often than not, poses a major challenge to the sustainability of a certain democratic system. Only if the impact of a certain event does not affect the groups' anticipation of success opportunities in the future can the democratic institutional arrangement operate in an enduring, stable fashion.

Realization of competitive democracy and cooperative game

Competition and great coalition effect

The actual operating effect of democracy, as a way to realize social cooperation, of course depends on its specific institutional arrangement. The typical way of implementing modern Western democracy is the system of free competitive election.

In other words, they exert control over collective affairs via competitive elections, thereby forming a great coalition encompassing all citizens and realizing social cooperation. Modern scholars on democracy generally believe that people cannot participate directly in running state affairs, but have to run them through their representatives. Therefore, as far as its essence is concerned, democracy is "an institutional arrangement that elites acquire leadership by competing for the people's votes".[3]

The basic principle of free competition originates from the successful practice that people use the market, a basic institutional arrangement, in their economic life. In the history of modern states, free competition has indeed played a crucial role in economic development; it is a fundamental institutional arrangement conducive to collective cooperation in market economy and has greatly boosted the economic efficiency of the state that is a great coalition. At least two conditions have contributed to the fact that competitive market economy can, to a great extent, realize cooperative game in the economic sphere: first, in terms of production, the competition between enterprises is efficiency oriented. For instance, if one enterprise stands out in the competition, the main measure it takes is to win over consumers either by improving the quality of its product or offering better service at the same price, or by reducing production costs and lowering the price. All these competitive measures are efficiency oriented; that is, more efficient enterprises will gain an edge in competition and thus beat less efficient ones. Secondly, from the angle of exchange, the premise for a transaction is that the two parties involved may complement each other's interests. Through trade, both sides' interests improve. Therefore, the market-centered arrangement characterized by free competition can improve the efficiency of the great social coalition economy-wise and is then complemented by a proper way of redistribution, thereby realizing cooperative game.

Now our question is: can free competition introduced into the political sphere fit with the realities of the political market, if it exists at all? Can political cooperation based particularly on free competition ensure the efficiency of the great coalition? In a competitive election, candidates win votes with administrative policies. They are somewhat like enterprises or producers in a market economy; voters are like consumers or buyers. If this competitive institutional arrangement works, candidates who can offer better public services at lower costs will come out winners in the competition. Now, let's analyze the intrinsic features of the political market to see if this is the case.

Behavioral analysis of voters' "choice"

Under the circumstance of serious asymmetrical information, voters' choice-making behavior features a loose connection between their preferences and candidates' policies. Voters lack adequate information and professional knowledge to assess the policies pledged by candidates; relevant research has indicated that their voting is not guided by performance, but favors better-qualified candidates;[4] more importantly, because of the information asymmetry, voters' preferences are susceptible to be influenced by other factors such as advertising and publicity campaigns.

Even if voters can make right judgments of the policies promised, they are still faced with the plight of collective action. Voting is a typical collective action. For every voter, the marginal revenue of one vote is nearly zero; it has so little influence on the outcome of the election that they believe it has no influence at all. Moreover, voting demands time and opportunity costs. Consequently, they may cast their vote arbitrarily or even waiver the right to vote.[5] The arbitrariness or randomness of voting gives the "elites" who enter into the election a crack to wedge themselves into, and more opportunities to wheel and deal so that they can win votes by irregular means.

There is also the issue of "preference aggregation". According to the public choice theory, there is not a universal way to aggregate every individual's preference and form a rational social preference. Therefore, the result of social choice formed by pooling together individual choices according to a certain package of rules and set of procedure may not truthfully reflect voters' wishes. For instance, in the 2000 presidential election of the United States, Al Gore got more votes than George W. Bush. However, due to the division of constituencies, the latter eventually won the campaign.

"Ineffective competition" in the political market

If we look at competing candidates, there is a serious issue of credibility concerning their commitments. The basic means by which candidates compete is to set forth better policies. We call this "prior commitment"; the promise will be implemented after the candidate wins the election. We call this "posterior commitment fulfillment". During the election, voters vote for a candidate on the sole basis of his commitment. That is, they are in fact "buying" the "commitment". It is obviously uncertain whether the candidate will fulfill the commitment after winning the election; this, to a great extent, depends on his "second choice". The reality is: in the electoral system of free competition, there is no effective responsibility mechanism to ensure the fulfillment of prior commitment. However appealing a candidate's prior commitment sounds in the campaign speech, he or she might discard it or go in the opposite direction after winning the election. Even if the "elites" place their personal interests or interests of the interest groups above those of the voters, the voters lack effective constraining measures, and law has ensured the rights of the elected "elites". The costs of impeaching them are very high. Because there is the issue of credibility concerning prior commitment, it becomes hard for candidates to win the election by promising better policies. Those candidates who are truly competent or can offer better public services do not naturally enjoy advantages in the competition.

Besides, does the contest of abilities or qualities enable better candidates to stand out? In the political market, there is a grave information asymmetry between supply and demand. Information concerning the competitors' true qualities and abilities cannot be accurately conveyed to voters. Thus candidates often try their best to maintain their public image by employing such marketing strategies as whitewashing and packaging so that they appear in front of voters in full regalia. Voters can only make their voting decisions on the basis of the candidates' speeches and speech skills, appearance, markings, educational background, and gossip leaked by the media. This, coupled with the above-mentioned features of voters' choice-making behavior, makes it hard for the contest of qualities between candidates to become the dominant factor in the election.

Realties have also shown that the competition in the political market, as represented by elections, often shows an obvious "ineffectiveness". The resources (particularly money) the candidate possesses and his campaign strategies tend to become the most important factors that influence the outcome of the elections. Even in the allegedly "most democratic" United States,[6] the control of American national power by eminent political families has never been interrupted in its history.[7]

Obligation competition: a basic model

To sum up, the competitive structure of the political market, troubled by the incredibility of prior commitment, information asymmetry, and the features of voters' choice-making behavior, causes the low efficiency of free-competition elections. The key negative factor is the incredibility of commitment. Therefore, our crucial task is to find a mechanism that ensures the candidates, after elected, honor their promises in their term and fulfill the prior commitment. Now, let's analyze the key elements ensuring an effective competitive election through a simple model.

Model description

Here we will build a simple dynamic game model. Suppose there is a competitive election. The participants are candidates and voters. We will focus on a representative candidate N and his interactions with voters. The game will be divided into four stages (as shown in Figure 4.1).

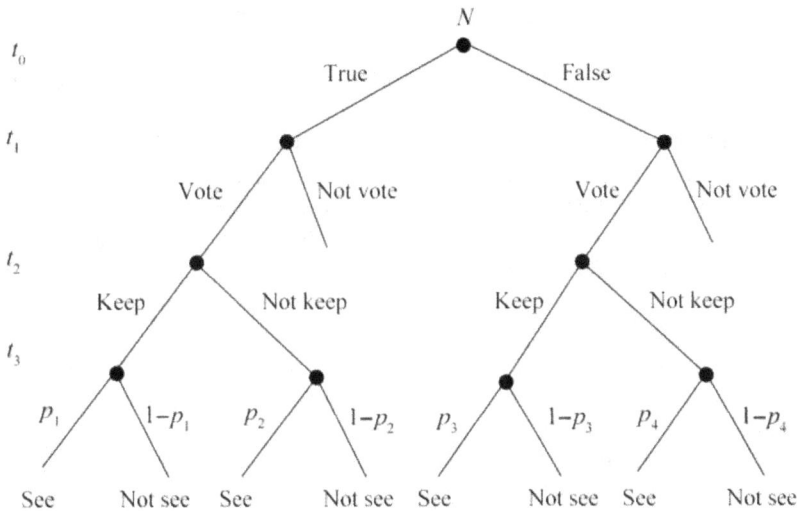

Figure 4.1 "Promise-choice" game

At moment t_0, candidate N's strategy is to win by making more appealing promises. We simplify these promises into a strategy set consisting of only two strategies, i.e., {true promises, false promises}. True promises are built on the true information the candidate has obtained, his abilities and resources and other actual situations, and are thus feasible; in contrast, false promises are not based on true information but made to please voters and win their votes, such as empty publicity promises.

At moment t_1, a voter makes his decision. The strategy set is {vote, not vote}. Between the voter and the candidate information is asymmetric, because the voter lacks the adequate information and is not a professional who can judge whether the candidate's promises are true or false. If the voter chooses not to vote, the game is over; if he chooses to vote, the candidate is elected and the game continues.

At moment t_2, the elected has to make the decision. The strategy set is {keep the promises, not keep the promises}. After he is elected by making false promises, he is likely to try to keep his promises under pressure or for other reasons. The cost for keeping the promises is C. If the promises he makes are true, the cost for the effort to keep them is C_1; if they are false, the cost of the effort to keep them under pressure is C_2, and $C_1 < C_2$.

At moment t_3, when voters check if the promises have been kept, there may be two results: they either see or do not see that they are kept. The scenario can be simplified into a set {see, not see}. In case of inadequate information, voters cannot accurately see how the promises are kept. If the candidate makes true promises at t_0 and keeps them at t_2, voters may see that they are kept at probability p_1 and that they are not kept at probability $1 - p_1$. If the candidate makes true promises but does not keep them, voters may see that they are kept at probability p_2[8] and that they are not kept at probability $1 - p_2$. If the candidate has made false promises but keeps them, voters may see that they are kept at probability p_3 and that they are not kept at probability $1 - p_3$; if the candidate makes false promises and does not keep them, voters see that they are kept at probability p_4 and that they are not kept at probability $1 - p_4$.

The candidate's gains are correlated with whether voters can see that the promises are kept. If voters see that the promises are kept, his gains are π_1; if voters fail to see that the promises are kept, his gains are π_2. And $\pi_1 > \pi_2 > C_j$. Then the function for the candidate's net gains is $E(\pi) = \pi i - C_j$. In the equation: $i = 1, 2, j = 1, 2$.

Voters' utility function is U (W), and it is only related to whether the candidate keeps his promises. If the elected tries to fulfill the commitment, whether voters observe his effort, it will benefit them; if the elected does not keep the promise, whether voters believe he keeps them nor not, the effect his effort has on voters is zero. The cost of voting is a constant R, and $R < w$.

Let's focus on analyzing how the two situations influence the outcome.

The first scenario is that the political market lacks a mechanism supervising and inspecting whether the elected honors his promises. In this case, $p_1 = p_2$. That is, the probability of voters' seeing or not seeing that the promises are kept has nothing to do with whether the elected has tried to keep his promises. We analyze this from two perspectives i.e., what the elected does to keep the promises and what his performance in office is like. On the one hand, due to the serious information asymmetry in the political market, voters lack the professional knowledge and can only get information that has been filtered and screened from the public media such as newspapers and television. Therefore, they are unable to judge the behavior of the elected. On the other, even if voters can perceive the administrative results in some aspects, because of the intrinsic features of politics, the results are subject to the influence of many factors. Now that system analysis and necessary information are absent, it is very hard for voters to judge whether the results have been caused by the effort made by the elected to keep the promises, or by other factors. Under these circumstances, the elected tends to choose "not to keep promises". And anticipating this, the voters tend to choose "not to vote", or their voting is not based on the promises of the candidates.

The second scenario is that in the political market there is a mechanism overlooking and inspecting whether the elected honors the promises. The responsibility for the supervision and inspection mechanism brings about two effects: first, $p_1 > p_2$. That is to say, the mechanism will reveal whether the elected has truly kept his promises. In this case, the probability that voters see the elected keep the promises when he or she does is significantly greater than the probability that they see the elected keep the promises when he or she does not.

Model analysis

Dynamic game should be analyzed with the backstepping algorithm. Let's "retrodict" what happened before moment t_3.

The candidate's decision-making at moment t_3

If the candidate makes true promises and keeps them after he is elected, the function for his expected gains is $E_1(\pi, \text{keep})$; if he does not keep his promises, the function for his expected gains is $E_2(\pi, \text{not keep})$.

$$E_1(\pi, \text{keep}) = p_1(\pi_1 - C_1) + (1 - p_1)(\pi_2 - C_1) \tag{1}$$
$$E_2(\pi, \text{not keep}) = p_2\pi_1(1 - p_2)\pi_2 \tag{2}$$

(1)-(2):

$$(p_1 - p_2)(\pi_1 - \pi_2) - C_1 \tag{3}$$

If the candidate makes false promises and is pressured by various factors to keep them, the function for his expected gains is $E_3(\pi, \text{keep})$; if he does not keep the promises, the function for his expected gains is $E_4(\pi, \text{not keep})$.

Then, $E_3(\pi, \text{keep}) = p_1(\pi_1 - C_2) + (1 - p_1)(\pi_2 - C_2)$ $\tag{4}$
$E_4(\pi, \text{not keep}) = p_2\pi_1(1 - p_2)\pi_2$ $\tag{5}$

(4)-(5):

$$(\pi_1 - \pi_2)(p_1 - p_2) - C_2 \tag{6}$$

Obviously, if the responsibility review mechanism is absent, function (3) <0 and function (6)<0; then, $E_1(\pi, \text{keep}) < E_2(\pi, \text{not keep})$, $E_4(\pi, \text{not keep}) > E_3(\pi, \text{keep})$. That is to say, whether the promises the candidate has made are true or false, he will choose "not to keep" them.

If there is a responsibility review mechanism for commitment fulfillment, $p_1 > p_2$, and $(p_1 - p_2)(\pi_1 - \pi_2) - C_1 > 0$ (suppose this condition is fulfilled when there is responsibility review), it is evident that (3)>0, (6)>0. That is, whether the promises he has made are true or false, he will choose to "keep" them.

The voter's decision making at moment t_2

If the candidate makes true promises, the function for the effect of the voter's vote when he votes is U_1 (w, vote), and the effect function when he does not vote is U_2 (w, not vote), then:

$$U_1 (w, \text{vote}) = p_1 w - R \tag{7}$$
$$U_2 (w, \text{not vote}) = 0$$

If the candidate makes false promises, the function for the effect of the voter's vote when he votes is U_3 (w, vote), and the function for the effect of the voter's vote when he does not vote is U_4 (w, not vote)

$$U_3 (w, \text{vote}) = p_2 w - R \tag{8}$$
$$U_4 (w, \text{not vote}) = 0$$

If the responsibility review mechanism is absent, since the elected will choose "not to keep" the promises at moment t_3, that is $q_1 = 0$ and $q_2 = 0$, then $p_2 w - R < 0$; the voter will choose "not to vote".

If there is a responsibility review mechanism, since the elected will choose to "keep" the promises at moment t_3, that is $q_1 = 1$, $q_2 = 1$, then $p_2 w - R > 0$; the voter will choose to "vote".

The candidate's choice of commitment at moment t_1

If there is not a responsibility review mechanism, because the voter will choose "not to vote" at moment t_2, neither true nor false promises can help him to win the voter's vote. That is to say, he cannot use policy commitment as a competitive tool. Consequently, political competition will be inefficient.

If there is a responsibility review mechanism, and the function of the candidate's expected gains is $E_5 (\pi, \text{true})$ when he makes true promises and $E_6 (\pi, \text{false})$ when he makes false ones, the voter will choose to "vote" at moment t_2 and the candidate will choose to "keep" the promises at moment t_3, then:

$$E_5 (\pi, \text{true})=E_1 (\pi, \text{keep})$$

That is:

$$p_1 (\pi_1 - C_1)+(1 - p_1)(\pi_2 - C_1) \tag{1}$$
$$E_6 (\pi, \text{false})=E_3(\pi, \text{keep})$$

Then

$$p_1 (\pi_1 - C_2)+(1 - p_1)(\pi_2 - C_2) \tag{4}$$

$(1) - (4)$:

$$C_2 - C_1 > 0.$$

That is to say, when there is a responsibility review mechanism, the candidate will tend to choose to make "true promises".

Theoretical implications

To sum up, if the responsibility review mechanism for promises is absent in the political market, the optimal decision to make for the candidate at moment t_3 is "not to keep" his promises, and the optimal decision to make for the voter at moment t_2 is either "not to vote" or "vote arbitrarily". Then at moment t_1, the candidate is unlikely to use policy commitment as a competitive tool. As a result, democratic politics will be "inefficient".

If there is a responsibility review mechanism for promises in the political market, the optimal decision to make for the candidate at moment t_3 is to "keep" the promises, that for the voter at moment t_2 is to "vote", and that for the candidate at moment t_1 is to make "true promises". Then, making promises will become an effective means in competitive elections. Therefore, the voter will vote according to promises that are made; and when the candidate is elected, he will keep his promises. The inevitable result will be: the candidate who promises better public services after elected will win out. The competition will make efficiency improve continuously.

Responsibility shift of the democratic system

From the above analysis it can be learnt that if a responsibility review mechanism is absent, the intrinsic features of the political market will lead to the ineffectiveness of ex-ante competition. Therefore, if we hope to truly achieve cooperative game in the democratic system by design, avoid the nominal democratic proce-dure, and achieve substantive democracy, the key is how to ensure the fulfillment of ex-ante commitments through some "ex-post" responsibility mechanism. We call this idea "the responsibility shift of the democratic system" and attempt to explain the feasibility of this "ex-post" responsibility review mechanism.

The "responsibility review" system here is different from the current account-ability system for officials at least in the following three aspects. Firstly, the sub-jects of initiating and launching the systems are different. Whereas the latter is implemented by superiors, the former stresses the embodiment of the "people's democracy" philosophy and is launched and implemented by the people or their representatives. Secondly, the pre-placement commitments are different in sig-nificance. As far as the current accountability system is concerned, whether the official makes commitments before he assumes office is not important, because the accountability system is directly concerned with the responsibilities of the administrative post he takes, rather than with the pre-placement commitments. The "responsibilities" the former reviews, however, consist not merely of the basic responsibilities of the post, but, more importantly, of his pre-placement promises or commitments; the responsibility review system officially makes them binding obligations. Lastly, the two systems are different in terms of the relationship of selection and posting with accountability. The official account-ability system stresses that the official must be held accountable for neglect of duty or his subordinates' neglect of duty; it is not the main basis for his posting (unless he was derelict of duty before). The responsibility review system com-bines ex-ante promises and ex-post review. First of all, it encourages candidates who are able to shoulder and fulfill more responsibilities to stand out; more-over, the responsibility review amid the official's term can provide the basis for his constantly rectifying his behavior. To meet the institutional requirements of responsibility review, the tentative idea is that at least the following basic insti-tutional arrangements should be made:

Election mechanism

Whether in theory or in practice, possible re-election may undoubtedly have factual effect on prompting the candidate to be committed in his career. There has already been a lot of literature discussing how re-election ensures that the candidate fulfills his commitments in the term after he is elected. As Arthur Lupia and John G. Matsusaka put it, to achieve this effectively, at least three conditions should be fulfilled: first, officials in office fulfill their commitments through policies and measures; secondly, ex-ante commitments are quantified as policies and measures, of which the implementation can be measured; and thirdly, policies and measures are hatched by their decision making rather than produced naturally.[9]

As discussed above, under the circumstance of a full-fledged responsibility review mechanism, the commitments made in elections become a key factor in the competition between candidates, and the election mechanism can thus perform its selective function, screening the candidate who is most likely to render the best service. Besides, this also requires that, in terms of specific election arrangements, more stress is laid upon the "circumspect review" of candidates' comprehensive qualities including professional proficiency and ethics and the thorough assessment of their integrity and ability to fulfill commitments. Relevant information will be made accessible to voters.

Evaluation mechanism

The evaluation mechanism is the basis and an important part of the incentive and constraint mechanism for officials. The evaluation of candidates' comprehensive qualities and abilities constitutes the fundamental basis for the selection; the scientific evaluation of post-election commitment fulfillment and the reasonable performance assessment are the important bases for incentive or constraining measures. The evaluation mechanism should, as designed, include the purpose, subject, contents, indices, index weights, standards, methods, and results of the evaluation. A scientific, full-fledged evaluation mechanism is not only the basis of responsibility review but helps voters learn about and supervise officials' work, alleviates the issue of information asymmetry, reduces officials' moral risks and adverse selecting, and improves the principal–agent relationship. In practice, the mechanism may work in different forms. For instance, it may manifest itself in multiple flexible forms of democratic appraisal, such as regular debriefing to public opinion representatives, who appraise officials' behavior and publicize the results, which have a direct bearing on officials' performance evaluation.

Remuneration mechanism

The performance evaluation of the remuneration mechanism is mainly based on the results of the joint appraisal of officials by voters and superiors. Whether they keep their promises, whether they have tried to keep them, their morality and ethics, their professional competence, etc. are all important subjects of appraisal. The officials' remuneration may include yearly salary, post allowances, merit pay, etc. or be designed with reference to the payment delay program in corporate management. The payment delay program means that part (usually 25 percent) of the permanent pay of officials who participate in the program will be automatically saved in an account and eventually paid to them in cash (usually with yields) when they retire or leave office. Payment delay is a long-term incentive, whose primary purpose is to encourage officials to focus on the long-term benefits of the state and voters, overcome short-term actions, and try to fulfill their duties. According to the theory on human resources management, the design of the remuneration mechanism should fit with the motive of taking office. The incentives should include not only cash, but also other incentives that can achieve other purposes so that officials are encouraged to perform their duties. Other incentives include: promotion, moral encouragement, reputation incentive, retirement plan, etc.

Reputation mechanism

According to modern theories on management and economics, the reputation mechanism is receiving more and more attention. The development of game theory and modern information economics has already furnished many approaches to giving play to the incentive role of the reputation mechanism. Holmstrom has built the agent reputation model in the context of the reputation theory and proves directly that reputation can serve as a substitution for the explicit incentive contract, thereby opening up new grounds for studies on the incentive effect of reputation.[10] Studies on the reputation mechanism in China mainly focus on the application of reputation as an incentive; they are mostly qualitative. When quantitative research is conducted, in most cases, the KMRW reputation model (designed by Kreps, Milgrom, Roberts, and Wilson) of repeated game is adopted or advocated.[11]

The reputation mechanism not only applies to corporate managers, but is also an important incentive mechanism for government officials. Reputation is especially important to the career of politicians. Their political careers are closely associated with the reputation formed accumulatively when they are in office. In the meantime, officials' social fame and reputation contribute to improving the social image of such public organizations like the government and boosting voters' trust of the government. The cumulative effect of reputation is a decisive factor determining the benefits government officials can expect after they retire. As far as officials are concerned, this is an important long-standing form of incentive. For many politicians, the pursuit of a good reputation is one of the goals of personal values. Therefore, in the architecture of a democratic system, if the effect of reputation can be brought to full play and a dynamic system of reputation accumulation can be built for officials on the basis of scientific appraisal, officials' ex-post moral hazards can be greatly lowered and they will be more active in fulfilling their ex-ante commitments.

Summary

Democracy is by nature an institutional arrangement for collective coordination and concerted action in human society. Through some specific rules, they pool decentralized individual will into collective will. Democracy, as an institutional arrangement of collective choice, has two basic functions: first, to make public power better serve the people. This function is intended to achieve collection rationality. It is the substance of democracy. Secondly, to combine different individual preferences into unified collective will when different preferences exist within the people. From the perspective of cooperative game, the first function is more important. It is the key to the assessment of the quality of democracy. Moreover, the second function should serve the first function. Just like the "majority rule", it is one of the procedural means to achieve collective rationality. When we discuss democracy, we should focus on the realization of substantive democracy, or collective rationality. Procedural democracy, that is, how to achieve collective rationality, should serve substantive democracy.

The key to the stable, orderly operation of a democratic system lies in whether all interest groups concerned can have "relatively" equal access to success or expectation of success when they visualize the future. From a long-term, dynamic perspective, a specific democratic system should not be based on a time or an event, but should be long-standing and conducive to the state's enduring stability. In the West, the means to this end is mainly to exert control over public affairs via free competitive election. The question is: does the introduction of free competition into politics fit with the actual situation of the political market? Reality has shown that competition in the political market, represented by elections, tends to show obvious "ineffectiveness". Therefore, if we hope to truly achieve cooperative game in the democratic system by design, avoid the nominal democratic procedure, and achieve substantive democracy, we must bring about the "responsibility shift of the democratic system". Furthermore, we should use the election mechanism, evaluation mechanism, remuneration mechanism, and reputation mechanism to ensure its success.

Besides, cooperative game also calls for information disclosure and symmetry, beliefs and institutional rules universally accepted by all parties concerned, mutual trust based on rules, as well as other conditions. They will be discussed in the next chapter.

In brief, the theory of cooperative game is indeed valuable in that it can lend some inspiration to China's future development of cooperative-harmonious democracy. Plus, some institutional designs it advocates are instrumental to the future development model of Chinese cooperative-harmonious democracy.

Notes

1 Part of this chapter has been published. See Liu Taoxiong and Zhou Bihua, "Democratic System in the Perspective of Responsibility: A Basic Model", *Comparative Economic and Social Systems*, 2012, 1.
2 To be accurate, the concept of value applies to the game involving one or more side payment systems. See Roger B. Myerson, *Game Theory: Analysis of Conflict*, Fei Jianping & Yu Yin (trans.). Beijing: Economic Press of China, 2001.
3 Wang Shaoguang, *Four Discourses on Democracy*. Beijing: SDX Joint Publishing Company, 2008.
4 When voters vote to elect officials, do they vote for better qualified candidates or better-performing ones? Some scholars have conducted empirical research on this subject. Data analysis reveals that voters tend to vote for better qualified officials. For professional politicians, it is not hard to demonstrate their "good qualifications". This is highly manipulable. For instance, they can hire an image consultant for image design and packaging.
5 There is another social phenomenon that attracts scholars' attention: that the voter has Rational Ignorance. Due to the high costs of information search, the voter is unwilling or unable to get all the information and knowledge needed in the complicated operation. Thus it is rational to acquire only some information and remain ignorant of other information. Besides, casting a vote has little influence on the outcome of the election or on the voter himself; or its influence is not determinable. Therefore, the voter is apt to choose not to vote or vote arbitrarily and become an ignorant voter by rational choice. Such ignorance is a testimony of rationality; it is a rational compromise with limited

knowledge and information, as well as an inevitable outcome of the improved efficiency of information substitution in the system of social division of labor.

6 Over 170 years ago, French writer Alexis de Tocqueville wrote vividly in his book *Democracy in America*, "The election becomes the most important and the all-engrossing topic of discussion. . . . The whole nation glows with feverish excitement; the election is the daily theme of the public papers, the subject of private conversation, the end of every thought and every action, the sole interest of the present. . . . One of the principal vices of the elective system is that it always introduces a certain degree of instability into the internal and external policy of the State. . . . The period which immediately precedes an election and the moment of its duration must always be considered as a national crisis. . . . It is impossible to consider the ordinary course of affairs in the United States without perceiving that the desire of being re-elected is the chief aim of the President; that his whole administration, and even his most indifferent measures, tend to this object." See Alexis de Tocqueville, *Democracy in America*, Dong Guoliang (trans.). Beijing: The Commercial Press, 1991, 141–153.

7 Arthur Lupia and John G. Matsusaka, "Direct Democracy: New Approaches to Old Questions", *The Annual Review of Political Science*, 2004, 7: 463–482.

8 For instance, because of some random events, under the circumstance that the candidate tries to fulfill his commitment, the voters still believe that the promises are kept. For example, the candidate has promised to curb inflation. After he is elected, he does not make an effort to do that. However, due to the evolution of the economic system or the influence of world economy, inflation is indeed contained and the voters observe that.

9 Arthur Lupia and John G. Matsusaka, "Direct Democracy: New Approaches to Old Questions", *The Annual Review of Political Science*, 2004, 7: 463–482.

10 Holmstrom and Moral Hazard in Team, *Bell Journal of Economics*, 1982, 13: 324–340.

11 Liu Huiping and Zhang Shiying, "A Study of the Reputation Theory-Based Dynamic Incentive Model for Chinese Managers", *Chinese Journal of Management Science*, 2005, 4: 79.

5 Transition to democracy from the perspective of cooperative game

A case study of Spain

The transition to democracy in Spain, which took place at the turn from the 1970s to the 1980s, has been much acclaimed – even dubbed "the Spanish model" – for its peaceful process of transition and consolidation without any detriment to the nation's socioeconomic development. Why is it that the founding of the Second Republic in the 1930s led to a brutal civil war, whereas a transition to democracy could be successful after thirty-six years of dictatorship by Francisco Franco? This question has sparked a great deal of thinking and research among political scientists. Some of them have offered explanations in terms of socioeconomic modernization and the change of the social structure,[1] while others have identified the strategic factors that contributed to the successful transition.[2] In this chapter, we will try to sum up the factors that can make cooperative game possible among various political forces during a transition to democracy as illustrated by the case of Spain.

A game-theory analysis of transition to democracy

Two perspectives of research

Structuralism and actor-oriented approach are two distinct perspectives most commonly employed in research into democratic transition. The structuralist perspective is interested in long-term, macro-structural socioeconomic and cultural factors, *inter alia*, that can affect the transition to democracy and its consolidation and development. Such factors are usually independent of individual will.[3] The actor-oriented perspective is more concerned with strategic acts between political forces during transition to democracy, including conflict, negotiation, and cooperation.[4]

The structuralist perspective emerged in the 1950s–1960s under the influence of the contemporary theory of modernization and behaviorism. One of the most influential among the early researchers was Seymour Lipset, who, based on empirical research, posited the famous hypothesis that wealthy societies are usually also more democratic.[5] He attempted to establish a theoretical nexus between a country's level of development and the probability of its becoming a democracy. In his opinion, industrialization, urbanization, the growth of the middle class, and the modernization of education, which are among the results of modernization, are all favorable conditions for democratization. Lipset's research sparked considerable controversy and was followed by increasingly extensive and profound comparative studies. The thesis he wrote in 1959 became one of the ten most frequently cited papers in *American Political Science Review*. Since then, many distinguished political scientists such as Huntington and Dahl have taken part in studies and debates on this issue, which has expanded the structuralist perspective on transition to democracy. In recent years, the statistical research based on large sample cross-sections and time series data by Przeworski and others have enabled a deeper understanding of the structuralist perspective.[6] While discussing the relationship between democracy and development, they raised an important question: does development bring democracy, or does it only help to sustain established democracy?

The structuralist approach links the features of the new starting point to those of the old terminal point. As summarized by Przeworski, this model is methodologically characterized by the linking of the generalized result, such as democracy or fascism, to the original conditions such as land hierarchy; in such reasoning, the result is unilaterally determined by conditions, for history would still develop this way even if no action were taken.[7]

However, criticism against the structuralist perspective has led to increasing dissatisfaction with its overlooking of the transition process and the proactive role of the participants. Moreover, determinism has become hardly tenable in light of the apparently uncertain link between economic development and transition to democracy as indicated by the new democratic wave in southern Europe in the mid- and late 1970s, Latin America in the 1980s, and eastern Europe toward the end of the 1980s. Researchers became more interested in in-depth study of specific cases of the transition process, with focus on the influence of the actor's strategy on the result. For instance, the study of O'Donnell and Schmitter is focused on the strategies of different actors and interprets the final outcome as the result of such strategies.[8] However, early strategy analysis was still a micro-analysis with an extensive use of macro-concepts like class and alliance. Yet to be introduced were formal and supra-historical methods like game theory.

Since the 1990s, game theory has been gradually adopted by democratic transition researchers. One of the first and most important pioneers is Przeworski. In *Democracy and the Market* (1991), he introduced a game theory model for the analysis of "how the results of democracy come into being". He was followed by Josep M. Colomer, a more enthusiastic proponent of game theory who used the formalized language of the theory to make a more detailed analysis of the democratic transition in Spain, as well as the transformation process in Russia and eastern Europe.[9]

Non-cooperative game and cooperative game

Game refers to "decisions with mutual influence made by individuals or organizations, the outcome of which not only depends on the actions of one individual or organization, but also on the corresponding actions of other individuals or organizations."[10] Game theory, which emerged in the 1940s, was extensively applied to economics first, and gradually to sociology and political science as well.

As mentioned before, there are two kinds of games in game theory – cooperative and non-cooperative. The major distinction is whether the participants can reach a binding agreement during the game process. Cooperative game highlights collective rationality, efficiency, justice, and fairness; non-cooperative game stresses the individual's rationality and optimal decision, the outcome of which can be efficient or otherwise.[11]

In the famous "prisoner's dilemma", which is a non-cooperative game, the two prisoners are not able to communicate and even less to reach an agreement. According to the Nash equilibrium, both of them will choose to confess and therefore produce the worst outcome for both. If they can communicate and reach a binding agreement, based on which they will keep silent and refuse to confess, the general outcome will be favorable to both of them.

A cooperative game often leads to better results for collective welfare. In the 1950s, cooperative game theory reached its apex. However, it was also realized that individual rationality and collective rationality are often contradictory. In the absence of effective enforcement by a third party, a self-enforcing binding agreement is quite unlikely to be achieved. This coincided with the groundbreaking study of non-cooperative game published by John Nash and Tucker's definition of the prisoner's dilemma in the early 1950s, which fueled the rapid growth of modern non-cooperative game theory. As a result, today's economists talk about game theory mostly in the sense of non-cooperative game rather than its counterpart.[12] This trend has also influenced other fields of social sciences. For instance, when political scientists introduce game theory into the study of micro-political behavior like voting, it is also mostly based on the non-cooperative variety.

Nevertheless, the cooperative game remains more useful in politics than in economics. On the one hand, political options differ from economic options in that consensus and ethics play a more fundamental role in the former. Non-consensual politics often lead to intense social conflict at tremendous social cost. Therefore, how to avoid political disaster in the face of a crisis can often become a consensual basis for cooperation. On the other hand, repeated political games are a norm in human society as a political community; they can alleviate information asymmetry between the participants, who, through political debate and communication, will better understand the pros and cons of the options and gradually cultivate a collective rationality and the acknowledgement of collective welfare. How to help consolidate democracy and prevent sociopolitical instability resulting from its collapse during transition to democracy has always been a major starting point for strategic study from the actor's perspective. Understanding the conditions for the cooperative game can help the actors to bring it about through consensus-based strategic choice and institutional design.

However, by definition, the cooperative game hinges on the reaching of a binding agreement, which is especially difficult in transition to democracy. The birth of democracy consists in the termination of the old regime and the formation and consolidation of a new democratic system. Reforms of the political system are often aimed at tackling the crises that occur under the old regime. If the crises are more than the old regime can handle and lead to revolution or other forms of collapse, society will face a new game between various political forces in the absence of an effective political authority. A new authority will be formed and a binding agreement will be reached in one of the three following scenarios:

1   One political force or political alliance stands out from the others and is able to restore order or impose an agreement by force.
2   No single political force or alliance can win on its own, and the unbearable social cost resulting from continuous anomie compels all the parties to reach a binding agreement based on the consensus of avoiding common ruin.
3   An external force, such as the international community or a foreign political force, intervenes.

If the old regime has the political authority to facilitate reforms and has both the authority and the ability to bring the political forces to a binding agreement based on negotiation when the crisis has yet to break out on a large scale and remains under control, a cooperative game will be more likely than in the first scenario. That was how the transition to democracy was achieved in Spain.

In the next two parts, we will first provide the basic facts about Spain and the process of her transition to democracy. Based on that, we will try to summarize the important strategies and institutional factors that contributed to the cooperative game during the transition in terms of the basic principles of cooperative game theory.

Spain's transition to democracy

Spain is located on the Iberian Peninsula in southwestern Europe. It covers an area of 506,000 km², slightly larger than that of Sichuan Province in China, with a mountainous terrain. By January 2008, it had a permanent population of about 46.16 million, slightly larger than that of Yunnan Province in China.[13] The population is rather unevenly distributed, with more than a quarter concentrated in Madrid and Barcelona. The predominant ethnic group is the Castilians, who account for about 73 percent of the population. The major ethnic minorities are the Catalonians (about 15 percent), the Galicians (nearly 7 percent), and the Basques (about 5 percent). Each ethnic group has its own language, with that of the Castilians (i.e., Spanish) being the official language of the nation. The geographic and demographic diversity of Spain, coupled with a long history of decentralized feudal despotism, have led to a wide gap in development between her different regions and a complex relationship between interest groups, among other challenges. At present, Spain has seventeen autonomous communities and fifty provinces.

The democratization of Spain, which started in 1976, has been widely acclaimed for its peaceful process without detriment to socioeconomic development. In fact, however, Spain had a rather checkered modern political history. She had always been at the mercy of foreign powers until her unification in 1492, soon after which she became a global empire with a significant impact on modern world history. The sixteenth century saw Spain's rapid rise and equally rapid decline. The enlightened despotism of the eighteenth century, which brought renewed prosperity, failed to stop the decline of the empire. Napoleon's invasion, coupled with the influence of the Enlightenment and the French Revolution, led the parliament in exile to draw up the Spanish Constitution of 1812 as Spain's first modern constitution. It became an important inspiration to the Spanish liberalists in their staunch resistance to the restoration of despotic monarchy in the nineteenth century. Nineteenth-century Spain was rife with wars and conflicts, reverting to the Restoration after the short-lived First Republic of 1873–74.

After her disastrous defeat in the Spanish-American War of 1898, Spain lost her last territory in America. This aggravated her domestic troubles and spawned political thoughts and factions demanding the reform of the government. These include anarchism and fascism, both of which gained currency in the early twentieth century. The bankruptcy of the government in 1939 led to seething public resentment, and the Second Republic (1931–1939) was founded after the king fled Spain following the Republicans' victory in the municipal elections. However, instead of bringing a stable democracy, this led to a brutal civil war (1936–1939), which caused a great number of casualties and a thirty-six-year dictatorship by Francisco Franco.[14]

The democratization of Spain began with the death of Franco on November 20, 1975 and King Juan Carlos I's accession to the throne two days later. In his inaugural address, the king enunciated a series of goals in political reform, including national reconciliation, an equal and just order, and reintegration into Europe.[15] However, King Carlos did not choose to go about the democratic reform in a radical way. He achieved a smooth transition of the supreme authority by retaining Carlos Arias Navarro, who had been handpicked by Franco, as his prime minister. In July 1976, he appointed Adolfo Suárez as the new prime minister in place of Arias, who had been unable to push through any substantive political reform. The new administration led by Suárez was mainly made up of the younger reformers in the Franco regime. Its assumption of power marked the real beginning of the democratic reform.

In the few years that followed, the Suárez administration made rapid progress in the transition to democracy by political and legal means. In November 1976, the congress, which was still dominated by the Francoists, voted through the Law of Political Reform. This act, by which "the congressmen voted themselves out to introduce democratic principles", marked a significant starting point for peaceful reform. The reform plan gained wider popular recognition and support when the Law was overwhelmingly ratified by referendum in December.[16] During the referendum, though, the opposition insisted on a "complete break" with the old regime; they did so by abstention instead of voting against the Law.[17]

What followed was the legalization of political parties and labor unions, which started in the spring of 1977. The greatest challenge during this process was the legalization of the communist party. Because of their memory of the civil war, many high-ranking military officials saw this as a provocation and a sign of the abandonment of the anti-communist principle of the Spanish government. As a result, none of them thought it was necessary for democratic reform. However, the arrest of the secretary-general of the Spanish communist party upon his secret return to the country sparked strong reactions among the public, with an obvious increase in skepticism, mistrust, and criticism regarding democratic reform. The Suárez administration found a tactical solution to this thorny issue. After the appeal to the Supreme Court for a decision on the legalization of the communist party was rejected, Suárez gave his approval by the issuance of a decree on a weekend (April 9, 1977). Though denounced by the military, this move did not trigger more violent acts of resistance.

This period also saw the mushrooming of political parties in Spain. By the general election in June 1977, after a dazzling flurry of reshuffling, uniting, or allying, they formed into right-wing conservative parties led by the People's Alliance (AP), left-wing parties led by the Spanish Socialist Workers' Party (PSOE), and the Communist Party of Spain (PCE), and a number of new left-/right-wing parties and local nationalist parties.[18] Prime Minister Suárez founded a central-right alliance of small parties called the Union of the Democratic Center (UCD). The first democratic election for the Congress of Deputies was held on June 15, 1977. The UCD, the PSOE, the PCE, and the AP won 39.9 percent, 28.8 percent, 9.2 percent, and 8.2 percent of the votes, respectively. This reflected the people's support for moderate parties and their opposition to radicalism. Besides, local nationalist parties and other small parties also gained seats according to the votes they received.

The new Congress of Deputies immediately set about redesigning the political system, especially the constitution. First of all, the new Congress passed a bill which required all the parties to cooperate with each other during the current congress. The Constituent Cortes was convened on July 26, and a widely representative panel was established for the drafting of the constitution. In October 1978, the new constitution was passed by the Congress; in December, it was overwhelmingly ratified by referendum. On December 29, it was officially promulgated with royal approval, and Suárez announced the dismissal of the Congress. In the new round of general elections in March 1979, the UCD won 168 seats, the alliance of the PSOE and the Socialist People's Party secured 121 seats, the PCE gained 23, and the AP got 9.

However, the successful adoption of the new constitution did not signify the end of the transition to democracy. On the contrary, it was followed by a spate of crises. Between 1979 and 1982, Spain went through a very difficult period in her democratic transition marked by sluggish economic recovery, growing unemployment, the rise of left-/right-wing radicalism and Basque terrorism, and rumors about a coup by the military. In 1980, the differences within the UCD, which was the party in power, came into the open. In May, the prime minister was impeached by PSOE congressmen at the Congress. The situation did not improve after Suárez reshuffled the cabinet in September. In January 1981, Suárez resigned.

On February 23, 1981, the Congress was about to vote on Calvo-Sotelo's takeover as prime minister when nearly 200 fully armed civil guards led by Lt

Col Antonio Tejero charged into the conference hall, interrupted the voting, and declared a coup. Tejero sought support from other members of the military and the king. However, King Carlos did not hesitate to uphold democracy and condemn the coup as an unconstitutional act. He ordered the perpetrators to surrender, and Tejero eventually complied. It was a critical moment for the thorough acceptance of democracy by the Francoists in the military.

However, after Calvo-Sotelo became prime minister, Spain soon relapsed into social and political crises. In August 1982, the UCD came to the brink of collapse when Suárez left the union to found a new party. Calvo-Sotelo decided to dismiss the Congress and hold a new general election.

The PSOE scored an overwhelming victory in the general election in October 1982, and Felipe González organized the first PSOE administration. The PSOE won the election again in 1986. This marked a smooth handover between political parties, which consolidated democracy in Spain.

Analysis of cooperative game in the Spanish transition to democracy and what can be learned from it

Cooperative game depends on a binding agreement. The essence is to eliminate information asymmetry through the agreement, plus dialogue, negotiation and repeated games, so that each player can fully understand the potential influence of the options on himself and the other players, who are all willing to cooperate in a collective game. Compared with the civil war in the 1930s, the success of Spain's transition to democracy in the late 1970s was not only based on socioeconomic development, but also attributable to the strategies and system choices that were instrumental in the cooperative game.

Basic political consensus was fundamental to cooperative game

One of the major causes of the civil war in 1931–36 was the lack of a basic political consensus among the various social strata and political forces. In fact, the whole country was deeply torn by ideological confrontation at home and political antagonism in the international arena. The civil war caused a terrible national trauma, and the lapse from war into dictatorship inflicted great pain on the Spanish people. Moreover, the military coup in the neighboring country of Portugal in 1974 and her democratization through violence also led the Spanish people to the consensus of preventing another civil war. Though burdened with the memory of the civil war and the dictatorship, they tried to look to the future instead of licking their historical wounds; they did not create a fact-finding committee or purge the officials of the dictatorial regime. These were also conducive to the forming of a consensus.[19]

On the other hand, universal education and opening to the outside world also helped to popularize democratic values among the people. A poll in 1978 showed that 77 percent of the Spanish people believed democracy to be the political system best suited to their country, whereas only 15 percent of them preferred an authoritarian regime.[20] As a result of the combination of such value factors, "during the transitional period, there was a high degree of consensus between the Spanish populace and the social elite, and a relatively moderate ruling class was willing to tolerate the presence of alliances and left-wing forces provided that they did not resort to violence."[21]

Apart from the consensus in political values during the transition, cooperative game was also supported by the government's efforts to bring about consensus on economic issues between the political parties and groups. One of the significant steps was the signing of the famous Pactos de Moncloa between the government of the major political parties and groups in October 1977. This brought various political forces to a consensus on the adoption of hard-line economic policy in the face of the economic crisis. The successful separation of political conflict from economic conflict played a considerable role in the consolidation of the new democratic framework in cooperative game.

Therefore, on the one hand, the forming of a basic political consensus prevented extremism in the political game (e.g., the exiled leaders of the Spanish communist party began to say they would give up attempts at armed overthrow of the current regime in the 1950s); on the other hand, it made political dialogue and negotiation possible.

Dialogue and negotiation were vital to cooperative game

Spain's transition to democracy is called a "transition by pact" or "transition through transaction", which clearly indicates the vital role played by dialogue, negotiation and agreement in peaceful transition. Dialogue and negotiation were helpful to the exchange of information and the forming of trust, which would reduce information asymmetry and enhance the likelihood of cooperative game.

Dialogue and negotiation were carried on throughout the democratization of Spain. To make dialogue and negotiation possible requires, first of all, channels for representing the interests of various groups of people and the inclusion of the representatives of the majority's interests in the negotiation process. In Spain, this took the form of the government's efforts toward the legalization of political parties, which would become the vehicle for the expression of principal political interests. The lack of organized channels of expression tends to reduce democratizing negotiation into populism or leave the populace to be mobilized by individual political parties. "The populace is destructive to smooth transition, and their mobilization is to be feared rather than blindly encouraged; a democracy resulting from transition through negotiation tends to be better than one born out of the destruction of the old regime."[22]

The democratization of Spain has also been much criticized for the fact that most of the negotiations were behind the scenes and between political elites. However, considering information cost and uncertainty, such behind-the-scenes negotiations were not unhelpful to narrowing down the options, increasing efficiency, and enhancing mutual trust between the participants.

The active role played by key political figures in cooperative game

King Carlos and Prime Minister Suárez have been much acclaimed for the essential role they played during Spain's transition to democracy. It is the general view that the king's open-mindedness is attributable to his family and education; as for Suárez, he knew that reform was the only way out, and he was also more skillful at finding the leeway for dialogue and cooperation in the old regime.

In terms of cooperative game, the consensus on democratization between the king and the prime minister motivated a voluntary top-down democratic reform. A vacuum in government authority was averted by the decision to carry out the reform when the old regime's governance had yet to fail completely and social crisis had yet to pose a fundamental threat to social and political order. As a charismatic leader, the king was able to play an indispensable role at critical moments for the reaching and enforcement of agreements in cooperative game and maintaining peace.

Summary

Despite the wide difference in national conditions between Spain and China, Spain's democratic transition and development may still be highly enlightening for us. From the perspective of cooperative game, what can be learned from it falls into three categories: a consensus for democracy is the foundation of democratic cooperation; dialogue and negotiation are an effective solution to differences; highly esteemed political leaders are important to a smooth transition to democracy.

Notes

1 Many scholars have made summaries of structuralist perspectives on the conditions for democracy and other issues. One of the relatively comprehensive summaries can be found in Vanhanen, *The Process of Democratization: A Comparative Study of 147 States 1980–1988*. New York: Crane Russak, 1990.
2 One of the proponents of this perspective is Josep M. Colomer, who made a detailed analysis of Spain's transition to democracy with a game theory model. See Josep M. Colomer, *Game Theory and the Transition to Democracy: The Spanish Model*. Aldershot, UK: Edward Elgar, 1995.
3 Josep M. Colomer, *Strategic Transitions: Game Theory and Democratization*. Baltimore, MD: The Johns Hopkins University Press, 2000.
4 Adam Przeworski, *Democracy and the Market: Political and Economic Reforms in Eastern Europe and Latin America*. Beijing: Peking University Press, 2005.
5 Seymour M. Lipset, "Some Social Requisites of Democracy: Economic Development and Political Legitimacy", *American Political Science Review*, 1959, 53(1): 75.
6 Adam Przeworski, Jose Antonko Cheibub, Michael E. Alvarez and Fernando Limongi, *Democracy and Development: Political Institutions and Material Well-being in the World, 1950–1990*. Cambridge: Cambridge University Press, 2000.
7 Przeworski, *Democracy and the Market: Political and Economic Reforms in Eastern Europe and Latin America*. Beijing: Peking University Press, 2005, 71.
8 Przeworski, *Democracy and the Market: Political and Economic Reforms in Eastern Europe and Latin America*. Beijing: Peking University Press, 2005, 72.

9 Josep M. Colomer, *Game Theory and the Transition to Democracy*. Aldershot, UK: Edward Elgar, 1995. Josep M. Colomer, *Strategic Transitions: Game Theory and Democratization*. Baltimore, MD: The Johns Hopkins University Press, 2000.
10 Cui Zhiyuan, *Game Theory and Social Sciences*. Hangzhou: Zhejiang People's Press, 1988, 3.
11 Zhang Weiying, *Game Theory and Information Economics*. Shanghai: Shanghai People's Publishing House, 1996, 5.
12 Zhang Weiying, *Game Theory and Information Economics*. Shanghai: Shanghai People's Publishing House, 1996, 5.
13 Sichuan Province covers an area of 481,400 km^2, with a population of 81.38 million (2008). Yunnan Province covers an area of 383,300 km^2, with a population of 45.43 million (2008).
14 For details of the historical process, see Jose M. Magone, *Contemporary Spanish Politics*. New York: Routledge, 2004, 1–26. The first chapter gives a most succinct description of the political history of Spain.
15 See Qin Haibo, "On the Democratic Reform in Spain (1975–1986)", *World History*, 2006, 3: 82–92. This article makes a comprehensive review of the process of Spain's democratic reform and the principal actions taken.
16 The turnout rate was 78 percent, with 94.2 percent of the voters in favor of the Law.
17 Qin Haibo, "On the Democratic Reform in Spain (1975–1986)", *World History*, 2006, 3: 82–92.
18 For more detailed studies of Spanish political parties, see Richard Gunther, Giacomo Sani, and Goldie Shabad, *Spain after Franco: The Making of a Competitive Party System*. Berkeley: University of California Press, 1986.
19 For studies on these isses, see Paloma Aguilar, "Justice, Politics, and Memory in the Spanish Transition", *The Politics of Memory and Democratization*, Alexandra Barahona De Brito, Carmen Gonzalez, Enriquez, & Paloma Aguilar (eds.). Oxford: Oxford University Press, 2001, 92–118.
20 Data as cited in Omar G. Encarnacion, "Spain after Franco: Lessons in Democratization", *World Policy Journal*, 2001, 2: 35–44. Such consensus on democracy was also reflected in the aforementioned referendum.
21 Anthony W. Pereira, "Democracies: Emerging or Submerging?" *Dissent*, Winter 2001, 48: 17–23.
22 Anthony W. Pereira, "Democracies: Emerging or Submerging?" *Dissent*, Winter 2001, 48: 17–23.

6 The design of institutional reform for Chinese cooperative-harmonious democracy

Based on a comparative analysis of Chinese and foreign theory and practice on democracy, we posit the concepts related to Chinese cooperative-harmonious democracy, which have been inspired by traditional ideas of "people-oriented" and "harmony and cooperation", in combination with the theory and methods of cooperative game as well as the historical experience of democratic transition and development in other countries. Next, cooperative-harmonious democracy must be taken beyond the conceptual level to institutional design, which would serve as the cornerstone for its construction. Institutions are the set of rules members of a society play by. They are the regulations or limitations designed for interactions among people, which help them to establish stable expectations in their dealings with others and facilitate cooperation for optimum results.[1] Though it is yet difficult to design an exhaustive system of institutions for cooperative-harmonious democracy, we should at least take into consideration the following issues.

Basic philosophy of institutional reform for Chinese cooperative-harmonious democracy

Conflict and cooperation are an eternal issue facing individuals, groups, and nations. While some individuals, groups, and nations benefit from fruitful cooperation, others are tormented by bitter conflict. Social scientists have long been trying to find out the fundamental causes for conflict and cooperation. The emergence and development of game theory have provided a new perspective on this issue. In game theory analysis, when taking purposeful and strategic actions, participants will consider their possible influence on others and, in turn, the possible influence of others' actions on them; then they will choose the optimum course of action for the maximization of benefits. All decision making in real life can be regarded as game. Game theory can be applied to the analysis of reconstructed interactions between people and that of important issues in social sciences.

Both the model of liberal democracy and that of socialist democracy have their raison d'être *per se*, but their way of dealing with political conflict is mainly based on the assumption of non-cooperative game. In fact, now we had better go beyond such assumption and apply cooperative game approach to a deep and systematic thinking about the construction of a model of Chinese cooperative-harmonious democracy. Each political process involves mutual influence between different interests and opinion holders, and the design of a political system is essentially a matter of power configuration. Therefore cooperative game can be a most fundamental approach to any attempt to transcend traditional studies of democracy and the reform of its political systems. Liberal democracy and traditional socialist democracy are located toward different ends of the horizontal axis (individual value vs. collective value), yet both fall into the category of non-cooperative game. Liberal democracy tends to underline democracy through competitive election for the protection of individual rights and interests, whereas traditional socialist democracy highlights collective democracy based on class struggle and conflict. Though still a form of socialist democracy, cooperative-harmonious democracy attaches more importance to cooperation and coordination between the diverse actors and elements of society and the construction of harmonious democratic relationships (see Figure 6.1).

The cooperative game approach is highly recommendable in the construction of cooperative-harmonious democracy.

First of all, it can help to achieve what is best for both the collective and the individual. To consider the construction of democratic politics in China from this perspective would help the whole nation to design the best democratic system and course of action for protecting the maximum interests of all political actors under the overarching goal of development.

Secondly, it can facilitate the laying of a stable organizational foundation. Cooperative game assumes that people will form alliances during their interaction, and one of the principal features of balance is the stability of such alliances, i.e., the existence of stable organizations in people's interaction and cooperation. Therefore, cooperative-harmonious democracy should incorporate collective behavior and organizational behavior into democratic theory on the basis of individual liberty and regard the relative stability, not instability, of political structure as one of the hallmarks of a scientific and feasible democracy.

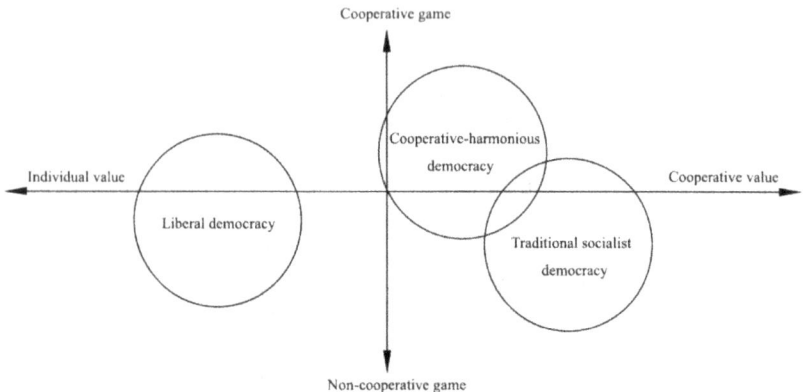

Figure 6.1 A two-dimensional diagram of different models of democracy

Thirdly, it is conducive to self-enforcement by the participants of cooperation. The capability of self-enforcement in an equilibrium state, as a basic concept, is one of the similarities between cooperative game and non-cooperative game. However, in cooperative game, this is extended to between organizations (i.e., alliances) and between organizations and individuals. Similarly, the institutional design for cooperative-harmonious democracy should aim for the voluntary choice of cooperation by the actors (including organizations and individuals) in a political process with a certain measure of institutional incentives and restraints. Therefore, the process and institutional design of cooperative-harmonious democracy based on cooperative game are more likely to strike a balance between what is best for individuals and what is best for collectives than the process and institutional design of democratic models based on non-cooperative game.

With regard to the realities in China, to achieve the goals of real cooperative game, cooperative-harmonious democracy requires the application of the cooperation-harmony concept and the cooperative game approach to the handling of all kinds of political relationships. These include the relationship between democracy within the Communist Party and people's democracy, between electoral democracy and deliberative democracy, between direct democracy and representative democracy, between centralization and local autonomy, between rule of virtue and rule of law, between the ruling party and the other parties, between the principal ethnic group and the ethnic minorities, between the mainstream groups and the marginalized ones, and between the three aspects of government – government of the people, by the people, and for the people (see Figure 6.2). The most important among these are probably the relationship between intra-Party democracy and people's democracy, between the ruling party and the other parties, between electoral democracy and deliberative democracy, and between rule of virtue and rule of

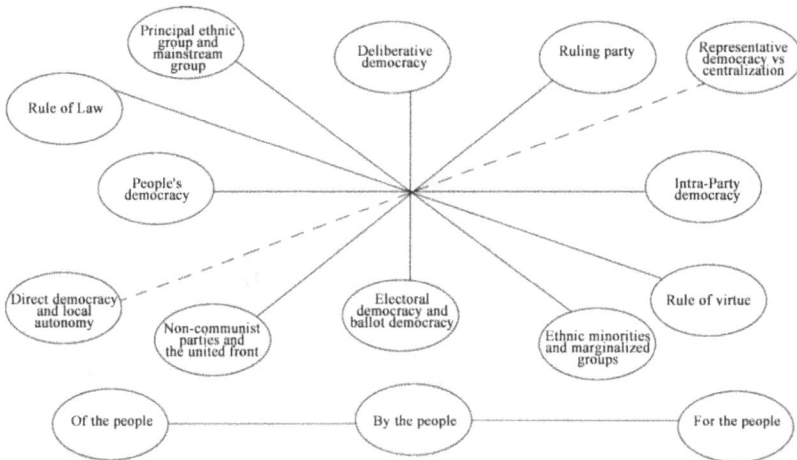

Figure 6.2 Major types of relationship to be coordinated for cooperative-harmonious democracy

law. Next we will further discuss issues related to these aspects. The settlement of these types of relationships through an institutionalized coordination mechanism would definitely facilitate the building of cooperative-harmonious democracy and a truly harmonious society.

The basic principles of institutional design for Chinese cooperative-harmonious democracy: an integration of people's democracy, the party's leadership, and law-based governance

To be recognized and accepted in China, cooperative-harmonious democracy must be combined with the existing democratic system. For democracy in China, the greatest emphasis is currently laid on this: "The most fundamental requirement in the development of socialist democracy is to integrate the Party's leadership, the people's role as the masters of the country, and law-based governance."[2] In fact, in terms of cooperative-harmonious democracy, the three aspects may take on new meanings. The Party's leadership means the power of authority, the people's role as the masters of the country is an expression of popular will, and the rule of law is an institutional arrangement and guarantee. In the institutional design of cooperative-harmonious democracy, we have to ensure an appropriate measure of well-regulated combination of and balance between the Party's leadership (authority) and the people's role as the masters of the country (popular will).

Election forms an essential part of democracy. The advance of the times has multiplied social strata, diversified people's interests and values, and awakened them to their civil rights. It can be safely stated that there is also a growing demand for election in China. The Communist Party of China (CPC), which advances with the times, should also learn to gradually lift the restrictions on election and tolerate the presence of alternative candidates within the system. However, the current development of democracy in China also has an explicit value orientation, which is a strong opposition to competitive election as practiced in the West. Under the current conditions, cooperative-harmonious democracy can pursue a type of election with a limited and moderate amount of competition, or what can be termed "semi-competitive election". Thus, within a manageable scope, direct election democracy can be gradually put into practice as the means by which the relationship between the givers and takers of power can be straightened out so as to enhance the legitimacy of the government. The strategy for developing this kind of cooperative-harmonious democracy is to prioritize grassroots election and, based on that, to gradually put into place local electoral democracy and eventually to introduce direct election on the central or national level.

However, in today's China, the CPC maintains its leadership in the selection and appointment of all types of leaders at various levels through its organizational and personnel system. There does exist some tension between this and bottom-up authorization implied by election.[3] Therefore, the following has to be taken into consideration in the institutional design of cooperative-harmonious democracy: during an election, too much emphasis on the role of the Party and the superiors would militate against a true reflection of public opinion unless it has been solicited by the Party before decision making; too much stress on the people's role as the masters of the country, with the voters managing the election entirely on their own without the Party's leadership, may lead to uncontrollable chaos and social instability. How to strike a balance between them is one of the key considerations in the institutional design of cooperative-harmonious democracy.

Basic forms of institutional design for Chinese cooperative-harmonious democracy: the integration of electoral democracy and deliberative democracy

How should cooperative-harmonious democracy be developed? On the one hand, we need to advance electoral democracy based on election and voting, with representative democracy as the principal institutional form, and deepen the reform of the electoral system, the representative system, and the representative conference system, in order to bring cooperative-harmonious democracy into existence; on the other hand, we need to develop deliberative democracy based on dialogue and communication, encourage direct participation by citizens, build public deliberative mechanisms, and promote the expression, coordination, and realization of diverse opinions and interests in society. In fact, electoral democracy and deliberative democracy can be essentially unified in popular sovereignty. They differ in form and scope of application, and each has its own strengths and limitations; they can be mutually complementary, with something of each in the other. In no country can the development of democracy rely on one form while excluding another. Therefore, Chinese cooperative-harmonious democracy cannot be an either-or choice between electoral democracy and deliberative democracy. The key to the sound development of Chinese cooperative-harmonious democracy in the future is the proper handling of the relationship between the two forms of democracy, the establishment of a model that integrates the two, and the maintaining of a proper measure of balance and tension between them.[4]

The application of electoral democracy in China

The reality in today's China seems to urgently demand the progress of electoral democracy. As long as democracy is developed in China, electoral democracy is eventually a threshold to cross, however great the challenges might be. In other words, it is impossible to postpone indefinitely the development of electoral democracy in China. This is because "[w]eak and problematic though elections often are, they now form a crucial step in the process of attaining political legitimacy throughout most of the world. [. . .] It may be true that in many countries democracy can barely live with elections, but in no country can it live without them."[5]

An ideal and true election should be characterized by the following: all the adults are entitled to vote; each vote has the same impact; the location and timing of the election and the interval between it and the next election are reasonable; all the seats are generated by the election; the election offers real options to the voters, and any major social group has the right to nominate its candidate; the candidates can freely express their political opinions with no fear and conduct a promotional campaign, and the voters can freely discuss such issues; the voters are entitled to free and secret ballot; all the candidates are impartially treated and the votes cast are respected; the winners of the election can hold public office until the end of their terms.[6] Democratic progress in many countries has been, to a large extent, toward an electoral democracy that lives up to these standards.

The electoral democracy currently practiced in China is lacking in a proper measure of competition; moreover, the scope and level of direct election democracy should be expanded and raised instead of being confined to the scope or level of the grassroots.[7] It is true, however, that before the adoption of real electoral democracy, we should pay more attention to China's economic, political, and social foundation, especially the degree to which electoral democracy is compatible with our historical legacy and current realities. We need to consider how to expand and enhance the scope, level, and quality of electoral democracy without getting out of state control so that the citizens can gradually come to enjoy a full right to vote. Therefore, how to promote electoral democracy with perfect timing is also an essential step for the development of Chinese cooperative-harmonious democracy.

The application of deliberative democracy in China

As a systematic theory of democracy, deliberative democracy was born out of the critique of Western electoral democracy with free competition. It cannot be equated with political consultation in China; nor can the latter be regarded as the only form of deliberative democracy. To avoid confusion, some scholars suggest that "deliberative democracy" be translated into *shenyi minzhu* instead of *xieshang minzhu*, which they believe is a misinterpretation.[8] Such argument may continue on an academic level to the benefit of scholarship. However, for the progress of democracy in China, we cannot afford to wait till the reaching of a consensus before we learn from the experience already gained in deliberative democracy. Despite the controversy on how to translate the term, scholars agree that the philosophy and institutional design of deliberative democracy can shed a great deal of light on how to develop democracy in China. Currently, the most crucial challenge is how to apply deliberative democracy to Chinese politics in a creative way. There are essentially two approaches worth considering:

1   Deliberative democracy in China should reflect its key concept, i.e., the emphasis on common citizens' direct participation in public decision making that has a bearing on their interests, with an expectation for consensus on controversial public policies during the deliberative process. Deliberative democracy has been widely used in public decision making and other areas in many Western countries with good results. For China in particular, it can also be used in public decision making, which is still largely dominated by elitism despite the emphasis on citizens' participation through improved mechanisms. As a result, public decision making is still largely the result

of interaction between and manipulation by political elites rather than that of interaction between citizens and the government.[9] Though this problem is attributable to many causes, the lack of ways to participate is a major restriction on citizens' right of participation.

Some people may argue that today's Chinese citizens have no shortage of channels for taking part in public discussion and decision making, such as reception days, symposiums, hotlines, mailboxes, and public hearings. However, in all these channels, citizens tend to play a passive role, with little real exchange and communication. Given the emphasis on citizens' right to know and participate, they should be accorded their due importance and offered opportunities to fully express their opinions and suggestions in democratic dialogues and public discussions on public decision making with experts and officials. In this sense, there is a shortage in the forms of participation offered to Chinese citizens. As an effective way to make public decision making more legitimate, deliberative democracy, in terms of its philosophy and institutional design, can be a source of inspiration for improving the mechanism for Chinese citizens' participation in public decision making. Not only can it help the government to improve transparency, legitimacy and the quality of decision making, but it can also help common citizens to enhance their interest in and capability of participation in public affairs as a virtue and acquire a deeper insight into policies.

2   Deliberative democracy has to be geared to the realities in China and undergo creative transformation. In particular, it needs to be combined with China's system of political consultation. In fact, since the advent of reform and opening up, interests and social strata have become diversified in China. As a platform for reflecting public opinion and political participation by various groups, the system cannot meet the people's growing demand for such participation without self-adjustment suited to the times. The reform of the political consultation system is of equal importance to the development of democracy in China. Therefore, "we need to persist in our effort to make multi-party cooperation and political consultation better institutionalized and regulated, with well-established procedures; based on that, we need to keep on analyzing new situations and challenges facing multi-party cooperation and seek new mechanisms and forms, in order to enrich and strengthen multi-party cooperation and political consultation led by the CPC in terms of scope, mechanism and procedures."[10]

During the combination of deliberative democracy and the political consultation system, it is necessary to highlight the strengths of the existing political party system and vigorously develop deliberative democracy on the level of political parties in order to make inter-party consultation more thorough, authentic, and effective. It is also necessary to introduce a well-developed consultation mechanism, and a feasible way to do this is to utilize the role of the People's Political Consultative Conference in the discussion of state affairs and borrow the institutional design of deliberative democracy in order to find out what public opinion really is. Therefore, the system of multi-party cooperation and political consultation led by the CPC can be regarded as a ready-made institutional platform for the application of deliberative democracy in China. To develop deliberative democracy, we need to make full use of the People's Political Consultative Conference as an institutional resource. In this way, through constant practice, we may indeed see deliberative democracy growing and improving in China someday.

The political report of President Hu Jintao to the 18th CPC National Congress voices an explicit demand for socialist consultative democracy:

> Socialist consultative democracy is an important form of people's democracy in our country. We should improve its institutions and work mechanisms and promote its extensive, multilevel, and institutionalized development. Extensive consultations should be carried out on major issues relating to economic and social development as well as specific problems involving the people's immediate interests through organs of state power, committees of the Chinese People's Political Consultative Conference, political parties, people's organizations and other channels to solicit a wide range of opinions, pool wisdom of the people, increase consensus, and build up synergy. We should adhere to and improve the system of multiparty cooperation and political consultation under the leadership of the Communist Party of China and make the Chinese People's Political Consultative Conference serve as a major channel for conducting consultative democracy. The Chinese People's Political Consultative Conference should, focusing on the themes of unity and democracy, improve systems of political consultation, democratic oversight, and participation in the deliberation and administration of state affairs, and deliver a better job in coordinating relations, pooling strength and making proposals in the overall interests of the country. We should strengthen political consultation with the democratic parties, make political consultation a part of the policymaking process, conduct consultations before and when policy decisions are made, and make democratic consultation more effective. We should conduct intensive consultations on special issues with those who work on these issues, with representatives from all sectors of society, and with relevant government authorities on the handling of proposals. We should actively carry out democratic consultation at the community level.[11]

The relationship between electoral democracy and deliberative democracy

Some Western scholars believe that "election-oriented" democracy should give way to "deliberation-oriented" democracy, and deliberative democracy does have its merits. However, for most countries, the current representative government cannot do without the legitimacy bestowed by electoral democracy. As a result, deliberative democracy cannot exist on its own; nor can it replace electoral democracy. It cannot survive without relying on activities and processes in the existing system of electoral democracy.[12] This also means that while electoral democracy can be independent of deliberative democracy, the latter can hardly survive without the former.

It is essentially possible to unify deliberative democracy and electoral democracy. Though the former was born out of the critique of the latter, both of them are aimed at putting into practice the Western concept of "popular sovereignty". While electoral democracy is a form of indirect democracy, with the voters delegating their right to govern to their deputies, deliberative democracy is a form of direct democracy – an attempt to restore the active role played by citizens in classical democracy, with emphasis on their direct participation in deliberations on public affairs. In China, both indirect democracy and direct democracy are fundamentally aimed at consolidating the people's role as the masters of the country. In this sense, therefore, both of them can be essentially unified in the concept of popular sovereignty.

In terms of their effects, deliberative democracy and electoral democracy are mutually complementary. The former lays more emphasis on communication and consensus, while the latter is inclined toward competition and resolution by the majority. Without electoral democracy, deliberative democracy would wear down the public's enthusiasm for participation if consensus cannot be reached; without deliberative democracy, the sole reliance on electoral democracy would give excessive weight to votes and widen the existing differences. Therefore, the two forms of democracy have mutually complementary roles to play.

Moreover, deliberative democracy is often necessary in the process of electoral democracy, and voting mechanisms can also be introduced into decision making in deliberative democracy.

Constructing a cooperative-harmonious democracy model that unifies electoral democracy and deliberative democracy

Electoral democracy and deliberative democracy can be essentially unified in popular sovereignty. In terms of function, each has its strengths and limitations. For the development of democracy, no country can rely too much on one while eschewing the other. Nevertheless, electoral democracy takes priority because its smooth functioning is the prerequisite for the authenticity of deliberative democracy. Therefore, China cannot make an either-or choice between the two. Instead, we need to integrate the two forms of democracy, with electoral democracy playing a leading role, and maintain proper balance and tension between them in order to construct a cooperative-harmonious democracy model in which they are integrated. At certain stages of democratic development, however, more importance can be attached to deliberative democracy.

In fact, this idea has been made clear in the CPC Central Committee's Directive on Strengthening the People's Political Consultative Conference, which was ratified in February 2006:

> The people can exercise their rights through election and voting; they can also conduct thorough deliberation before the making of any important decision in order to reach consensus on issues of common interest whenever possible. These are two major forms of socialist democracy in our country.

This has expanded the theoretical and practical space for the construction of a Chinese cooperative-harmonious democracy model. However, while integrating electoral democracy and deliberative democracy, we must bear in mind the differences between China and the West in history and discourse. We must avoid mechanical imitation, which would set up unnecessary barriers to the development of democracy.

The basic ingredients of institutional design

In the institutional design of cooperative-harmonious democracy, it is necessary to grasp the essential spirit of democracy, which is the role of the people as the master of their country. We need to highlight traditional ideas of "people-oriented" (*minben*) and "harmony and cooperation" (*hehe*) and employ cooperative game approach. We must consider institutional design in terms of cooperation between individuals, between organizations, between individuals and organizations, and among individuals, organizations and the country, and enable all the interest groups and political groups in society to have the opportunity for full participation, so that conflicts of interests and differences in opinion can be institutionally resolved. To this end, with respect to the current realities and future development, we believe that the following issues are worth considering in the institutional design of cooperative-harmonious democracy.

Institutional design should be reflected in the electoral institutions and party institutions related to power structure

Direct election and moderately competitive election should be introduced in a planned and systematic way for the election of party representatives and deputies to the People's Congress at all levels as well as the election of local party leaders and administrative leaders. Within the framework of the existing party system, we may promote pre-election communication and deliberation between the parties and social groups, institutionally evade the negative side of electoral competition, create well-regulated channels of cooperation and competition between the parties and effective incentives, construct a stable and lasting multi-party cooperation system led by the CPC, and enhance leadership by one party and government by a multi-party coalition. In fact, the idea of coalition can be traced back to *On Coalition Government* (1945) by Mao Zedong, who outlined the plan to establish such a government for cooperation as well as check and balance between political parties, which would essentially be a government by a multi-party coalition. To develop cooperative-harmonious democracy is to develop this important idea under today's conditions, in a way suited to the times and the growth of diverse political groups. We need to design a more inclusive party system that would raise the status of the non-communist parties, offer them more opportunities to participate in government by coalition, and enhance their capability of doing so, so that more leaders from such parties could assume leading posts in state organs at various levels, with more institutionalized channels to take part in the making and execution of major state policies.

The differentiation of interests in today's Chinese society is becoming more and more complicated. On the one hand, the CPC can expand and enhance its representativeness and include emerging major interest groups and political forces in controlled political participation; on the other hand, it is also necessary to expand the representativeness of non-communist parties and include particular new interest groups and political forces in the discussion of state affairs. We need to raise the status of non-communist parties from participants in governance and political consultation to participants in a coalition government similar to what they used to be during the early years of the People's Republic of China. This would definitely stimulate their enthusiasm and initiative and enable them to play their special role more effectively in the existing system for the development of democracy. This can be a truly effective and proactive way to avoid the drawbacks of the one-party system and the multi-party system. In particular, it can eliminate what can be taken advantage of in the name of democracy over the issue of China's democratization by reactionary political forces at home and abroad. Moreover, it can improve the image of democracy in China and propel the overall harmonious development of the Chinese society.

Institutional design should be reflected in the reform and improvement of horizontal and vertical state power relations

On the horizontal level, we must continue to adhere to and improve the CPC's leadership of state organs and straighten out the relationship between the CPC and such organs. The CPC must exercise self-discipline, propel people's democracy through intra-Party democracy, and conduct all its activities within the scope of the constitution and other laws. Moreover, we must adhere to the People's Congress system and the principle of democratic centralism, and protect and raise the status and role of the People's Congress as the only organ of state power; we need to strengthen the check and supervision on the executive and judicial organs by the People's Congress and prevent the abuse of power and corruption. Vertical-wise, we shall adhere to the unitary system of centralization while adopting local decentralization and autonomy in economic development and relevant areas of public affairs in order to give full play to the role of local government and grassroots organizations.

Institutional design should also be reflected in public governance

On the level of public governance, institutional design is mainly reflected in the emphasis on the introduction of actors like citizens and stakeholders into the management of and decision making about public affairs for controlled participation in various types of deliberative democracy:

> Nowadays, an important change has taken place in the way public decisions are made by the government. People can no longer accept the view that the government's public policies are made by the few leaders who hold power

and claim to represent public interests but reject participation by citizens. Nowadays, policy-makers must attach great importance to citizens' demand to participate in government decision making. Otherwise, such decision making would prove to be meaningless if most of the public are indifferent, unresponsive or even strongly opposed to the public policy process.[13]

Generally speaking, elitism still plays a prominent role in the selection of and decision making on topics of public discussion in China. Public decision making is largely a result of interaction between and manipulation by elites within the political system instead of that of interaction between citizens and the government.[14] Despite the variety of causes for such a limited degree of public participation, it is the institutional flaws that have restricted citizens and stakeholders' deliberative rights to a large extent. There is still an inadequacy in the institutional forms for placing citizens and stakeholders on an important position for real democratic dialogue, public discussion, and deliberation. In the discussion of how to improve socialist consultative democracy, the report of President Hu Jintao to the 18th CPC National Congress emphasizes the importance of improving its institutions and work mechanisms, promoting its extensive, multilevel, and institutionalized development, and conducting intensive consultations on special issues with those who work on these issues, with representatives from all sectors of society, and with relevant government authorities on the handling of proposals as well as democratic consultation at the community level.

Institutional design may be challenging, yet such challenge can be overcome. Moreover, it must keep abreast of the times so that instructional changes could be brought about in a strategic way along with the change in philosophy. So long as we follow the correct philosophy and adhere to the truth-seeking spirit and cooperative game approach, the designing of cooperative-harmonious democracy would be feasible.

Basic steps of the development of Chinese cooperative-harmonious democracy

Chinese cooperative-harmonious democracy cannot be successful overnight; it must develop step by step. At first, we may carry out reform on the community and local level toward the direct election of Party representatives, deputies to the People's Congress, and executive leaders, and promote institutional innovation and experiment in certain aspects of electoral democracy such as intra-Party democracy and the reform of inter-party relations. After that, we may share the experience from the success in local areas and certain sectors and wait for the right timing and conditions to carry it upward in a planned way. This can ensure that the development of democracy would not have too much negative impact on political stability.

Additionally, some practices of deliberative democracy in public governance, such as democratic symposiums and decision hearings, usually involve changes in the structure, process, and ways of public governance rather than changes in the state power structure, with little direct impact on political stability. Therefore, they can be popularized in a bottom-up way, or carried out in a top-down manner.

Notes

1 Douglas North, *Institutions, Institutional Change and Economic Performance*. Shanghai: Shanghai Joint Publishing Company, 1994.
2 See the Political Reports of the 16th–18th CPC National Congresses.
3 Pan Wei and Wang Shaoguang, "Academic Symposium on Contemporary Issues of Chinese Political Reform", *Sun Yat-sen University Political Science Review*, Xiao Bin & Guo Zhonghua (eds.). Guangzhou: Sun Yat-sen University Press, 2005, 286–288.
4 Ma Ben and Peng Zongchao, "Integration of Deliberative Democracy and Ballot Democracy: Models of Democratic Development in China", *Theoretical Studies*, 2009, 4.
5 Thomas Carothers, "How Democracies Emerge: The 'Sequencing' Fallacy", *Journal of Democracy*, 2007, 18(1): 21.
6 Cai Ziqiang, "Electoral Systems and Voting", *New Perspectives on Political Science: Western Theories and Chinese Experience*, Zheng Yushuo & Luo Jinyi (eds.). Hong Kong: The Chinese University Press, 1997, 171–172.
7 For details, see Peng Zongchao, *Authorization by Citizens and Representative Democracy: A Comparative Study of Systems for the Direct Election of People's Deputies*, Chapter 6. Zhengzhou: Henan People's Press, 2002.
8 Jin Anping, "'Deliberative Democracy': Misinterpretation, Coincidence and Possibilities of Creative Transformation in China", *New Vision*, 2007, 5: 63–67. The Chinese translation of "deliberative democracy" was also discussed at the symposium on "Deliberative Democracy and Its Practice in China" jointly held by The World and China Institute, 21ccom.net, and the Democratic Symposium Office of Wenling City, Zhejiang Province on December 14–15, 2012. See the website on the symposium at http://www.21ccom.net/special/xieshangminzhu.
9 Hu Wei, *The Government Process*. Hangzhou: Zhejiang People's Publishing House, 1998, 255.
10 The CPC Central Committee's Opinions on Further Strengthening Multi-party Cooperation and Political Consultation Led by the CPC (ZF [2005] 5).
11 Hu Jintao, *Firmly March on the Path of Socialism with Chinese Characteristics and Strive to Complete the Building of a Moderately Prosperous Society in All Respects: Speech at the 18th CPC National Congress*. Beijing: People's Press, 2012.
12 Michael Walzer, "Deliberation, and What Else?" *Deliberative Politics: Essays on Democracy and Disagreement*, Stephen Macedo (ed.). Oxford: Oxford University Press, 1999, 59.
13 John Clayton Thomas, *Public Participation in Public Decisions: New Skills and Strategies for Public Managers*, Sun Baiying (trans.). Beijing: China Renmin University Press, 2005, 1.
14 Hu Wei, *The Government Process*. Hangzhou: Zhejiang People's Publishing House, 1998, 255.

7 A case study of Chinese cooperative-harmonious electoral democracy

It cannot be denied that China has made great progress in democratic practice since the beginning of reform and opening up. Local democracy has been developed through bold and proactive explorations, including experiments in the direct election of the township heads or party secretaries in some places, and intra-party reform in other places. However, democratic practice in China is now facing great difficulty, for it has reached a bottleneck. This is mainly reflected in the difficulty we have in incorporating the direct election of township heads into the existing institutional arrangement. Some people even believe that, if allowed to go unchecked, this practice will pose a threat to the ruling party's authority and the power structure. Therefore, without democratic innovation, grassroots democratic experiments, however numerous they might be, cannot make a breakthrough, nor can they be institutionalized. In this chapter, we will conduct a case study of the direct election of the head of Shiping Township in Yunnan Province from the perspective of cooperative-harmonious democracy.

Literature review

There are three major points of view in current research into the direct election of township heads:

1   This practice is of great significance and should be popularized. Li Fan made some case studies of the direct election of township heads in Nancheng Township of Meishan City, Sichuan Province (December 1998), Buyun Township of Suining City (December 1998), Pingba Town of Chengkou County, Chongqing City (2003), and seven townships in Shiping, Yunnan (2004). He found out that, since the introduction of direct election, the local officials have changed their attitude toward farmers. They have become more attentive listeners to farmers' needs and would like to spend more time with them. In fact, direct election has changed the tradition of officials being accountable to their superiors only. Since the advent of direct election, appeals from local farmers to higher authorities for help have disappeared or significantly decreased, and the political tension in rural areas has been eased in those places. The direct election of township heads has laid a solid foundation for

the further expansion of political reform and the further progress of grassroots democracy. Such reform is highly meaningful and has, in its own right, marked a step forward for grassroots democracy.[1]

Huang Weiping sees the reform in the election of township heads as a new practical source of growth and motivation for the democratization of Chinese politics. The success of the new model is helpful for consolidating local governments' foundation of governance and enhancing the legitimacy of grassroots political power. Now that the leaders of grassroots governments are elected by their voters, who have the right to appraise or even dismiss them, they need to rely more and more on the latter's votes for their legitimacy. This, in turn, will cause a profound change in their relations with the higher levels of government. With the development of local democracy, a lower-level government will have a proportionally higher degree of legitimacy derived from a fully quantified popular foundation. Such enhancement of legitimacy may boost the growth of democracy and bring Chinese politics to a new stage of beneficial interaction. However, the reform in the way to elect township heads can also be impeded by psychological barriers, wrong perceptions, and institutional restrictions.[2]

Lai Hairong attributes competitive election at the township level to the attempt of authorities at the county level and above to ease the operational difficulty of townships, reduce their debt burden, or enhance their operational efficiency. Therefore, this kind of election is actually a decentralization campaign at the county level and below. It is a policy vehicle for governance at the county level and above rather than the free election that some people have generally expected. Instead, it is a limited and prudent adjustment to our political system. Gradual as it is, it does have the effect of stimulating the growth of democracy because: (i) competitive election in townships have eased their operational difficulty to some degree; (ii) the party-state system has become more open and more transparent at the township level; (iii) the masses have come to take a conspicuously more active part in political processes of townships, with the ability to restrain their power; (iv) county-level Party committees' right to appoint or dismiss township officials has been diluted to some extent and apparently decentralized; (v) township Party committees' right to appoint or dismiss village cadres has been considerably diluted or completely devolved.[3]

Yang Xuedong is of the opinion that the direct election of township leaders has expanded the scope of public participation and enabled more common villagers to know how the principal leaders of townships are generated. However, there are certain limits upon democratization within this system, and there is some conflict between open participation and the limited institutional channels. We cannot be sure as to when such direct election can lead to an institutional change because election at the township level is significantly different from village-level election; it has a wider and deeper impact, and its destiny hinges on the political leaders' resolve and confidence regarding political reform. Nevertheless, it is just a matter of time before the scope of direct election is expanded and its level raised.[4]

2   The experiments in the direct election of township heads are to be opposed because such election is unconstitutional. The holders of this opinion argue that such election is essentially an attempt at a radical constitutional change. The focus of reform should be on the election of deputies to the People's Congress in order to address the weaknesses in the existing electoral system, such as the lack of competitiveness in such elections and too many levels involved in indirect elections above the township/county level. However, it is utterly unnecessary to change the election of township heads by the People's Congress to direct election by citizens at the cost of breaking the constitution. Such experiments are bound to be without value or practical significance.[5]

3   Under the current conditions, prudence is to be exercised in the nationwide adoption of the direct election of township heads. The holders of this opinion argue that such direct elections require human, material, and financial input and are therefore too costly for townships in economically backward regions. Even if it is put into practice in such regions, it would not be sustainable. Such elections are limited to a certain size of population, so appropriate candidates would be hard to choose in heavily populated townships. The sustainability of this institutional innovation may rely on whether it can be conducive to political stability, the effective enforcement of the Central Government's policies and decrees, and socioeconomic development. However, the current situation suggests that it is unlikely to be extensively adopted, at least not in the near future. Nevertheless, these people are not against the direct election of township heads. Instead, in their opinion, for the areas that meet the above two preconditions (enough investment and limited population), the Central Government should allow and advocate this practice, discuss related issues, and summarize experience in order to be prepared for the upward extension of direct election at an appropriate time.[6]

The literature review above shows the different attitudes of researchers, which range from positive to negative, about the role and future of direct election of township heads. The focus of our research, however, is not to refute or critique their opinions. On the contrary, it is based on such opinions, which can help us to better analyze and understand the issue of the direct election of township heads in China. However, it should be noted that the existing research into this issue is mostly focused on the pros and cons of election itself. In particular, in terms of the relationship between this issue and the prospect of China's democratization, people often argue that direct election *per se* is a major progress in grassroots democracy and should be pursued as an impetus for China's democratization. However, it is necessary to find out the initial direction of such development under a macro-framework of democratic theory. Otherwise, the expansion of such direct election can only produce limited results; worse still, it might become an obstacle against the further development of democracy. Because of this, we shall posit the cooperative-harmonious democracy model as a framework for analyzing the future trend of democracy in China in the hope that tentative research can be made under this framework into the relationship between the direct election of township heads and the prospect of China's democratization.

Basic framework

Democracy is good, but it is likely to be troublesome if the relationship between conflict and cooperation cannot be properly handled in its institutional arrangement. From the perspective of cooperative-harmonious democracy, the most essential task in the democratic practice in China is to properly handle the legal relationship between the CPC's leadership (collective authority) and people's democracy (civil liberty).

The CPC's leadership and people's democracy are essentially in accord with each other, with the former serving to achieve the latter in a more effective way. However, in actual practice, unnecessary conflict may arise if the relationship between the two is improperly handled. As shown in Figure 7.1, if too much emphasis is laid on the CPC's leadership, it might annihilate people's democracy under extreme circumstances, with the Party replacing the people as the master of the country. Such would be a false kind of democracy, with non-cooperative game between the two, which is likely to cause conflict. If, on the other hand, too much emphasis is laid on people's democracy, it might annihilate the CPC's leadership under extreme circumstances. This kind of democracy might lose a stable leadership and jeopardize social order. There will also be non-cooperative game, and consequently conflict, between the two.

Cooperative-harmonious democracy underlines the necessity to establish a virtuous cycle between the CPC's leadership (collective authority) and people's democracy (civil liberty) through cooperative game for the development of democracy in China. This is because long-term partnership is easier to maintain than cooperation on a single occasion; even parties whose short-term interests are in serious conflict can strike a cooperative balance through repeated games. This also indicates that, for a long time to come, the development and stability of democracy in China cannot be possible without the legal combination of the CPC's leadership and people's democracy (see Figure 7.1).

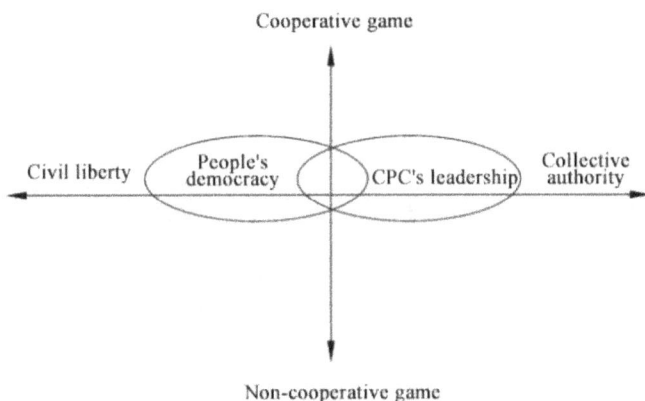

Figure 7.1 Framework for analyzing electoral democracy

A case study of the direct election of township head candidates in Shiping

Introduction

According to the current Chinese constitution and related laws, township heads should be elected by the People's Congress at the township level. If the Party monopolizes the right to nominate and choose among the candidates, the deputies to the People's Congress would have hardly any right to express their will and make their choice. Thus the election of township heads is to a large extent merely a formality. Though it guarantees the Party's management of its cadres, it falls short of the demand of popular will.

Since the late 1990s, motivated by the election of village committees, some areas have conducted bold experiments and made institutional innovations in the generation of township heads. This is mainly reflected in the augmentation of the role of popular will in the generation of candidates, the design of competitive election, and the substitution of direct election for indirect election. The most noticeable practice is the direct election of township heads by township citizens despite the legal constraints. The earliest case of the direct election of township head candidates that was reported by the press took place in Buyun Township in the Central District of Suining City, Sichuan Province in 1999.[7] The elected people were merely the *candidates* because the constitution says that a township head must be eventually elected by the township People's Congress.

Between February and April 2004, direct elections of township head candidates were held at seven townships in Shiping County, Honghe Prefecture, Yunnan Province. More than 100,000 voters took part in it, marking a major breakthrough in the history of electoral reform in China. Between March 25 and 28, 2009, we conducted a field interview and study of the direct election of township head candidates in Shiping. How should we consider the practical effects of such election? What limitations does it have? We shall analyze this case and see what it means for the future of democracy in China.

Analysis of the direct election of township heads in Shiping

Basic facts

Between February 1 and April 25, 2004, an experimental direct election of township head candidates by voters was carried out at seven of the nine townships in Shiping County. Before the introduction of the direct election of township heads, a new round of election of deputies to the People's Congress had already been held at two of the nine townships. As a result, the experiment could only be conducted in the remaining seven townships, which had seventy villagers' committees and a total population of 151,200. It was probably the first direct election of township head candidates on such a large scale in almost the whole county.

The basic procedure

1   Preparatory stage, which mainly consisted in drafting the plans and regulations (e.g., "Tentative Procedures for the Direct Election of Township Heads by Voters" and "Deliberative Procedures at the Joint Conference") and appointing the Election Committee.
2   Motivating and training the masses: telling the citizens the policy for the direct election and encouraging them to take an active part in it.
3   Registration: registering the qualified voters.
4   Electing deputies to the township People's Congress and convening a session of the People's Congress, which would pass a resolution on the direct election of the township head candidates and adjourn.
5   The election committee of each villagers' committee would recommend their candidates. Of the 140-plus candidates recommended by the seven townships, 77 would be retained, with 11 representing each township. A preliminary candidate could be recommended by a group of at least thirty voters, and he/she could be outside or within this group.
6   Each township would select two preliminary candidates during the Joint Conference (JC). The JC would be attended by over 100 people, including community representatives, deputies to the People's Congress, township leaders and people from all walks of life. During the JC, each candidate would have to make a speech on his/her platform and be ready to debate or answer questions about it.
7   The two preliminary candidates selected at the JC would deliver campaign speeches all over their township. They would start with expressing their opinions on how to govern the township, and then answer questions from villagers. The process would be broadcast live on TV.
8   The voters would directly elect the township candidate, with three persons in charge of one mobile ballot box. After that, the votes would be counted at the seat of the township government and the results would be announced on the same day. The person gaining more than half of the votes, or more votes than the other preliminary candidate, would be elected the official candidate nominated to the township People's Congress.
9   The township People's Congress would resume its session to examine the legality of the electoral process and select the township head among the candidates. The head-elect would then nominate the vice township head subject to approval by the People's Congress.

Participation in direct election and the casting of votes

The seven townships elected seventy-seven preliminary candidates, consisting of sixty-nine males and eight females. These included township cadres, principals and school teachers, farmers, technicians, and village cadres. By social status, they comprised twenty-three Party/government leaders at the section level or above, twenty common cadres/employees (including laid-off workers), thirteen school teachers, six members of village committees, fourteen farmers, and one self-employed person. By educational background, they were composed of nineteen college graduates, forty-three junior college graduates, and fifteen senior high school/technical secondary school graduates. The total number of voters taking part in the direct election all over the county was 103,581, with a turnout rate of 97.1 percent.

Findings of our study (by field interviews in 2009)

PEOPLE'S DEMOCRACY WOULD BE IMPOSSIBLE WITHOUT DIRECT
COMPETITIVE ELECTION[8]

Our field interviews and survey revealed a generally positive view on the competitive direct election among citizens and government officials alike. The opinions cited below indicate that people's democracy would be impossible without competitive election.

Citizens' enthusiasm for participation was effectively aroused[9]
It was an opportunity of public education in democracy and law. In the past, we used to cast our votes randomly because the election was indirect. This time few of us did so because we all hoped to choose a really capable person. (I)

I took part in the whole process as a staff member. Even old people in their seventies or eighties came to the election. Each candidate's speech, plus the questions and answers that followed, lasted more than one hour. The people were very active in raising questions, and all of them were about their own village, such as the building of a road. In the past, we could not even see the Party secretary and the township head. Now we are familiar with them, and will turn to them for help if there's any problem. Whoever is elected will lead us toward a better future. (P)

Direct expression is real democracy, and voting is the only way to show what we really want. It's true democracy. The people are enthusiastic about it and are ready to take an active part in it. (S)

Theoretically it has enriched the forms of democracy. Direct election is the only way for people to show what they really want. It's better than indirect election. (T)

The distance between citizens and township heads was shortened
It has shortened the distance between the government and common citizens. We hadn't seen the township head in eight years. Now, after the election, how the head plans to go about his work is crystal clear to us, and it can be brought in line with what we think. (J)

It has been a rewarding experience for myself and brought me closer to common citizens. Now I have a deeper and more thorough knowledge of what is going on in the rural areas. (L)

The people have chosen their own leader. They are familiar with the head they have elected. They regard him as one among them and believe he will work for them. (H)

The government has become more responsible
The elected person will think about fulfilling his promises all the time. If he does, he will be heading a responsible government; if he is open and aboveboard about it, he will be heading a transparent government. (J)

The results were very good. The cadres have become more responsible and the people trust them. Now they are really caring about the common citizens. (S)

Through the competitive debate, the plans of development were combined with the local realities. As a result, policy has been better geared to reality, and the cadres have changed their working style in a way that brings them closer to the people. (V)

THE PARTY'S LEADERSHIP IS THE FUNDAMENTAL GUARANTEE FOR THE
ORDERLY DEVELOPMENT OF DIRECT COMPETITIVE DEMOCRACY

The Party's leadership serves to guarantee people's democracy rather than replace the people's role as the master of the country. Therefore the crux of the issue is the maintaining of a relationship of cooperative game between the two. The Party's leadership should be reflected in institutional support for election instead of the imposition of the Party's will on the people.

Since the way in which the township heads gain their power is changed through direct-election democracy (from appointment by the superior Party committee to reliance on the voters' trust), the way in which they use their power has also changed accordingly. In the innovation for the direct election of township heads, the Party's leadership (especially the power of superior Party organizations) is worthy of our attention. Since the direct election of township heads as practiced today is carried out under the direction or with the tacit consent of the Party (or superior Party organizations), failure to demarcate the limits of the Party's (or superior Party organizations') power would render such election perfunctory and lacking in the reflection of what the citizens really want. Generally speaking, during the election in question, the Party was quite judicious in its leadership, focusing on procedural justice. However, in a couple of townships, the superior Party organizations exercised their power improperly sometimes. As a result, the citizens have been disgruntled about the fact that the leaders they elected ended up being transferred before the end of their term. In fact, however, this is understandable because it was after all an experimental election.

The directly elected leaders were frequently transferred during their term. None of them stayed more than three years before they were moved to another post by the superior Party organization. The people are quite unhappy about this. (J)

The recommendation process, with 30 nominees, was fair in terms of procedure. However, the organizational department expected the original head to win.

The Party committee leaders had their intentions; at least they were not quite impartial. (Q)

The direct election of township heads in Shiping as carried out this time had its flaws. It was not purely competitive. The superior Party organization's agenda was somewhat obvious. Some elected persons were transferred before the end of their term, so they were unable to fulfill their promises. The people are unhappy about this. (Q)

The direct election of township heads and the prospect of China's democratization

PROGRESS AND HIDDEN PROBLEMS

In the past ten-odd years, a succession of experiments in the direct election of township heads have been carried out in China in what is hailed as the real beginning of China's democratization.[10] In fact, however, these are merely isolated events. They have not met with any positive reaction from the Central Government or the state, and the superior authorities have mostly taken an ambiguous attitude of "no publicity, no encouragement and no promotion". The National People's Congress is of the opinion that the constitution and the Local Organizations Law have clearly defined how township heads are to be generated and the procedures of their election; that is to say, township heads and vice heads are to be elected by secret ballot through the township People's Congress from among the candidates nominated by the presidium of or deputies to the Congress. The direct election of township heads by voters as practiced in some places, where it is perceived as an attempt to expand grassroots democracy, is against the constitution and the related laws. The election of township heads must be carried out in strict accordance with the constitution and the Local Organizations Law to prevent the occurrence of similar direct elections.[11] Despite this, however, the experience and progressive ideas gathered from the decade-long practice should not be devalued.

Currently there is no sign yet of any institutional arrangement for promoting the direct election of township heads in China. The main reason may lie in the essential difference between the direct election of township heads and that of villagers' committees, which are merely organizations for mass autonomy instead of organs of political power. The direct election of villagers' committees, therefore, would not have any impact on China's fundamental political structure and the status of the CPC. The township government, in comparison, is the lowest organ of political power. Its democratization is closely related to the democratization of political power in China. If township heads can be directly elected, it would lead to the inevitable demand for the direct election of the leaders of counties, provinces, and even the Central Government. In particular, the progress of the election of villagers' committees has caused conflict and tension between the Party and the government or governance (i.e., between the village Party branch and the villagers' committee) and between the upper level and lower level (i.e., between the township authorities and the villagers' committee). This would naturally lead to the concern that the direct election of township heads might cause similar tension between the township Party committee and the township government and between the county authorities and township authorities, and consequently threaten the CPC's system of governance centering around the People's Congress.

Besides, while clan influence can effectively motivate the people for participation in the direct election of village committees, it can hardly function so well in direct election on a township scale, which involves a more extensive geographic area, a larger number of people, a wider range of interests, and, consequently, fiercer competition. Under such circumstances, effective motivation of the voters would require the force of organization as an electoral vehicle. This is very likely to give rise to organized political activism, which might endanger the political establishment. This indeed makes it difficult for the authorities concerned to make up their minds about the direct election of township heads.

However, mere concern is far from enough because the mounting pressure of public opinion suggests that direct election will be an inevitable outcome of the progress of democracy in China. The crux of the issue is to find innovative ideas and institutional arrangements for democracy in line with the Party's leadership, the people's role as the master of the country, and rule of law. In this connection, cooperative-harmonious democracy may offer an approach to tackling the issue.

HOW SHOULD THE DIRECT ELECTION OF TOWNSHIP HEADS
CONTRIBUTE TO CHINA'S DEMOCRATIZATION?

This question will be answered from the perspective of cooperative-harmonious democracy, with details as follows:

The necessity of guidance by a macro-theory of democracy   The direct election of township heads as practiced in the past ten-odd years in China was mainly motivated by open-minded local CPC organizations and daring leaders. At each place, the election has been carefully designed by the superior Party organization, so the result was essentially predictable. Generally speaking, the practice has been sporadic and unsystematic. Admittedly, the noncommittal attitude of the Central Government has its benefits, such as evasion of ideological constraints and leftist attacks. However, it has also led to the lack of proactive planning and adaptation to the reform. The practice still falls far short of well-conducted electoral democracy. In particular, the absence of guidance under the framework of a macro-theory of democracy might make it even more unlikely to progress in a sustainable way.

Therefore, the development of democracy in China calls for guidance by such a theory and reflections on how to incorporate elements of the competitive direct election of township heads in terms of the political structure instead of "crossing the river by feeling the stones". Concern for direct election should be translated into a macro-theory on the practical development of democracy, which should have a preliminary orientation in high-level theory. Otherwise, the expansion of the direct election of township heads can only produce limited effects, or even become a barrier against the further progress of democracy.

Anyone who respects the reality in China would find it impossible and impermissible for the design of this theory to follow the path of Western liberal democracy. However, if it is only based on the current Chinese theory of democracy, it can hardly overcome the barriers against the development of democracy. A relatively feasible way is to combine the two models of democracy and to advance democracy in China through the cooperative-harmonious democracy model. It should be conceded that this research project is incapable of building a complete theory of the cooperative-harmonious democracy model, which would require more effort from our colleagues in academia. Nevertheless, this book may at least propose a new framework for consideration.

The necessity of a scientific and innovative overall institutional design   Democracy requires a well-developed overall institutional design, in which election is merely one of the essential parts. It is an unsound democracy, to say the least, that focuses only on election. Despite the benefits, the direct election of township heads can hardly be incorporated into the existing institutional arrangement if it endangers the ruling party's legitimacy and structure of governance. Therefore, the progress of democracy in China calls for a scientific and innovative overall institutional design for a more effective unification of the Party's leadership and the people's role as the master of the country.

However, democracy is not a windfall; it needs to be propelled and practiced. Yet democratization is only possible if there is a system that can offer reasonable hope that the interests of the main political actors would not be seriously affected in democratic competition and that the resources would still be under their control.[12] The most important task at present is to combine the direct election of township heads with a macro-theory of democracy in China and to think in a whole about how to design a cooperative-harmonious democracy system for this practice. This would be the only way to find out where this practice should be going.

Cooperative-harmonious democracy emphasizes overall institutional design, which is to reflect the philosophy of cooperative game. However, the institutional support for the direct election of township heads in China is insufficient. The question of how to make a scientific and innovative institutional design can be generally considered in terms of the ideas and institutional principles advocated in cooperative game. Firstly, in terms of the electoral system, reforms in the constitution and electoral law are to be carried out to provide the necessary legal latitude for the direct election of township heads. Additionally, the candidates' overall quality, including moral standards and professional ability, should be judiciously examined, and their integrity and ability to fulfill their promises should be fully assessed, with the results made available to the voters. Secondly, in the construction of the competitive system, the "reputation effect" should be fully utilized to form a dynamic mechanism for the accumulation of reputation. This could effectively discourage officials from taking the moral risk while encouraging them to honor their commitments. Thirdly, in terms of the political party system, well-regulated channels and effective incentives should be created for electoral cooperation between parties, and an effective system of multi-party cooperation should be established to offer more opportunities for non-communist parties and people with no party affiliation to participate in political affairs and enhance their capability of doing so.

The necessity of the Party's leadership and support   China is facing mounting pressure for the growth of democracy. Whether or not such pressure can be translated into motivation for reform hinges on the CPC's daring and resolution. No reform can be carried out in China without the CPC's leadership, and the development of democracy is no exception. Without the Party's leadership and support, the democratic reform could not start and the direct election of township heads would be confined to sporadic experiments.

However, the CPC's resolve to lead this reform won't come from nowhere; in fact, it may result from social pressure. When its rule is seriously threatened, it will have to seek new sources of social recognition and legitimacy, which would be the advance of democracy. For the ruling party, one of the safest ways to do so is to incorporate the direct election of township heads into its agenda so as to gain experience and buy time for the development of democracy.

The CPC has always been a pragmatic party capable of keeping abreast of the times. It should consider what theory of democracy to use for the incorporation of the electoral reform. It should also consider the establishment of a democratic mechanism that can guarantee a proper degree of competition and harmonious cooperation in the direct election of township heads – an institutional structure that can tolerate different opinions and maximize the interests of all parties involved through interaction and mutual trust. The Party's leadership remains a vital element in the institutional arrangement for such election. For the development of democracy in China, a virtuous cycle must be established between the Party's leadership (collective authority) and people's democracy (civil liberty) through cooperative game. However, in terms of the current course of development, how to advance people's democracy through intra-Party democracy is also an issue that must be dealt with.

To sum it up, the study of the direct election of township heads in Shiping reveals that the value of such a practice is worth considering, though it is still confined to sporadic experiments. Analyzing this case from the perspective of cooperative-harmonious democracy theory, we may say that:

> In terms of the integration of the Party's leadership, the people's role as the master of the country, and the law based governance, the second element was highlighted, with the people being very hopeful about the direct election; the Party's leadership also played a prominent role because it was the leadership of the superior Party organization that provided the impetus and political support for the election; regarding the rule of law, institutional support was insufficient despite the existence of some rules and regulations.

In terms of the spirit of cooperative-harmonious democracy, an essentially cooperative and harmonious state was achieved between the above three elements in the Shiping case.

However, it should also be noted that, in the absence of a macro-theory of democracy and institutional innovation, the direct election of township heads is unlikely to be carried on in a widespread and sustainable way and the latent concern about this practice remains.

Summary

The case discussed above is a practice in the democratic reform of grassroots election based on election by ballot, with representative democracy as the principal institution. It was a very effective practice, for a balance was stricken in a cooperative-harmonious democracy model between the democratic rights of citizens/Party members and the Party's leadership and organizational leadership. It has provided incipient proof of the feasibility of the cooperative-harmonious democracy model advocated by us. However, it has also revealed some deficiency in legal and institutional support for democratic reform. In particular, the reform in Shiping also involves the institutional restrictions of the constitution and the electoral law. In the long run, apart from new democratic ideas and political resolve truly geared to practical need, whether cooperative-harmonious democracy reforms can be sustained also hinges on legal and institutional progress on the superior level and concrete support from specific operational norms on the subordinate or practical level.

Notes

1 Shi Xuelian, "Minutes of the Symposium on Grassroots Democracy and the Election of Township Party and Government Leaders", *Background and Analysis*, 2009, 2(2): 181. http//www.world-china.org/newsdetail.asp?newsid=2423.
2 Huang Weiping, "The Reform of the Election of Chinese Township Heads: Significance and Predicament", *Marxism and Reality*, 2001, 5: 50–54.
3 Lai Hairong, "The Development of Competitive Election at the Township Level in Sichuan Province", *Grassroots Democracy and Innovation in Local Governance*, Yang Xuedong, He Zengke, Lai Hairong & Gao Xinjun (eds.). Beijing: Central Compilation and Translation Press, 2004, 51–108.
4 Yang Xuedong, "From Competitive Selection to Competitive Election? An Initial Analysis of Township Election", *Grassroots Democracy and Innovation in Local Governance*, Yang Xuedong, He Zengke, Lai Hairong & Gao Xinjun (eds.). Beijing: Central Compilation and Translation Press, 2004, 109–139.
5 Tong Zhiwei, "Prudence Is Needed in the Re-justification of Unconstitutional Reform: the 'Experiments' of Direct Election of Township Heads in the Past Few Years", *Jurists*, 2007, 4: 93–102.
6 Jin Taijun, "Prudence Is Needed in the Introduction of Direct Election of Township Heads", *Study Monthly*, 2007, 2: 33–34.
7 See Li Fan, Shou Huisheng, Peng Zongchao and Xiao Lihui, *Innovation and Development: Reforms in the Election of Township Heads*. Beijing: Orient Press, 2000.

8 This election is called "direct competitive election" here because the process is characteristic of this kind of election, as distinct from free competitive election in the West.

9 What follows is quoted from interview records, with the interviewees' names represented by English letters. The same is true of the subsequent sections.

10 Since the village committee is not an organ or political power, the direct election of village committees hardly touches upon the essential system and structure of Chinese political power. Townships, in contrast, are the lowest organs of political power, and therefore the direct election of township heads is of vital importance due to its bearing on the democratization of Chinese organs of political power.

11 Sheng Huaren, "Carry out the Election of Deputies to the People's Congress at the County and Township Levels According to Law", *Qiushi*, 2006, 6: 37–42.

12 Adam Przeworski, "Democracy as a Contingent Outcome of Conflicts", *Constitutionalism and Democracy*, Jon Elster & Rune Slagstad (eds.). Cambridge: Cambridge University Press, 1988, 79.

8 A case study of Chinese cooperative-harmonious deliberative democracy

Political participation in modern times is mainly conducted on two levels – rule and governance. The former is reflected by election and party politics, while the latter consists of the making and implementation of decisions for daily public administration. Deliberative democracy is a "policy science of participatory democracy", as distinct from the policy science in which the policy process is controlled by the elite and the "policy science of liberal democracy" in which decisions are made by simple majority and benefits are distributed among interest groups according to their political strength.[1] As a form of participatory democracy, deliberative democracy encourages citizens to take part in public decision making on an equal basis. This means that, during the deliberative process, each citizen must have the opportunities for free attendance (as participants in deliberation), argument, debate (claims for challenge or defense), and final decision (with impact on the collective consensus).[2] Since the advent of reform and opening up, China has made great progress in the democratic practice of participation in governance through deliberative democracy. A case in point is the Democracy Symposium that originated in Wenling, Zhejiang Province.

General institutional design of deliberative democracy

Deliberative democracy can take a variety of forms, such as Citizens Conference, Deliberative Poll, Citizens Jury, Scenario Workshop, and Deliberative Day. Unlike traditional forms of public participation, these institutional designs extend access to discussions on public policies to common citizens.[3] These five forms will be described as follows in terms of their ingredients and operational procedures.

Citizens conference[4]

What is Citizens Conference?

Citizens Conference, or Consensus Conference, can be traced back to the model of Danish citizens' participation in the making of decisions on science and technology in the mid-1980s. It is the most fundamental institutional design for deliberative democracy. From a traditional point of view, decision making on science and technology is the private domain of professionals and off-limits to common citizens, who should be excluded on account of their "ignorance". However, with the advance of science and technology, the making of such decisions began to involve more and more issues about ethics and social risks, which necessitated participation by the public. On the one hand, such issues could not be simply settled by science and technology, so the experts' knowledge does not entitle them to any superiority. On the other hand, by the principle of "popular sovereignty", citizens affected by such decisions have the right to take part in assessing consequent issues about ethics and social risks. Denmark attaches great importance to such participation; her law prescribes that, for any decision on science and technology related to ethics or social issues, the public must be consulted and given the chance to express their opinions.[5] The Board of Technology, which was founded in 1987 as part of the Parliament, is tasked with assessing how such decisions might affect the citizens and encourages them to take part in discussions on topics related to science and technology. A Citizens Conference is one of the principal mechanisms for doing so. This Danish-style model of public participation embodies the philosophy of deliberative democracy.[6] Since 1990s, it has been introduced into other countries and constantly improved through practice. Now it has become an essential way for common citizens to take part in discussions on public policies.

The procedure

1   *Selecting the topics.* Topics to be discussed at the Citizens Conference should reflect social concerns, be controversial, and demand responsive decision making by the government. They are selected by the organizer, which can be an official organization (e.g., the Board of Technology) or a non-governmental/academic institution deputed by the government. To ensure that the discussion is focused and easy to carry on, the scope of such topics should neither be too extensive nor too narrow. A "moderate" scope would be most desirable.

2   *Creating the Executive Committee.* When the topic has been chosen, the organizer will select appropriate persons as the members of the Executive Committee for organizing and supervising the Citizens Conference. Balanced composition will be considered during the selection process. Since the topic reflects social concern and is controversial, there is bound to be conflict between different opinions, all of which must be allowed to be presented during the discussion. Because of the vital role it plays in selecting the participants of the Conference, providing data to it and controlling the agenda, the Executive Committee should include representatives of different opinions so as not to be biased for any particular opinion that might otherwise dominate the agenda. Generally speaking, the Committee members would include experts, business representatives, NGO members, common citizens, and the organizer's plan executor.

3   *Picking the participants.* Once established, the Executive Committee is tasked, among other matters, to select the citizens who are to attend the Conference as members of the Citizen Panel. The organizer will put advertisements in newspapers and on radio, TV, and the Internet for stating the purpose and topic of the Conference and recruiting citizens. Except for the age limit (voting age), all citizens who are willing to understand the topic with an open mind may sign up. When recruitment is done, the Executive Committee, acting upon the principle of heterogeneity and pluralism, will select the members of the Citizen Panel according to age, gender, educational background, occupation, and domicile.

4   *Preliminary conference.* This is convened before the Citizens Conference for the members of the Citizen Panel to interact and get familiar with the topic they are going to discuss. There will be a period of time devoted to lessons during which they will read and discuss topic-related background materials selected by the Executive Committee. These materials usually include different opinions on the topic. Through reading and discussion, the Panel will have some understanding of the topic and form the questions they are going to discuss and pose to the experts at the Citizens Conference.

5   R*aising the questions and selecting the experts.* The members of the Citizen Panel raise the questions they are interested in, which usually touch upon all the important aspects of the topic. In response to these questions, the Executive Committee will offer a list of the experts familiar with the topic. However, the Citizen Panel has the final say about the list, with the right to add or remove names from it. When the list is finalized, the organizer will ask the experts to prepare oral and written reports in response to the questions, which are to be phrased in such way as to be comprehensible to common citizens.

6   *Public forum.* The Conference takes a form similar to a public forum. It is open to the media as well as members of the Parliament and common citizens interested in the topic. At the first stage, the experts give explanations on the questions prepared by the Citizen Panel and answer questions posed by the Panel on the spot. At the second stage, the Panel cross-examines the experts, asking individual experts to elaborate on their opinions; additionally, members of the Panel explore the controversial issues on which they hold different opinions. After the cross-examination, the Panel members have a discussion among themselves and prepare to draft the final report. In this report, they will try to reach consensus on the controversial issues, but they will also point out the parts on which they cannot do so. At the final stage, the Panel shows its report to the experts, the audience, and the media. Before the official release of the report, the experts have a chance to clear up misunderstandings and correct factual errors, but they cannot sway the opinion the Panel wants to express. In Demark and other countries, the conclusion report of the Panel will be sent to all the Parliament members as reference for decision making. Such reports usually draw nationwide attention.

Under the principle of equality, openness, transparency, mutual respect, and voluntary participation, the Citizens Conference offers a platform to exchange and debate different opinions and values. Such exchange is not one-way communication from government officials and experts to citizens. Instead, it will create a dialogical public forum that enables common citizens, experts, and government officials to gain necessary knowledge through discussion; on the basis of information disclosure, they can have thorough discussions on highly significant yet controversial topics and reach consensus wherever possible. The convening of the Citizens Conference would be a public event with informative and educational effect. Participation in it can enhance the willingness and ability to take part in public affairs among common citizens. Democratic participation within the system can encourage positive interaction and help to deepen and consolidate democracy.

So far dozens of Citizens Conferences have been held, in the US, New Zealand, Denmark, Canada, South Korea, Japan, Argentina, and China's Taiwan region. All these conferences have demonstrated positive effects. In 1998, for example, the first Citizens Conference was held in South Korea, on the topic of the Safety and Ethics of Genetically Modified Foods. Despite some bewildering moments, the citizens found the discussions highly beneficial. EU research has revealed that in Denmark, where Citizens Conferences are frequently held, the citizens show a deeper understanding of and a greater willingness to accept their country's public policies than the other European countries.

Deliberative poll[7]

What is a deliberative poll?

A deliberative poll is an institutional design for deliberative democracy developed by Professor James S. Fishkin, Director of Stanford's Center for Deliberative Democracy. In Fishkin's opinion, despite the progress toward more direct democracy in America in recent years, which has expanded direct participation by citizens to the benefit of the pursuit of equality, direct participation hinders deliberation as valued in democracy and can only be considered a partial realization of democracy. A complete democracy has to fully guarantee equality and deliberation at the same time. It is the difficulty in striking a balance between the two that a deliberative poll is mainly designed to overcome.

Inspired by the selection of judges or lawmakers by drawing lots in ancient Athens, Fishkin believes that, in a modern country, some of the citizens can be randomly selected as a microcosm of the country and assembled for face-to-face discussions. This can give common citizens an opportunity to be ideal citizens, for their voices would be heard rather than drowned in the voices of thousands of people. A deliberative poll is a process for practicing deliberative democracy. It provides a milieu for discussion in an attempt to understand public opinion as shown in an ideal state with sufficient information that allows citizens to deliberate and debate with each other. The procedure is as follows:

First, make a random selection of the citizens to be polled;
Second, poll these citizens for the first time;
Third, assemble them for dialogues with government officials and experts, and ask them to have judicious and rational discussion based on the relevant knowledge;
Finally, poll the citizens again on the original topic.

It can be said that a deliberative poll is a combination of town meetings in the US, quasi-experimental research design, survey research, the focus-groups method, and statistical analysis. In practice, a group of citizens are randomly selected from the matrix (society) as a microcosm of society and equal participants in politics; they are then enabled to have face-to-face discussions to represent deliberation in the whole society. The basic assumption of a deliberative poll is that the deliberative process may influence the individual's attitude and opinion. The main purpose of a deliberative poll, therefore, is to find out if the participants in the discussions have changed their attitude toward the issue after deliberation. A strict procedure has to be followed in practice to ensure that the desired effect is achieved.

The procedure

1   *Preparations.* A committee is jointly established by the media, government agencies, a common poll center, and a deliberative democracy poll center. The media conduct promotion and broadcast citizens' dialogues with officials and experts. The common poll center designs a questionnaire and conducts preliminary interviews with the participants regarding their choices. The deliberative poll center designs the activities and conducts quality control. The committee will maintain neutrality in its operation to gain trust from citizens.
2   *The selection of participants and preliminary interview.* The organizer draws a random national sample and interviews the members face-to-face or by telephone according to the questionnaire regarding their readiness to join the group discussions.
3   *Symposium.* When the pre-discussion questionnaire is completed, the citizens ready to discuss are invited to discussions in focus groups (the organizer has distributed the briefing materials representing different positions to the participants before the symposium). After the groups have discussed the various topics, experts, opinion leaders or government officials are invited to dialogues with the citizens on those topics so as to deepen the latter's understanding and thinking. Some of the group discussions and dialogues may be broadcast via television or other media.
4   *Post-discussion questionnaire.* The citizens who have participated in the discussions form the Experimental Group, whereas those who were interviewed but did not join the group discussions are the Control Group. A deliberative poll typically involves one Experimental Group and two Control

Groups.[8] When the discussions are finished, apart from the comparison between the Experimental Group's attitude before and after the conference, the results are also compared with the two Control Groups in order to strengthen the intrinsic validity.

To sum up, a deliberative poll is just one of the institutional designs that can help to achieve political equality and deliberation at the same time. It offers common citizens an opportunity for face-to-face discussion and communication and enables them to take part in deliberations on issues on a politically equal basis. The results are normative because they are the voices of the citizens who have a chance to reflect on the topics. Being prescriptive rather than predictive, such results must include opinions that are worth listening to. The institutional design of a deliberative poll can be applied not only to the American political system, but also to any other country in the world with an intention to expand citizens' participation and deliberation in a democratic reform program.

The deliberative poll as conceived by Fishkin has been held a dozen times, with more than six nationwide experiments conducted in the UK, the US, and Australia. Denmark conducted its first deliberative poll regarding the joining of the EU. At least nine local experiments have been conducted in the US. Greece had its first deliberative poll on June 4, 2006 regarding the candidates for the mayor of a city. The practices in these countries have shown that a deliberative poll has achieved what it is designed for.

Citizens Jury[9]

What is the Citizens Jury?

The Citizens Jury, which derives from the American jury system, has been advocated since the 1970s. It was invented by Ned Crosby of Jefferson Center in the US. A similar method has also been developed by Professor Peter Dienel of Wuppertal University in Germany at his Research Institute for Citizen Participation and Planning Methods. The Citizens Jury is to be created by an official committee, which selects experts, witnesses, and randomly picked jurors and facilitates dialogues between citizens, witnesses, and politicians. The Jury's meetings and the issues they discuss will be made available to the public in order to put government policies in a broader social context. After deliberation, the Jury will draft a resolution or make a recommendation in the form of a citizens' report. Normally the department that initiates the Jury will be asked to make a response, either following the recommendation or stating the reasons why it is rejected.

The procedure

1   *Preparations.* The topic of public deliberation is usually selected by the organizer – the Central Government or a local government – which will then entrust the operation to an independent agency. The latter will first of all set up an Advisory Committee made up of professionals familiar with

the topic. The Committee is responsible for important matters like the agendas, the preparation of materials, and the invitation of experts with different opinions. To find jurors fully representing demographic features, the agency will draw a random sample of citizens willing to join the jury based on geographic location, gender, age, ethnic group, and educational background. At this stage, the organizer, the independent agency, and the invited citizens must sign a contract which requires the organizer to give a certain amount of reward to each juror and to respond to the results of the jury's discussion within a definite period of time.

2   *Discussion.* The sampled citizens have a four- to five-day discussion on the selected topic. On the first day, the organizer divides the topic into sub-topics. After hearing analysis by experts with different opinions and government officials' explanations on the basis of the related policies, the jurors will raise questions and have enough time to deliberate over the topic. On the second and third days, the jurors discuss the economic, environmental, and social impact of the topic with citizens concerned with the topic, policy stakeholders, scholars and experts, and government representatives. The core value of the issue will be sought through reciprocal questioning and debate. During the discussion, cross-examination of various stakeholders will be conducted; if necessary, the same experts or stakeholders (or new experts or stakeholders, if these are found to be untrustworthy) can be re-invited or invited to clarify some issues.

3   *Consensus and conclusion.* During the discussion on the last day, having deeply discussed all the sub-topics, the jurors will see if they can reach a consensus on the issues involved. They will make recommendations regarding these issues and draft a report, which will be submitted to the organizer by the independent agency. The organizer must respond to the recommendation although it is not legally binding.

Since it was founded in 1974, Jefferson Center has applied the Citizens Jury method to the discussion of 30-odd major public policy issues, such as national health care reform, budgeting priorities, and environmental protection. Besides, the UK, Denmark, Spain, and Australia have also developed similar institutions suited to their own conditions and conducted a number of experiments.

Scenario Workshop[10]

What is a Scenario Workshop?

A Scenario Workshop, which was also developed in Denmark, is a form of public participation reflecting the philosophy of deliberative democracy. It enables government officials, scholars and experts, interest groups, and common citizens to seek solutions to common problems through discussion, questioning, and criticism and develop visions about the future. In a plural society, people face some common problems yet hold different opinions on what is the best solution owing to discrepancies in values and interests. Sometimes this may even lead to a deadlock of conflict. Therefore, to solve such problems requires the integration of knowledge and information from all quarters and cooperation between people with different interests and values. A Scenario Workshop, as an attempt to create a milieu for dialogue, is expected to promote interaction and mutual understanding between the actors involved and find a solution through brainstorming; it is expected to develop visions for common actions through communication between different groups; it is also expected to enhance the quality of decision making through the exchange of knowledge, information, and experience between those groups.

The procedure

1   *Description of scenarios.* Before the Workshop is conducted, relevant data and materials describing different scenarios are provided to the participants. At the beginning of the conference, government agencies or experts will give a lecture on the status quo of the topic to be discussed and plans for the future so as to familiarize the participants with the topic.
2   *Role playing and scenario construction.* The participants are divided into groups according to the categories of government representatives, scholars and experts, interest groups, and common citizens. The groups will then discuss, question, or criticize the plans and propose scenarios related to the topic. Then, at the plenary meeting, each group will report its scenario, which is to be discussed by all the attendees. The discussion should be focused on these questions: Which scenarios are viable? Which are relatively difficult to carry out? What is in common between these scenarios? What are the differences? After the meeting, the key similarities between the scenarios will be summarized as the basis for the next stage of discussion.
3   *Plans of action.* The participants are divided into groups by subject and have discussions on how to realize the common scenario. During each group discussion, every person will propose a plan of action and explain its importance. Then all the plans of action will be voted upon. The top five plans of action will be submitted to the plenary meeting.
4   *Selection and assessment.* During the plenary meeting, the plans of action proposed by the subject groups are arranged in sequence. After each group has explained its plan, the attendees will assess its viability and vote on it. They will grade the ideas put forward by all the groups except their own on a five-point scale (the ideas can be marked separately or as a whole). Then the five plans with the highest points will be announced, with their purposes explained by their authors.
5   *Common plan of action.* The participants discuss the top five plans of action with the following focus: Are they viable? What opportunities and methods can make them viable? How shall we draft a more specific plan of action as a policy recommendation? They will reach a consensus through discussion and formulate a plan of action for realizing the scenario.

6   *Announcing the conclusion.* The conclusion reached by the Scenario Work-shop, including the common scenario and plan of action, will be reported to the government organizations concerned, the public, and the media as reference for decision making.

The Plan of Action developed by the Scenario Workshop, as an embodiment of consensus from various circles, reflects equal consideration of different values and interests and therefore enhances the legitimacy of decision making. Besides, rational discussion, communication, and criticism make it possible for the partici-pants to express and exchange their diverse opinions. To refer to the conclusion that results from such judicious deliberation will greatly improve the quality of decision making. The Scenario Workshop can also facilitate dialogue and mutual understanding between the groups involved, break the stereotypes about particular groups, and encourage the solution of problems on the basis of consensus. All these will improve communication, mutual trust, and cooperation between the government, society, and various social groups. Because of its effects, the Scenario Workshop is widely used by government departments, businesses, and NGOs to seek solutions to problems and develop plans of action. Examples include the European Awareness Scenario Workshop initiated by the European Commission for a social environment more favorable to innovation and the Scenario Workshop program carried out by the Danish Board of Technology to discuss technological subjects and urban planning issues.

Deliberative Day[11]

What is Deliberative Day?

Deliberative Day was proposed by Professor Bruce Ackerman of Yale Law School and Professor James S. Fishkin, Director of Stanford's Center for Deliberative Democracy. Based on the empirical results of previous deliberative polls, they believe that common citizens are more than willing to play the role of active citi-zens under a particular institutional design, though the existing institution restricts this role. They hope that Deliberative Day can incorporate the philosophy of deliberative democracy into the formal political process in order to overcome the weaknesses of competitive democracy as it is practiced, i.e., the atrophy of public participation, media-dominated public opinion politics, and the election process manipulated by election PR agencies and poll experts.

The operation of Deliberative Day is carried out by a government organization set up for this purpose, which will invite citizens to public deliberation during a two-day holiday before a national election. To prevent interference with business activities and the life of common people, the designers have selected the Presidents Day[12] for this event, when citizens from around the country can deliberate on major national issues before voting. Citizens are free to sign up for Deliberation Day activities. To give a chance to the disadvantaged, the government will pay $150 to each participant.[13] On that day, the participants can register at the nearest of the schools or institutions selected by the Organizer for one-day discussions.

The procedure

1   *Watching a televised debate.* The Organizer will ask the participating citizens to watch a televised debate on political opinions between the candidates of the two parties. Unlike the traditional election debate, in which experts can raise questions at will, this debate will be about two most important issues faced by the nation, which have been selected by the two candidates respectively and discussed in groups by 500 randomly selected citizens from around the country.

2   *Group discussion.* Questions are posed to the candidates of the two parties during the debate to find out the differences between their major policies. After watching the national debate, the participating citizens will be randomly divided into groups and have face-to-face discussions. During the group discussion, the local citizens will form questions to be discussed during the subsequent local debate with regard to the issues not yet clarified during the televised debate.

3   *Local debate.* Following the group discussion, this will be the occasion on which the local leaders of different parties answer the questions formed by the citizens during the group discussion. After two rounds of group discussion and face-to-face local debate, the citizens will have the final group discussion. However, the purpose of this will not be consensus or decision by voting, but the sharing of opinions and the discussion of public issues not yet addressed during the debates.

Though Deliberation Day offers no final solution to the problems with Western democracy, Professor Ackerman and Professor Fishkin believe that it can be a channel for institutionalized participation by common citizens. Through public deliberation, it can reshape the current political process and prevent citizens from over-reliance on information provided by the political elite when making judgments; it will weaken the influence of special interest groups and common polls on policies and enhance citizens' interest in politics and sense of the role they can play; it will also facilitate the exchange of opinions and improve citizens' understanding of election issues. This innovative concept and its institutional design can be a source of enlightenment for the pragmatic proponents of democratic reforms and the managers of public inquiry.

Practice and development of Chinese deliberative democracy

The Chinese institution of political consultation is a type of deliberative democracy with Chinese characteristics. Besides, China has adopted the institutional form of deliberative democracy for public decision making. Since the 1980s, and especially since the 1990s, not only have elections been instituted in both rural and urban areas, but many new deliberative institutions have come into being. These have become important means for knowing public opinion, making public policies, and improving local governance. With the rise of Western deliberative democracy and thanks to advocacy by some scholars, such native-born institutions have drawn more and more attention. One of the most typical examples is the Democratic Forum in Wenling, Zhejiang Province.

We do not build an institution after we realize its merits, for it already exists in people's lives before such realization. Similarly, the application of deliberative democracy in China took place before, not after, the realization of its virtues. Since the 1990s, some forms of deliberative democracy have been spontaneously innovated, such as the Democratic Forum, the Citizens' Council,[14] the Community Council,[15] and the Community Discussion Center.[16] They have certain features in common: citizens are encouraged to participate and speak up before conclusions are drawn; the participants have a little, albeit insufficient, time to take part in discussions; the participants are required to exchange different opinions on the basis of mutual respect during deliberation.[17] The most influential of such innovative forms is the Democratic Forum in Wenling, Zhejiang Province. An analysis of it can help us to appreciate the existence of a practical foundation for deliberative democracy in China apart from the theoretical assumptions. It is such native-born practices that offer realistic resources for the application of deliberative democracy in China.

The Democratic Forum originated from the Rural Modernization Education Campaign launched in Zhejiang in 1999. To make it more effective, Songmen Town of Wenling City held the Rural Modernization Education Forum, which took the new form of face-to-face communication between officials and common citizens. Though the forum was designed to promote government policies, the inclusion of an opportunity for common citizens to speak up led to an unexpected outcome. "They haven't had any chance to speak like this in twenty years." Some of the leaders of Wenling City have not only maintained the practice, but they have also spread it to the other townships in the city, giving rise to various forms of democratic exchange and dialogue. The Rural Modernization Education Forum can be said to be the forerunner of the Democratic Forum. As the democratic dialogue went deeper, leaders of Wenling City came to see it as a new form of grassroots democracy that breaks the latter's limitation to the stage of election and makes it more substantial. In 2000, Wenling City held a conference at Songmen Town, at which "Democratic Forum" was adopted as the standard name for the Public Opinion Forum, the Villagers' Democracy Day, the Farmers Forum, and so on developed in various areas. It would be a new vehicle for the development of democracy in the city and a new approach to grassroots democracy in the new situation.

Some scholars have divided the progress of the Democratic Forum into three stages. At the first stage, the Forum originated from efforts to improve the relations between officials and common citizens. The leaders of Wenling wanted to change the apathy and tension between the two sides and get closer to common people. At first, however, they did not have any specific policy or refined method to follow. The Forum became a channel for communication between the masses and officials. In terms of the guiding principle, this practice was subsumed into the discourse of "political and ideological work". At the second stage, the "decision making consultation" function emerged and developed as a logical extension of the previous stage. When the officials had listened to the masses and understood their concerns, the next step would be to think up solutions. This pushed the Forum toward the role of decision-making consultation. Instead of being confined to routine communication between officials and the masses, it took "policy issues" related to the people's interests as the basis for exchange and dialogue and began to explore corresponding ways of decision making. Based on the summing up of experience, the Forum came to assume an increasingly well-designed form. At the third stage, the Forum began to transform into the Democratic Hearing. With the progress of practice, the name "Democratic Forum" became too narrow for new elements, and new practices went beyond the ambit of the term "political and ideological work". As a result, the Forum gradually evolved into a hearing for decision making by grassroots governments. At this stage, apart from the formal change, a new variable was added, namely the inclusion of deputies to the People's Congress at the town level and the designation of the Congress as the final decision maker in order to fit the role of the Congress defined in the current political system.[18]

With the progress of the Forum, Wenling City has developed it toward a better-regulated institution with refined procedures and made it a must for the making of decisions on important matters in villages, towns, and functional departments of the municipal government.

1 *Establishing leaderships for the Forum.* A leading group for the Forum headed by the Party secretary has been set up in each township and each department directly under the municipal government. It is mainly tasked with selecting the topic, time, and location of each session, presiding over the Forum, and providing the participants with relevant information.

2 *Improving institutions.* These include: (a) regular meetings for refining the implementation of the Forum and examining important matters concerning the socioeconomic development of the whole township; (b) discussion of important recommendations made by the Forum and subsequent decision making for enhancing the Forum's educational and service functions and democratizing the decision-making process; (c) the listing and delisting of cases[19] at the Forum for expanding the channel of communication, solving hot and thorny issues for villagers, and further improving the relations between officials and the masses; (d) feedback supervision for understanding and supervising the execution of the Forum's recommendations.

3 *Prescribing the procedures.* Each kind of Democratic Forum follows a specific set of procedures.[20]

"The Democratic Forum is actually a public hearing for decision making by the government, an equal dialogue between officials and citizens, and a meeting for coordination and communication between interest groups."[21] Its main purpose is to solicit citizens' opinions on some public policies and find solutions to issues of common concern. It has played a vital role in defusing tension between officials and the masses, reconciling the interests of various groups, and maintaining social stability. In fact, similar forms of democratic decision making involving common citizens have long existed in China, albeit under names such as the Democratic Forum. Some scholars have fully acknowledged the importance of such institutional innovation. For instance, in 2002, Professors Wang Puju, Li Jingpeng, Xie Qingkui, Zhang Xiaojin, Jing Yuejin, and Yu Xunda visited Wenling to observe the Democratic Forum and each of them subsequently wrote an article praising it as a democratic innovation.[22] However, common citizens' participation and discussion as emphasized in the Forum are still limited to the context of improving the relations between officials and the masses and developing grassroots democracy. Despite the importance attached to participation and deliberation by common citizens, such forms have not yet risen to the level of deliberative democracy.

Later, inspired by the paradigm of deliberative democracy, some scholars began to apply this concept to the analysis of such democratic practices as originated from within China. In November 2004, about fifty scholars and officials from at home and abroad attended a symposium on the Theory of Deliberative Democracy and Local Democratic Practices in China. This marked the official connection between deliberative democracy and such practices. Since then, the former has been more consciously used by some scholars to analyze such forms as the Democratic Forum.[23] The philosophy of deliberative democracy is implied in such forms, which have been subsumed into its paradigm.

The concept of "socialist consultative democracy" was put forward for the first time in President Hu Jintao's report at the 18th CPC National Congress, which also established deliberative democracy as a socialist democratic institution with Chinese characteristics. On December 14–15, 2012, the World and China Institute, 21ccom.net, and the Democratic Forum Office of Wenling City, Zhejiang Province jointly initiated and hosted a symposium on Deliberative Democracy and Its Practice in China. Three subjects were discussed at the symposium: (a) the theory of deliberative democracy, including the translation of the term, its rise and development in the East and the West, its basic relationship with election democracy, and the room for its progress after the 18th CPC Congress; (b) Democratic Forum in Wenling and participatory budgeting, which involved a detailed analysis of the form of deliberative democracy in the Forum; (c) deliberative democracy practices in various areas, which involved an analysis of such practices at other places in China. Speeches and discussions on this subject were made by scholars from the mainland (Chen Yimin, Li Fan, Pu Xingzu, Zhang Qianfan, Chen Jiagang, and Jia Xijin, etc.) and Xu Sijian from our Taiwan.[24]

However, in comparison with the institutional designs for Western deliberative democracy, the forms and practices developed in China, including the Democratic Forum, have yet to be diversified and enriched. Since deliberative democracy is still at the initial stage of development in China, the scope and depth of practice are yet to be expanded and increased. Anyway, such local practices in China, being somewhat characteristic of deliberative democracy, have encouraged participation by citizens, enhanced their consciousness of citizenship, nurtured public reason, and expanded citizen oversight as a way to put into practice the idea of "popular sovereignty". The evolution of such grassroots deliberative institutions has helped to improve democratic governance in China.

Chinese deliberative democracy in budgetary participation[25]

Public budgeting, as part of public governance, is the material foundation for the operation of all levels of government and the nucleus of benefit distribution between state and society, and between government and citizens. Any political power is ultimately represented by budgetary powers, and any institutional change will first and foremost involve an adjustment of such powers. For instance, democratic reform of township budgeting has been carried out in some places. Though the reform of public budgeting has been going on for a decade in China, the issue of public participation during the budgeting process has not yet been effectively resolved. The proper approach is to increase participation by all types of actors during the process and turn the single game in elections into long-term, multiple games in budgetary participation, thereby solving such problems as information asymmetry, the shortage of incentives, and the lack of professionalism. Here we will make a new analysis of the model of budgetary participation, as illustrated by some cases, in the practice of deliberative democracy in the area of Chinese public governance from the perspective of cooperative-harmonious democracy.[26]

Literature review

It is generally believed that modern research into budgetary participation originated from the creation of the New York Bureau of Municipal Research in the early twentieth century. The forms of such participation have been broadly defined as voting, lobbying, and direct public participation, with the former two increasingly found to be underrepresenting the public.[27] Current foreign research into participation in the budgeting process has gone beyond the forms to the object of participation, namely participation matters, with inquiry into uncontrollable matters, budget allowances, and long-term plans. In such research, participatory budgeting (PB) is a popular issue, with the study conducted by the World Bank being the most systematic.

In China, research into budgetary participation has also drawn attention from academia. Since it is at the initial stage, most of the literature is introductory or summaries of specific cases in China.[28] There are also some discussions with a broader scope and from various perspectives. For instance, under the second subject in *Toward a "Budgeting Country": Governance Democracy and Reform* compiled by Ma Jun, Tan Junjiu, and Wang Puqu, there is an analysis of budgetary democracy and transparency, which involve the discussion of the reform of budgeting oversight by the People's Congress, the reshaping of the power of local People's Congress, citizens' participation in public budgeting, and practices in foreign countries.[29] There are also collections of research and data for reference, such as *From Democratic Forum to Participatory Budgeting* by Hu Xiaowen, which makes a detailed summary of the development of the Democratic Forum in Wenling, institutionalized participation, the making of public policies by the local government, the process of decision making on public affairs and budgetary participation, and the experience gained from that.[30]

Generally speaking, however, current research into participation in budget at home and abroad share the following features: (a) equating participation in budgeting with public participation and emphasizing the role of the former in enhancing the legitimacy of public budgeting, without adequate attention to its role in making budgeting more rational and professional; (b) focus on technical issues such as polls, public meetings, and computer networks; (c) orientation toward the model of participatory budgeting.

Contemporary public budgeting needs to address two issues – legitimacy and rationality. The former means that the distribution of budgeting resources should fit the popular will, whereas the latter refers to the scientific distribution of resources through budgeting. Legitimacy is fundamental to budgeting and rationality guarantees its efficiency. Due to information asymmetry and the private interests of deputies, the outcome of the deputation chain (people→people's representatives→legislative bodies→administrative bodies) always deviates from the purpose of deputation. The discrepancy between the expression of public opinion at the beginning and governance by administrative bodies at the end would result in the loss of legitimacy. On the other hand, contemporary budgeting is much more complicated and professional than it used to be, which has rendered the public much less able to give their opinions on budgetary outlays due to their limitations in knowledge and specialty. As a result, control over budgeting tends to shift toward specialized officials and experts.[31]

Therefore, for budgetary participation, we must not ignore the technicality of budgetary power while considering how to enhance its legitimacy. The proper approach is to increase participation by all types of actors during the process and turn the single game in elections into long-term, multiple games in participatory budgeting, thereby solving such problems as information asymmetry, the shortage of incentives, and the lack of professionalism. In future institutional designs, legislative bodies and executive organs will not have unsupervised monopoly over the budgeting process; nor should people's representatives and the bureaucracy be the only actors in the process. Instead, there should be ways and means for participation by the general public, experts, and other types of actors. This is also the logical foundation for the reestablishment of legitimacy and rationality in budgetary reforms.

Conflict and cooperation: theoretical framework for the relationship between participants

Budgetary participation will involve actors with different value orientations, such as administrative bodies, legislative bodies (parliament/congress) and their members, the public, experts, political parties, and interest groups. Different interest relations and participation models will be formed on the basis of game relationships (conflict or cooperation) between them in the two dimensions of professionalism and representativeness (Figure 8.1).

Non-representative

Public type: experts   Public type: general public
Budgetary model: expert   Budgetary model: public
                     participation   participation

Specialized   Non-specialized
                     Cooperative-
                     harmonious
                     democracy model

Government type: administration   Government type: legislative
Budgetary model: administrative   bodies
                     control   Budgetary model: representative
                                                             democracy

Representative

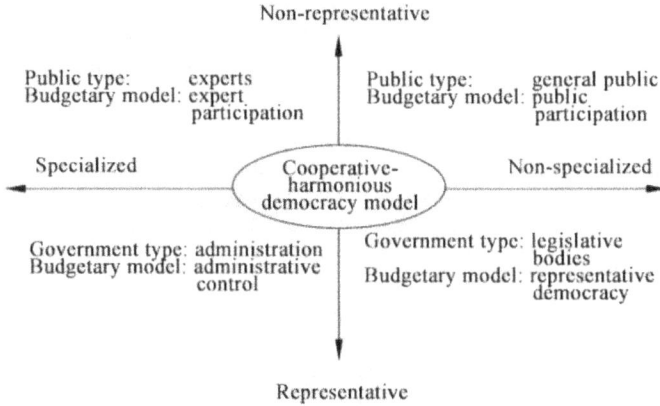

Figure 8.1 Models of participation in the budgeting process

Types of interest relationships between actors

The legitimacy of budgetary power mainly comes from: the public, legislative bodies, and representatives of the public. The legitimacy of budgetary power lies in its reflection of the popular will, with the degree of legitimacy determined by the degree of such reflection. The relationships among the public, legislative bodies, and representatives of the public has been viewed, in sequence, in terms of deputation, representation, and conflict game.[32] Among these, the "conflict game" view is the closest to reality. It can help us to understand the model and pattern of interactions between representatives and voters. General concord and cooperation between them can be eventually guaranteed by better designing the rules for the game between them and the related institutions.

The power of budgetary decision making, execution, and supervision is the ebb and flow of control over budgeting between the government's legislative and administrative branches. Budgetary power can be divided into the powers of decision making, execution, and supervision/assessment, with the decision-making and assessment powers held by the legislative branch and the execution power held by the administrative branch. At first, budgetary revenues and expenditures were relatively simple and there was little information asymmetry between the two branches. As a result, the parliament and the representatives had more control over budgeting. However, as public revenues and expenditures grew more frequent and complex, the budget executors became superior in information and technology. This gave rise to the encroachment of the execution power upon the powers of decision making and supervision, which is similar to "insider control" in business administration. This problem has occurred in many countries.[33]

Budgetary participation by non-governmental actors: difference between experts and the general public in the capability of budgeting control. Public policies work on two levels – values and facts. While experts participate on the fact level to address the issue of "what it is", the public do so at the value level to resolve the issue of "what it should be". However, if experts made choices in place of the public, or the public made decisions on technical issues in place of experts, the result would be chaos.

Administrative power in the budgeting process is the difference between the public and administrative bodies. The public, people's representatives, legislative bodies, and administrative bodies make up a complete power chain. Though administrative power has been delegated to administrative bodies by the public, this does not mean that this power no longer belongs to the public. Such delegation is limited, and the public can still share this power with administrative bodies.

Models of budgetary participation determined
by interest relationship between actors

The model of budgetary participation is determined by the relationship between participants. It can be divided into two categories, governmental and non-governmental, by the degrees to which different actors represent the popular will. Non-governmental actors refer to various types of the public whose opinions are non-representative because they are the direct reflection of the popular will. Legislative bodies and administrative bodies are deputed by the public, and their opinions are generally representative of the popular will. Different actors can be divided by specialized actors (officials and experts) and non-specialized actors (the public and its representatives). Officials' tendency toward specialization and technicality give administrative personnel, along with experts, an advantage in the specialization dimension (Figure 8.1). Combinations in the two dimensions form different budgetary structures.

1   *The representative democracy model.* This is characterized by leaders' reception of people's votes in regular and free elections. To maintain the stability of democracy, most people's participation in politics does not go beyond the minimum level of operation of the means to sustain democracy (the electoral mechanism).[34] In this model, the parliament made up of deputies selected by the public holds the budgetary power and makes budgetary policies. The public's budgetary participation is not independent but carried out through influence on elections and deputies.

2   *The expert participation model*, with focus on the involvement of economic and technical factors in the budgeting process. Experts play a decisive role in the determination of budgetary items. For instance, nowadays experts make decisions on Chinese government procurements by secret ballot, and experts' opinions are referred to as the basis for budgetary choices in some places.

3   *The administrative control and expert participation model.* In this model, little importance is attached to public participation because the emphasis on administrative rationality excludes the legitimacy value from public decision making. Due to the stress on the role of administrators and experts, budgetary

control is shifted to administrative bodies.[35] Due to the complexity of modern budgeting, the execution of budgets has increasingly become the province of administrators and a complicated technical process controlled by technocrats and technical experts along with administrators and politicians.

4   *The public participation model.* With quickening administrative reform and growing transparency in many countries, the progress of e-government has also facilitated budgetary participation by the public. Additionally, the rise of the deliberative democracy theory has offered theoretical support to participatory budgeting. In fact, the participatory budgeting model has grown out of this theory, which is characterized by an emphasis on legitimacy, openness, and accountability. During the budgeting process, the participants achieve a consensus for decision making by persuading others or modifying their own preferences.

The budgetary participation model based on co-administration under cooperative-harmonious democracy

All the four models above are non-cooperation games due to the lack of common interests under information asymmetry conditions. In practice, we should go beyond the assumptions of non-cooperative conflict game and, based on traditional Chinese thought of "people-oriented" and "harmony and cooperation", make a comprehensive, systematic, and profound analysis of the relationship between various actors based on the assumptions of cooperative game, in order to develop a budgetary model with Chinese characteristics better geared to the needs of the present and the future.

The practicality of cooperation in games is denied in non-cooperative games, which highlight the common damage of the results. A classic example is the Prisoner's Dilemma. In cooperative game, however, it is believed that the actors can conduct effective communication and coordination in terms of information and incentives through mechanism design and therefore achieve the goal of maximizing individual interests, overall interests, and long-term interests.[36] Inspired by traditional Chinese thought of "people-oriented" and "harmony and cooperation" and grounded in the basic assumptions of cooperative game, cooperative-harmonious democracy emphasizes the introduction of citizens and related interest groups and opinion holders into the administration of and decision making on public affairs of the state and society for orderly and effective communication and participation; it also aims to make cooperative game possible on the rule and governance level through the creation of a mechanism for long-term interaction. It can benefit from the creation of institutions for petition, complaint, hearing, expert consultation, and e-democracy. Compared with the budgetary model based on conflict game, the cooperative-harmonious democracy budgetary model based on cooperative game is more likely to strike a balance between what is best for individuals and what is best for the collective.

The public budgeting model under cooperative-harmonious democracy highlights the achievement of real harmonious governance through negotiation and cooperation between stakeholders by legislative bodies, administrative bodies, the general public, and experts, who can give full play to their strengths during the game for the distribution of public budget resources. In terms of the representation of the popular will in public budgeting, this model lays more stress on cooperation between the government and the civil society in making government budgets more reflective of the popular will in order to satisfy the demand for legitimacy. In terms of the professionalism of public budgeting, it emphasizes cooperation between experts, professional officials, the general public, and representatives of the public, in order to make budgeting more scientific and therefore meet the demand for legitimacy (Figure 8.1).

The evolution of the budget system in China

In terms of budgetary participation, the evolution of the budget system at home and abroad is related to the change of the actors in public budgeting in the two dimensions. Such evolution is a self-circulation during constant change in those dimensions. A glimpse of such evolution can be caught in the development of budgeting in China (Figure 8.2). In recent years, two relatively typical models of public participation in budgeting have formed during the reform of public budgeting in China.

Changes in the Chinese budget system

In terms of budgetary participation, there have been two periods of major institutional change since the founding of the People's Republic of China. One was the administration-led budget model that existed between 1955 and 1998, and the other was the change from the previous model to the expert model that began in 1998.

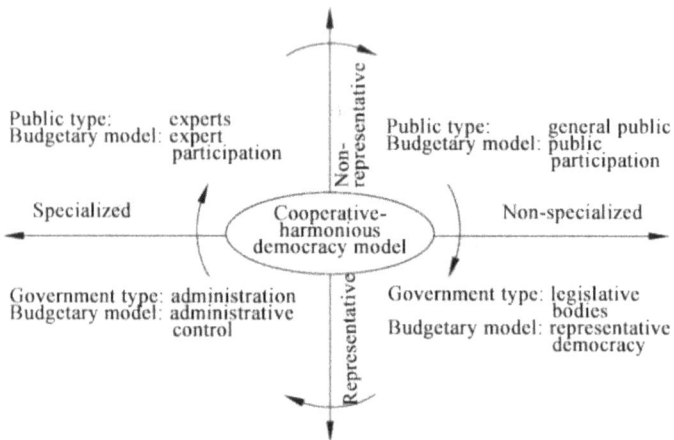

Figure 8.2 Evolution of the budgetary participation model

1 The administration-led model period can be further divided into three stages by the degree of control over budgetary power:

   a 1955–1980, with highly centralized, administration-led budgetary power. Budget was defined as an "overall plan for state revenues and expenditures formed out of the distribution and utilization of resources according to the state's administrative policies and construction plans."[37] The Central Government played a leading role in budgeting, with little participation in budgetary decision making by other actors.

   b 1980–1992, with the budgetary power gradually devolved from the Central Government to local governments, and the separation of the government's budgetary power from that of businesses. This was accompanied by "administrative decentralization", or the division and adjustment of the government's budgetary power between various levels of local government. Nevertheless, local budgetary power was still dependent on that of the Central Government. As a result, local governments' budgetary participation was still limited.

   c 1992–1998, with adjustment of the power over budgetary revenue. A well-designed system of tax distribution was put into practice between the Central Government and local (mainly provincial) governments. This gave a legal guarantee to local governments' sharing of budgetary power, and the budget system began its transition from the planned economy model to the market economy model.

2 The administration-led model underwent a transition to the expert budgeting model. In 1998, the establishment of a public fiscal system was proposed as a goal of reforms, with focus on the reform of the budgetary expenditure system. In recent years, budgeting has become more transparent thanks to budgetary reforms in departmental budget, national treasury centralized payment, government procurement, and the separation of revenues from expenditures. Besides, the practice of bid evaluation by experts has been introduced into government procurement, with the results of evaluation determined by experts' appraisal. In the reform of performance budgeting, the help of experts in the related professions is enlisted and performance indicators are established. In some places, experts and the public are even invited to participate in the budgetary decision stage.

Trend of China's reform of her operating
mechanism of budgetary power

A retrospect of the reform process from the perspective of budgetary participation can reveal that it shares certain similarities with the common course of development of budgetary control around the world.

1 *Wider range of players in budgetary power*. At the beginning of the People's Republic of China, budgeting was solely conducted by the Central

Government to the exclusion of local government. Reforms gradually led to the vertical sharing of budgetary power between the Central Government and local governments; horizontally, the government's budgetary department has authority over quota distribution and supervision, while other departments have the authority to formulate budgetary items and carry out budgets.

2 *More transparency in public budgetary power.* Fiscal transparency of the government requires easy access to information for the public and the openness of budgetary planning, execution, and reporting.[38] In recent years, greater budgetary transparency has been achieved thanks to budgetary reforms, actions to make government affairs public, and law enforcement publicity. In many places, budgetary transparency has been institutionalized.

3 *Improvement of public budgeting techniques and procedures.* Through the reform in the classification of governmental revenues and expenditures, expenditures are divided by types of public service and how the costs are spent into functional categories and economic categories. This is in keeping with the System of National Account (SNA), a lingua franca for international communication.[39] Most of the reforms before 1998 were designed to make incentives effective, with technical and procedural measures making up the vast majority. Since 1998, though expenditures have replaced revenues as the main focus of budgetary reforms, such reforms, due to inertia, have remained highly technical and procedural. There was the lack of a rational decision mechanism for fiscal expenditure items and quantities, and the lack of a rational mechanism for public evaluation of the effects of expenditure. In recent years, some places have actively promoted evaluation of the performance of fiscal expenditures and have indeed reviewed the performance of some expenditures; they have even added or reduced departmental expenditures according to such performance. However, due to the persistent failure to resolve the rationality of budgetary decisions and the evaluator of budgetary performance, the fundamental issue of the legitimacy of the form of budgetary power remains prominent.

4 *Practical reforms of China's budget system.* In recent years' public budgeting reforms, the pattern of change in budgeting model described above has been reflected by the emergence of a type distinct from the administrative control model, i.e., the social participation model involving actors other than administrative bodies. This model falls into two categories – the expert participation model as typified by the budgetary reform at Nanhai District in Foshan City, Guangdong Province,[40] and the public participation model as represented by the budgetary reform at Xinhe Town of Wenling City, Zhejiang Province.[41]

The Nanhai model with expert participation

The authorities of Nanhai District believed that the root of the problem was the lack of information about budgetary performance as the basis for budgeting. At the beginning and toward the end of 2004, they asked experts to evaluate the information technology application projects of 2004 and 2005, and substantially added/

reduced budget amounts and items. This marked the first introduction of actors outside the administrative system into budget decision power, which is central to budgetary power.

The budgetary reform at Nanhai District mainly involved the following:

> The fiscal department of the government will ask some experts to analyze and determine the performance indicators as the criteria for evaluating project budgets. Then, according to these indicators, the experts will examine the necessity of budgetary funds before the budgets are approved. After that, they will keep track of the performance of budgets during their execution. When this is over, they will make an evaluation of the effects as the basis for budgeting for the next year. In the budgetary reform at Nanhai District, the evaluation of performance was focused on the appropriateness, feasibility, and fund effectiveness of projects.

The Nanhai model is mainly characterized by the following:

1 *The introduction of experts into administration-led budgetary decision making.* There has always been much expert participation in public budgeting, in terms of fiscal and accounting management, the development of fiscal information networks, and bid evaluation by experts in government procurement. However, such participation has mostly focused on technical and procedural affairs. Nanhai district's reform involves experts' direct participation in budget decision, supervision, and the evaluation of budgetary power. In particular, the introduction of experts into budget decision, which is central to budgetary power, constitutes the most salient feature of Nanhai's reform.

2 *Self-discipline by the government's fiscal management department in the operation of budgetary power.* This department deputes the actual evaluation process to the expert panel instead of taking part in it by itself. For the next step, it is envisioning the deputation of budgetary evaluation to an intermediary agency and the involvement of the public in this effort.

3 *Combination of budget decision and the evaluation of budget performance.* The traditional budgeting process lacks necessary evaluators and evaluation mechanisms. Performance budgeting is defined as the central task of Nanhai's budgetary reform, which is known as the "reform in performance budgeting for special fiscal expenditure items".

4 *Change of the operating procedure of budgetary power.* The distribution of fiscal funds under the traditional system follows this process: application by a work unit → examination and modification by the financial department → feedback from the applying unit → making an overall plan → submitting the plan to the government and the People's Congress for approval → allocation of funds. The post-reform new procedure features the addition of four stages – appraisal by experts, in-process performance evaluation, ex-post performance evaluation, and the using of the results as the basis for budgeting for the next year.

Evaluation of the Nanhai model of "expert governance":

> It is a typical model of expert participation in the budgeting process. Today, with the highly refined division of labor, public administration and public service have become highly institutionalized, specialized, and technological. In some areas of public affairs, "expert participation" shows some superiority to participation by common citizens, who are unlikely to have adequate knowledge and full rationality for judgment, choice, and expression. At the value level, expert governance is a more advanced concept, and the intellectual elite's involvement in public choices is an important step toward enlightened politics. Nowadays, with the diversification of stakeholders, expert governance has to some degree become an essential way to cope with special interest groups. Some practices in China's fiscal reform, such as consultation with experts for decision making on fiscal expenditures, voting by experts for government procurements, and voting by experts for budget items in Nanhai District, are, to a large degree, reflections of this concept in public affairs.

The Xinhe model of public participation

Public participation in budgeting is another type of social participation. It is mostly practiced at Xinhe Town in Wenling City, Zhejiang Province; Huinan Town in Nanhui District, Shanghai; Wuxi City, Jiangsu Province; and Harbin City, Heilongjiang Province. The most representative is the practice in Xinhe Town.

In July 2005, the deputies to the People's Congress, cadres, and common citizens of Xinhe Town discussed the town's budget plan through the "Democratic Forum" for the first time, and the town government modified the budget according to the recommendations. This marked the beginning of public participation in budgeting. In November 2005, the town held a second Democratic Forum to evaluate the execution of the budget. As a result, the Forum has become a regular form of public participation with the authority to supervise the execution of budgets.

The main practices of the Xinhe model: The budgetary reform at Xinhe mainly involves the following: under the Party committee's leadership, the deputies to the People's Congress and the public participation in the making of all the budgets for personnel funds, public funds, and project funds as well as the whole budgetary process including budgetary decision, execution, and evaluation. In terms of budgetary power, public participation is focused on the determination of budgets, which is a crucial stage. However, the public has also intensified supervision of the execution of budgets through the creation of a financial work group.

The main characteristics of the Xinhe model: like the Nanhai model of expert participation, the budgetary reform at Xinhe is a model of social participation in the public budgeting process by actors outside the administrative system. However, it has its own characteristics:

1   *Participation in the budgeting process by the people's deputies and the common public under the local Party committee's leadership.* It was not motivated

by the administration, but by the local Party's committee and the People's Congress; the direct participants are the local government, people's deputies, the public. People's deputies and the common public have the chance to participate in the budget process so that it is a combination of representative democracy and direct democracy.

2   *Whole-process and all-round participation.* In the Nanhai model, experts mainly take part in the budgeting of project funds. In the Xinhe model, however, the public plays its role in the making of all the budgets for personnel funds, public funds and project funds. Admittedly, though, such comprehensiveness has something to do with the fact that Xinhe, being merely a town, is way inferior to Nanhai District in budgetary scale and complexity.

3   *The existing power structure and institutional platform of the People's Congress as the foundation.* All the several Democratic Forums since 2005 have been closely linked to sessions of the town's People's Congress, with the participants mainly consisting of the deputies to the Congress. Though the town has made separate rules on budgetary democratic forums, the regulations of the People's Congress are still adopted as the basic norms.

4   *The designing of scientific and detailed deliberative process and rules of procedure, which have institutionalized public participation in public budgeting.* The institutional design of the Democratic Forum is highly feasible thanks to attention to procedural details (e.g., the rules on secret ballot and those on the selection of participants). Besides, the previous budgetary process has been tailored to the needs for public participation. For instance, the previous process was: application by a work unit → examination and modification by the financial department → feedback from the applying unit → making an overall plan → submitting the plan to the government and the People's Congress for approval → allocation of funds. The new process features the addition of two stages – Democratic Forum by the people's deputies and the public, and recommendations for modification; examination by the financial department has been replaced by the drafting of an overall plan, and "feedback from the applying unit" has been omitted.

5   *Enhancement of the public's consciousness of their rights and political participation awareness through budgetary participation.* The practical public participation in budgeting has offered the people vivid examples of civil rights and democracy as an informal type of democratic education. Participatory budgeting has effectively improved the people's capability of democratic deliberation and decision making.

Evaluation of the Xinhe model: in previous governmental governance, democratic mechanisms were generally perceived as unique to public institutions. Early classical democracy even saw the selection of political figures through direct voting as the main manifestation of democracy. Albert Hirschman has unified all kinds of organizations, ranging from states and governments to companies and families, into a single framework of interpretation from the perspective of intrinsic mechanism. This framework is based on voice, the most essential manifestation of democracy, as the fundamental way to maintain the effective operation of all kinds of organization. In his opinion, the exit mechanism as a market force in the economy mainly has its effect on the market; the voice mechanism as a non-market force in politics is a concrete manifestation of democracy.[42] An institution should be designed that can enhance the will for and efficiency of the use of voice and lower its cost. The same issue of voice exists in the democratic manifestations of political life in China. The Xinhe model has been effective because it has reformed the previous administration-controlled budgetary model in terms of the increase of the common public's basic right of voice.

At the beginning of reform and opening up, the need for economic growth pushed economists to the forestage of history. Economics became a distinguished branch of learning, and economists played a leading role in all reforms. However, in economist-led theory and practice, public budgeting is mostly perceived as a purely technical and procedural process; the ignoring of the fact that public budgeting is essentially a process of the political distribution, selection, and evaluation of interests makes it difficult to recognize the true nature of public budgeting in China.[43] The budgetary participation by people's deputies and the public at Xinhe is a kind of social participation in budgetary power by actors outside the administrative bodies. Participation by people's deputies is a form of representative democracy within the system, whereas public participation is a form of direct democracy outside the system. Public participation has made public budgeting more reflective of the popular will and enhanced its legitimacy. The inclusion of people's deputies and the general public falls into the category of "enhancing the legitimacy and representativeness of the budget" in the budgetary evolution/circulation model (see Figure 8.2).

Financial revenue and expenditure are typically the most direct reflection of the relationship between state interests and the people's interests. In terms of values, democratic mechanisms should be the leading model of financial decision making. Though the understanding of budgetary democracy may vary according to difference in values, relatively common criteria do exist, such as:

1   Budgetary transparency should consist of information about governmental budgets available to the public at relatively low cost. This is one of the basic prerequisites for cooperative game.
2   Standard procedures for budgetary participation during the budgeting process – how to generate participants in decision making, guarantee their representativeness, and process their recommendations – should be specified and standardized.
3   Budgetary power should take the form of division at various levels by the scope of benefit from and burden of public services.
4   The creation of necessary incentives is another prerequisite for cooperative game.

Competition will arise between local governments for the different public services they provide. This will give rise to the "voting with feet" effect, as Charles Tiebout called it, by which the public can express their will by choosing to exit.

Contrary to expert governance, the legitimacy of democratic decision making is indisputable. The public choice school has also proven the rationality of democratic selection procedures in maximizing benefits in terms of Pareto Optimality. However, democratic decision making is not always related to rational decision making; the refinement of the division of labor and the specialization of technology in public services, and the consequent complexity and professionalism of public budgeting, also pose some challenge to the rationality of the public choice process.

The prospect of budgetary participation reform in China

The analysis above can lead to the following conclusions:

1   Legitimacy and rationality are the two basic requirements for public budgeting. Legitimacy is the degree to which budgets reflect the popular will, while rationality refers to the scientificity of budgets themselves. Budgeting can be divided into five models by the reflection of legitimacy and rationality in different actors in the dimensions of representativeness and specialization, as well as the relationships among the four actors in these two dimensions. Based on cooperative game, cooperative-harmonious democracy theory can effectively resolve the tension in public budgetary power in the two dimensions (see Figure 8.1) by stimulating enthusiasm in budgetary participation by the four major types of actors – legislative bodies, administrative bodies, experts, and the general public. The evolution of budgeting is one of the circulations in the models of evolution of budgetary power (see Figure 8.2).

2   Through many years of budgetary reform, China has made considerable progress in public budgeting management in terms of budgeting techniques and budgeting procedures. She is narrowing the gap between herself and other countries in these respects, and great improvements have been made in scientificity and rationality. However, public budgeting in China is in the "administrative control" model, i.e., budgetary decision, supervision, and evaluation are still under the control of administrative bodies, with the lack of a mechanism that reflects public opinion. This has resulted in great room for improvement in legitimacy.

3   Some places have begun to reform the "administrative control" model for public budgeting and build a social participation model. The reform has given rise to two distinct models – expert governance and public participation, represented by the Nanhai model and the Xinhe model, respectively. They share the common ground of a wider range of participants in budgeting, but they differ in the types of participants. The departmentalization of the distribution and utilization of budgetary funds as an essential public power is the source of all malpractices in public budgeting. The substitution of experts for departments in budget decisions represents great progress, but public budgeting must reflect the common preference of the public in further reforms.

Worldwide, performance budgeting characterized by expert participation originated from the New Public Management reform by European and American governments since the late twentieth century, whereas participatory budgeting characterized by public participation derived from the attempts at social reform by the Workers' Party in Brazil. Though both models have borne fruit in some countries, there have been few instances of complete success, due to obstruction by interest groups and the ambiguity of the benefits of public projects. The budgeting models adopted by most countries are actually a compromise between them, with equal stress on the role of experts and public participation. The budgetary reform in China in the new period should be based on the ideas and methods of cooperative-harmonious democracy theory and cooperative game in the paradigm of traditional culture of harmony and cooperation. To this end, we make the following policy recommendations:

1   We should reform the current model of administrative budgetary power. Within the system, the legislative bodies' control over the public budgeting process should be strengthened; outside the system, experts and the general public should be allowed to participate in the process as two social forces. The purpose is to combine the administrative and legislative power over budgeting with expert governance and public participation.

2   The model that lays too much stress on the technical and procedural reform of public budgeting by all levels of government, from central to local, should be altered. The priorities of reform for some time to come should be modulated to give real rights to people's deputies and the general public, reflect more of public opinion, and enhance budgetary legitimacy.

3   Budgetary participation should be more professional and scientific in public budgeting by the higher levels of government, with more experts included in the process. Compared with the Central Government and the governments of provinces/autonomous regions/municipalities, local governments' budgets have a more direct bearing on the public, and more stress should be laid on public participation. In contrast, the role of experts should be more valued for non-fixed, complicated expenditures for political, military and diplomatic purposes from the higher levels of government, which are typically beyond the understanding of the general public.

4   Improve the selection of budgeting participants and the processing of their recommendations. Mechanisms should be improved for the generation of budgeting participants (including experts, the public, and people's deputies), secret ballot, and compliance with resolutions. More mechanisms should be created for online participation in public budgeting, polling, budgetary hearing, and committees of the public so that budgeting can reflect the needs of all social strata and participation in public budgeting would not become a mere formality.

5   Based on improved project management, make the transition toward performance evaluation of departmental budgets. We need to further improve the budgetary project library, accumulate experience in project evaluation, and refine project

indicators and assessment methods to lay a foundation for selection by experts and the public. The evaluation of any department should be based on the quality and quantity of the public services it provides through its budgets, which would make our government more democratic, transparent and accountable.

Summary

As administrative power keeps "colonizing" public power, people have begun to ask why the bureaucrats, being neither elected by the people nor appointed, should have the right to make authoritative value distribution for society. In other words, the focus of democracy is turning to the area of administration. In the past, democracy was thought to have been practiced in opposition to despotism, which was embodied by the king, members of the nobility, and high priests. Gradually, however, political rule has become impersonal; what democracy strives to overcome nowadays is not real political resistance, but the systematic imposition of a separate administration.[44] Thus one of the trends of democracy today is the vigorous development of administrative democracy. How democratic a country is should be measured not only by the actual operation of her representative democracy, but also by the degree of administrative democracy, i.e., the degree to which citizens can take a direct part in public decision making and the management of public affairs. Amid the wave of civic engagement, deliberative democracy has critiqued liberal democracy and believes that no public decision making can be legitimate without dialogue, communication, and discussion among citizens. Recent years' application of deliberative democracy in China has blazed a new trail for civic engagement in public decision making.

Notes

1 Jonn S. Dryzek, *Discursive Democracy*. New York: Cambridge University Press, 1990, 114–123. As cited in Xie Zongxue, "Internet Democracy and Deliberative Democracy in Practice: A Utopia in Information Society?", *Information Society Studies*, 2003, 4: 98.
2 Carolyn Hendriks, "Integrated Deliberation: Reconciling Civil Society's Dual Role in Deliberative Democracy", Hao Wenjie & Xu Xingjian (trans.), See Chen Jiagang, *Deliberative Democracy*. Shanghai: Shanghai Joint Publishing Company, 2004, 134.
3 Carolyn Hendriks, "Integrated Deliberation: Reconciling Civil Society's Dual Role in Deliberative Democracy", Hao Wenjie & Xu Xingjian (trans.), See Chen Jiagang. *Deliberative Democracy*. Shanghai: Shanghai Joint Publishing Company, 2004, 134.
4 For Citizens Conference, the following literature has been referred to: Lin Guomin and Chen Dongsheng, "Citizens Conference and Deliberative Democracy: Civic Engagement in Universal Health Insurance", *Taiwanese Sociology*, 2003, 6: 61–118. Lin Guomin and Huang Dongyi, "Models of Civic Engagement and Their Use", *Third Stage Technical Report of the 2nd Generation Health Insurance Planning Group of the Executive Yuan*, 2004. Hendriks, Carolyn M., "Consensus Conferences and Planning Cells: Lay Citizen Deliberations", *The Deliberative Democracy Handbook: Strategies for Effective Civic Engagement in the Twenty-First Century*, John Gastil & Peter Levine (eds.). San Francisco: Jossey-Bass, 2005, 80–110.
5 Ida-Elisabeth Andersen and Brigit Jaeger, "Danish Participatory Models", *Science and Public Policy*, 1999, 26(5): 331–340.

6 The models adopted by the Danish Board of Technology fall into five categories: (a) citizen consultation, including citizen conference, citizen summit, perspective work-shop, interview meeting, and voting meeting; (b) stakeholder involvement, including future research, policy exercise, and Scenario Workshop; (c) expert analysis, including work groups, conference and workshop, and structured brainstorms; (d) advisory func-tion, including parliament hearings, future panel, and early warning and briefings; (e) public debate, including local debate fund and debate products/www. See Fu Kairuo, *Interactions between Members of a Public Deliberative Group, as Illustrated by the Citizens Conference at Yilan Base of Hsinchu Science Park*. Taipei: Association for the Publication of Papers on Civic Engagement by the Youth, 2005, 4. For the description of ways to participate at the Board of Technology's website, see http://www.tekno.dk/ydelser/?lang=en [accessed December 22, 2012].

7 For Deliberative Poll, the following literature and websites have been referred to: Huang Dongyi, "Deliberative Poll: Research Methods and Feasiblity Assessment", *Poll Quar-terly*, 2000, 1: 123–143. Lin Guomin and Huang Dongyi, "Models of Civic Engagement and Their Use", *Third Stage Technical Report of the 2nd Generation Health Insurance Planning Group of the Executive Yuan*, 2004. He Baogang, "The Methods of Delibera-tive Democracy", *Study Times*, February 13, 2006. James Fishkin and Cynthia Farrar, "Deliberative Polling: From Experiment to Community Resource", *The Deliberative Democracy Handbook: Strategies for Effective Civic Engagement in the Twenty-First Century*, Jonn Gastil & Peter Levine (eds.). San Frandcisco: Jossey-Bass, 2005, 68–79. The website of Stanford's Center for Deliberative Democracy: http://cdd.stanford.edu/ [accessed December 22, 2012].

8 To avoid the possibility that other reasons than participating in the Symposium lead to changes in the attitude, two "Control Groups" must be formed. One contains the national sample which did not take part in the first poll; the other contains the sample which took part in the first poll but did not participate in the Focus Groups, namely the Symposium.

9 For Citizens Jury, the following literature and website have been referred to: Graham Smith and Corinne Wales, "Citizens' Juries and Deliberative Democracy", *Democracy as Public Deliberation: New Perspectives*, Maurizio Passerin D'Entreves (ed.), & Wang Yingjin, Yuan Lin, Liu Xianglin, Lin Yunjuan, Wang Wenyu & Wang Yongbing (trans.). Beijing: Central Compilation and Translation Press, 2006, 100–118. Lin Guomin and Huang Dongyi, "Models of Civic Engagement and Their Use", *Third Stage Technical Report of the 2nd Generation Health Insurance Planning Group of the Executive Yuan*, 2004. He Baogang, "The Methods of Deliberative Democracy", *Study Times*, February 13, 2006. Crosby, Ned and Nethercut, Doug, "Citizens Juries: Creating a Trustworthy Voice of the People", *The Deliberative Democracy Handbook: Strategies for Effective Civic Engagement in the Twenty-First Century*, John Gastil & Peter Levine (eds.). San Francisco: Jossey-Bass, 2005, 111–119. The website of the Jefferson Center: http://www.jefferson-center.org [accessed December 22, 2012]

10 For Scenario Workshop, the following literature is referred to: Lin Guomin and Huang Dongyi, "Models of Civic Engagement and Their Use", *Third Stage Technical Report of the 2nd Generation Health Insurance Planning Group of the Executive Yuan*, 2004.

11 For Deliberative Day, the following literature and website have been referred to: Huang Dongyi, "Deliberative Day: A Utopia of Governance or a Practical Democratic Innova-tion?", *Public Administration Journal*, 2006, 18: 137–142. Bruce Ackerman and James S. Fishkin, "Deliberation Day", *Public Opinion Quarterly*, 2004, 68(4): 641–650. Ack-erman and Fishkin, "Deliberation Day", *Deliberative Democracy*, Tan Huosheng (ed.), & Yuan He (trans.). Nanjing: Jiangsu People's Press, 2007, 124–145.

12 The Presidents Day, which derived from Washington's Birthday, is an American statu-tory holiday on the third Monday of February. Ackerman and Fishkin have criticized the current Presidents Day for having lost its meaning and been overcommercialized, with most citizens spending it on resting, shopping, or other recreational activities. In their

opinion, Presidents Day can be shifted from February to the month before the presidential election so that common people could do their duty as citizens for democracy in America. This might awaken citizens' appreciation of the hard-won democracy and endow Presidents Day with a new meaning with greater democratic implications.

13 They have analyzed the necessity of giving $150 to each participant in terms of the political economy of citizenship. Apart from raising the attendance rate, this can give a chance to the disadvantaged and break the dominance of the middle class and well-educated, well-paid citizens. Faced with skepticism, Ackerman and Fishkin believe that such expenses can be justified in two ways: (a) Deliberation Day offers new democratic legitimacy to the funds allocation structure; (b) Deliberation Day can help to address weaknesses in the current theory and practice of democracy. See Ackerman and Fishkin, "Deliberation Day", *Deliberative Democracy*, Tan Huosheng (ed.), & Yuan He (trans.). Nanjing: Jiangsu People's Press, 2007, 141.

14 Citizens' Councils have appeared in many cities and rural areas. They are intended to give common people a chance to evaluate the performance of local officials. A Citizens' Council is typically divided into three stages: (a) local leaders and heads of departments make presentations on their performance; (b) citizens raise questions, comment on the presentations, exchange opinions, and participate in the discussion of the leaders' performance; (c) citizens are asked to fill out an evaluation form, also known as a vote of confidence. The results of the evaluation will affect the political prospect of local leaders and other officials. See He Baogang, "Participatory and Deliberative Institutions in China", *The Development of Deliberative Democracy*, Chen Shengyong & He Baogang (eds.). Beijing: China Social Sciences Press, 2006, 98–99.

15 Since the beginning of the reform and opening up, with the relaxation of the state's direct control over society through work units, communities have become the basic space of social life for members of society. Some of them have established councils to improve democratic autonomy and protect their members' rights to know, manage, and supervise community affairs. Examples include the Community Council of Jing'an in Shanghai, the Residents' Council of Dejia Community in Hangzhou, and the Community Council of Yantian in Shenzhen. The Community Council is a form of governance by which citizens can participate in community decision making. Functioning like a "residents' conference", it has the rights of discussion, proposal, and supervision. See Liu Ye, "Public Participation, Community Autonomy and Deliberative Democracy: Analysis of Public Interactions in an Urban Community", *Fudan University Journal* (Social Sciences Edition), 2003, 5: 39–48.

16 The Community Discussion Center is a mechanism for discussion of community affairs by all community members through council meetings, complaint/suggestion boxes, the conference hall, and bulletin boards. Through complaint/suggestion boxes, a community can collect problems and difficulties its members have met in their daily lives and their comments and suggestions on community work. Through bulletin boards, it can announce to its members the issues being discussed, the process of discussion, and the feedback. Council meetings discuss solutions to hot issues and major challenges; the attendants are invited by the Community Residents' Committee according to the subject under discussion. The conference hall is where council meetings are held and visitors are received, a venue for the discussion of affairs by residents. See "Guiding Residents toward the Democratic Autonomy of Communities through Community Disscussion Centers", at the website of Chinese Urban Communities at http://www.cucc.org.cn/bencandy.php?fid=73&id=2134.

17 He Baogang, "Participatory and Deliberative Institutions in China", *The Development of Deliberative Democracy*, Chen Shengyong & He Baogang (eds.). Beijing: China Social Sciences Press, 2006, 94.

18 Jing Yuejin, "Administrative Democracy: Significance and Limitations, as Illustrated by the Democratic Forum at Wenling", *The Democratic Forum: A Creation by the People of Wenling*, Mu Yifei (ed.). Beijing: Central Compilation and Translation Press, 2005, 47–48.

19 This requires the staff to sort out, classify, number, and register the issues raised at the Forum as well as issues reported by other means, and submit them to the principal town leaders, who would give their comments and instructions. Thus these issues would become "listed" cases, and each of them is to be promptly and justly dealt with by the person(s) assigned to the task. If the results are found to be satisfactory by the person(s) concerned, the case can be "delisted"; if not, it has to be dealt with all over again until satisfaction is attained. See Xie Qingkui, "Expansion of Grassroots Democracy: Democratic Forum at Wenling City", *The Democratic Forum: A Creation by the People of Wenling*, Mu Yifei (ed.). Beijing: Central Compilation and Translation Press, 2005, 26–27.

20 "Opinions of the Party Committee of Wenling City on the Development of Grassroots Democracy through Deepening the Democratic Forum", *The Democratic Forum: A Creation by the People of Wenling*, Mu Yifei (ed.). Beijing: Central Compilation and Translation Press, 2005, 208–216. Lang Youxing, "Deliberative Democracy and Chinese Local Experience: The Democratic Forum in Wenling City, Zhejiang Province", *The Development of Deliberative Democracy*, Chen Shengyong & He Baogang (eds.). Beijing: China Social Sciences Press, 2006, 204–218.

21 Guo Yukuan, "Innovation in Local Political Reform: The Democratic Forum in Wenling, Zhejiang", http://news.sina.com.cn/c/2004–02–17/18172886523.shtml.

22 Mu Yifei (ed.), *The Democratic Forum: A Creation by the People of Wenling*. Beijing: Central Compilation and Translation Press, 2005, 1–93.

23 Wu Lezhen, "The International Symposium on Deliberative Democracy Theory and Practices of Local Democracy in China: A General View", *Zhejiang Social Sciences*, 2005, 1: 220–222.

24 For details, see the Symposium on Deliberative Democracy and Its Practice in China, http://21ccom.net/special/xieshangminzhu/ [accessed February 16, 2013]

25 The contents of this part have already been published. See Peng Zongchao and Li Ming, "A New Perspective on China's Public Budgeting Reform: Cases and Approaches of 'Cooperative-Harmonious Democracy'", *Reform*, 2008, 9.

26 Budgetary participation in the narrow sense only refers to public participation in the budgeting process; in the broad sense, it includes participation in the process by all actors outside the government (the legislative, judicial, and executive branches). By "budgetary participation" we mainly refer to the latter, i.e., the broad sense.

27 Hendrik T. Nieuwland, "A Participatory Budgeting Model for Canadian Cities", MA thesis submitted to the School of Policy Studies, Queen's University, Kingston, Ontario, Canada, July 2003.

28 Chen Jiagang and Chen Yimin, "Participatory Budgeting in Local Governance: A Case Study of the Reform at Xinhe Town in Wenling City, Zhejiang Province", *Public Administration Journal*, 2007, 3: 76.

29 Ma Jun, Tan Junjiu and Wang Puqu (eds.), *Toward a "Budgeting Country": Governance Democracy and Reform*. Beijing: Central Compilation and Translation Press, 2011.

30 Hu Xiaowen (ed.), *From Democratic Forum to Participatory Budgeting*. Beijing: World Affairs Press, 2012.

31 Gerald J. Miller and Lyn Evers, "Budgeting Structures and Citizen Participation", *Journal of Public Budgeting, Accounting and Financial Management*, 2002, 14(2): 233–272.

32 Peng Zongchao, "Cooperation or Conflict: Theories on the Relationship between Voters and Representatives", *Beijing Administrative College*, 2000, 6: 9–10.

33 Peng Jian, *The Evolution of Government Budgeting Theories and Institutional Innovation*. Dalian: DUFE Press, 2005, 77–127.

34 Carole Pateman, *Participation and Democratic Theory*. Shanghai: Shanghai People's Press, 2006.

35 An Weifu, "Technocracy: A Value-free Instrumental Rationality", *Seeking the Truth*, 1999, 5: 35–37.

36 Fei Jianping, "Academic Contributions by the Three Recipients of the Nobel Prize for Economics in 2007", *Economic Perspectives*, 2007, 11: 3.
37 Yin Wenjing, *National Finance Studies*. Shanghai: Shanghai Lixin Books and Accounting Supplies Press, 1953, 365.
38 IMF, *Fiscal Transparency*. Beijing: People's Press, 2001, 6–7.
39 Meng Chun and Li Ming, "Deepening the Reform in the Classifiication of Governmental Revenues and Expenditures, and Furthering the Efforts for Fiscal Transparency and Performance Evaluation", *References for Economic Research*, 2007, 37: 2–6.
40 Tang Min, "Actual Effects Valued in Budgeting Reform", *Outlook Weekly*, 2007, 34: 34–35.
41 Chen Jiagang and Chen Yimin, "Participatory Budgeting in Local Governance: A Case Study of the Reform at Xinhe Town in Wenling City, Zhejiang Province", *Journal of Public Management*, 2007, 3: 76.
42 Albert O. Hirschman, *Exit, Voice, and Loyalty: Responses to Decline in Firms, Organizations, and States*. Cambridge, MA: Harvard University Press, 1970, 15.
43 Ma Jun and Yu Li, "Public Budgeting Studies: An Area to Improve in Political Science and Public Administration in China", *CASS Journal of Political Science*, 2005, 2: 108.
44 Jürgen Habermas, *Between Facts and Norms: Contributions to a Discourse Theory of Law and Democracy*. Tong Shijun (trans.). Beijing: SDX Joint Publishing Company, 2003, 627.

9 A case study of Chinese cooperative-harmonious intra-Party democracy[1]

"Intra-Party democracy is the life of the Party." In 1988, the Organization Department of the Communist Party of China (CPC) Central Committee piloted the system of Party congresses with fixed terms (changed from its past functioning only once every five years to functioning at least once every year) in some counties and cities, with the purpose to reform the mechanism of the exercise of power and reinforce Party members' subject status in the Party. This is an important practice in extending intra-Party democracy. However, only a few pilot counties and cities persevered. In 2002, the 16th CPC National Congress approved this exploration. The report says, "Extend the piloting of the system of Party congresses with fixed terms in cities and counties." In 2007, President Hu Jintao's report at the 17th CPC National Congress takes it further, "We should improve the system of Party congresses . . . implement and improve the tenure system for delegates to Party congresses, experiment with a system of Party congresses with a fixed term in selected counties and county-level cities and districts." The resolution of the 4th Plenary Session of the 17th CPC Central Committee approved the pilot program and decided to advance the experiment and "continue experimenting with a system of Party congresses with a fixed term in selected counties and county-level cities and districts".[2] It can be said that after more than ten years' development and practice, the CPC Central Committee has affirmed the value of intra-Party democracy at the level of practice, made it an important content of the development of Chinese democratic politics, and attempted to promote the development of the people's democracy by this means.

As reported by *China Organization and Human Resources News*, 27 provinces (autonomous regions and municipalities) have promulgated the interim provisions on the tenure system for delegates, and 365 cities (autonomous prefectures) and 2,684 counties (county-level cities and districts) established the supporting systems concerning delegates' making proposals, conducting surveys, attending important meetings, contacting and serving Party members and ordinary people; 20 provinces (autonomous regions and municipalities), 174 cities (and autonomous prefectures), and 780 counties (county-level cities and districts), which account for 64.5 percent, 46.5 percent, and 27.9 percent of their respective totals, have established delegate liaison agencies of the Party congress. All across the country, 313 other counties (county-level cities and districts) continue to pilot the system of Party congresses with fixed terms, as do 2,982 other towns and townships. In 2009, when 363 community Party organizations of Nanjing changed personnel upon completion of tenure, all leaders of the Party organizations in question were determined via "public recommendation and direct election". In 2010, all the Party organizations at the village and community level in Guangxi changed personnel upon completion of tenure via "public recommendation and direct election".[3]

What are the main contents of democratic practices inside the Party? How are the practices evaluated? Where are some reflection and consideration about the practices and future developments required? This chapter will study the case of Ya'an and attempt to explore some questions related to intra-Party democracy, particularly questions concerning intra-Party elections.

What is especially worthy of attention is that this model of democratic reform is unlike the aforementioned direct elections of township and town heads in Shiping County, Yunan, which is pure reform of the democratic system; neither is it like pure deliberative democracy in Wenling. Instead, it involves various aspects of intra-Party democracy, including elections, the representative system, meeting system, deliberative system, etc. However, we believe that it is a comprehensive democratic reform based on intra-Party election reform and combining a variety of democratic factors. Therefore, we will discuss it here separately.

Literature review

A query was made in the CNKI China Academic Journal Network Publishing Database with intra-Party democracy as the search term. By 27 January 2013, we had retrieved 4,246 results, of which near 4,000 entries date after 2002. After September 2009, the relevant literature increased most steeply in amount – by near 2,000. However, there have been few academic investigations or case studies of the democratic practice within the Party in Ya'an.[4] The few entries are mostly descriptive reports. As a matter of fact, since the report of the 16th CPC National Congress stresses intra-Party democracy, it has gradually become a focus among scholars, and the tendency is still on the rise. Particularly after the 4th Plenary Session of the 17th CPC Central Committee made intra-Party democracy a key subject, studies on it have received a fresh round of attention in the academic and practice circles. The research literature so far is concerned with the following several aspects.

As far as the meaning of intra-Party democracy is concerned, Gao Fang summarizes the lessons that can be learnt from the fall of the communist parties in the Soviet Union and Eastern European countries because of the absence of intra-Party democracy and believes that intra-Party democracy is an indicator of a party's prosperity; particularly for the CPC, the exercise of intra-Party democracy does concern the security of its ruling status.[5] He also believes that the model of Chinese democratic politics should be improved from three aspects: intra-Party democracy, inter-Party democracy, and the people's democracy, and that the development of intra-Party democracy should be a top priority.[6]

As for the relationship between intra-Party democracy and social democracy, Hu Wei holds that as long as the CPC keeps its unique leadership, China's process of democratization will depend on it. If a fresh start is made outside the CPC, either it is completely unlikely or the costs will be too dear. Therefore, if the CPC can achieve intra-Party democracy, it will fuel the development of the entire democratic process in China. Therefore, as China moves towards democratization, it is much better to take a path within the existing system than outside it. The constructive and feasible design of the development of Chinese democratic politics should not change the leadership of the CPC but improve it and vigorously advance intra-Party democracy.[7] This is the universal belief in the political and academic circles that intra-Party democracy can be employed to drive social democracy.

In terms of the development direction and institutional design of intra-Party democracy, Wang Guixiu believes that inflexible rules should be laid to ensure Party members' rights; that the Party congress system should be reformed and improved, with the system of Party congresses with fixed terms implemented, and it is even necessary to establish a permanent body of Party delegates, i.e., the Party delegates' committee; that the Party committee system should be improved to truly realize collective leadership, collective discussion, and collective responsibility; that the intra-Party election system should be reformed and improved, or specifically speaking, direct elections expanded, multi-candidate elections improved, candidate nomination standardized and competitive elections implemented; and that the intra-Party deposal system be established.[8] Cai Xia thinks that the intra-Party power architecture should be constructed properly on the basis of ensuring Party members' rights, special efforts made to improve the operating mechanism, great attention paid to such key issues as procedure, and the institutional construction of intra-Party democracy advanced on the three levels of system, mechanism, and procedure.[9]

On the process of intra-Party democratic reform, Zheng Yongnian holds that an intra-Party representative mechanism should be set up. The intra-Party democratic mechanism should not only resolve the problem of excessive power concentration, but also prevent the Party itself from becoming an interest group and coordinate the interests of different classes.[10] Besides, in the process of implementing intra-Party democracy, though voting and the voting procedure are very important, the concept of the voting system should be transcended with the purpose to further intra-Party democracy. "That is to say, intra-Party democracy should not be simply equated with the voting system. Voting is merely an instrument, through which leaders are elected. However, intra-Party democracy is more than just electing people; but more importantly, it is about making policies. Leaders are important, so voting is employed to select or elect competent people. Policies are more important and candidates' policy orientation and their executive ability are crucial. Ideally, democratic competition is competition between different policies rather than between people. Competition between people is mainly about whether specific candidates have the abilities to implement their policies."[11]

On case studies of intra-Party democracy practices, the book edited by Wang Changjiang conducts a comprehensive, systematic, and in-depth case study of the experiment of intra-Party democracy with "public recommendation and direct election" conducted by the town and township Party committees in Pingchang County, Sichuan Province. It also compares and investigates the innovative practices of community-level intra-Party elections in different areas; and, lastly, conducts in-depth analysis of the issues of intra-Party democracy from theoretical and international perspectives and reveals the development tendencies of the innovations of the community-level democratic system within the Communist Party of China.[12] In recent years, Wang Changjiang has also analyzed the three types of intra-Party democratic practices in China: perfunctory type, practical type, and patterned type, and shown special concern and approval for the intra-Party democratic practice at Lügang Township, Shanghai.[13]

On the implementation of intra-Party democracy, Ren Jiantao clearly states that three aspects should be implemented: first, conceptual revolution should be implemented so as to truly realize the ideological shift from that of a revolutionary party to that of a ruling party; secondly, institutional innovation should be implemented, with the priority being the introduction of the full competition mechanism, procedural arrangement, and open evaluation; and thirdly, the step-by-step strategy should be implemented – there should not only be sporadic reforms, but, more importantly, top-down and comprehensive design, and the path of progressive reform should be taken.[14]

This literature of Chinese intra-Party democracy has different focuses. However, it should be noted that so far there are more macro-context studies of intra-Party democracy than micro-case studies, more descriptive studies than evaluative ones, more approving studies than reflective ones. Particularly the development of intra-Party democracy still lacks the guidance of a theory on democratic development; that is, the reform of intra-Party democracy calls for the standardization and guidance of a high-level theory on democracy. Otherwise the expansion of intra-Party democracy can only produce limited effect. On the basis of drawing on relevant literature on democracy, this chapter will mainly adopt the analytical approach illustrated by Figure 9.1, focus on whether the guarantee of Party members' rights

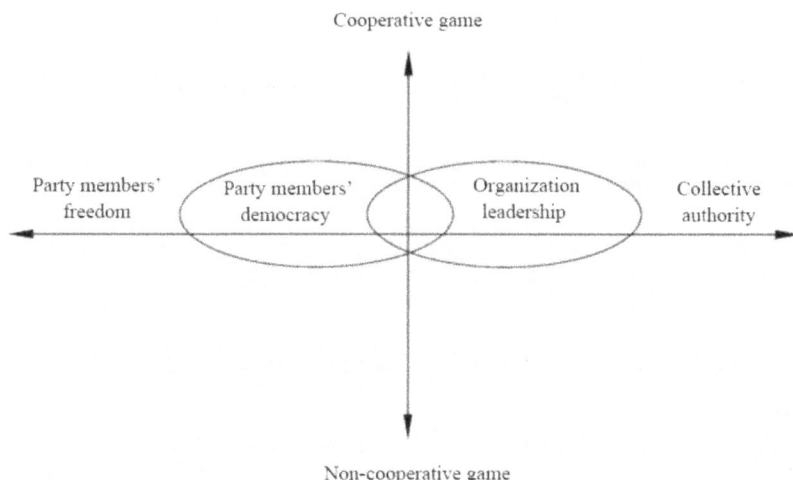

Figure 9.1 Analytical approach to intra-Party democracy

and organizational leadership can be seamlessly combined. The stress on one of the two might be beneficial in some special situation, but will definitely be problematic in the long run. Based on the interviews about intra-Party democracy in Ya'an in early September 2009, we conduct some analysis and evaluation of the case of Ya'an in terms of intra-Party democracy and think about the possibilities of its future developments; then we try proposing the target of the development of intra-Party democracy in China, i.e., cooperative-harmonious democracy combining democracy for Party members and organizational leadership.

History of Chinese intra-Party democracy

The stress of the CPC on intra-Party democracy can be traced back to the revolutionary period. However, in the harsh circumstances of revolutionary struggle, more emphasis was laid upon top-down control, rigorous organizational discipline and unified will. The 8th National Congress of the CPC in 1956 saw the theory and practice of intra-Party democracy reach a historical high and make such creative decisions as changing the Party congresses at national, provincial, and county levels to fixed terms, imposing strict effective intra-Party supervision, implementing the Party leadership tenure system, and protecting and expanding Party members' democratic rights.[15] Unfortunately, in the next over twenty years, intra-Party democracy was gradually seriously damaged. The resolutions of the 8th CPC National Congress on intra-Party democracy were not continuously and steadily implemented. It was not until 1978 that it recaptured attention, though intra-Party democracy remained restricted only to some areas of intra-Party political life. However, these areas helped usher in the period of reform and opening up.[16] The 3rd Plenary Session of the 11th CPC Central Committee restored and promoted intra-Party democracy, restarting the democratization within the Communist Party.

The report of the 13th CPC National Congress convened in 1987 points out that advancing the people's democracy gradually with intra-Party democracy as the breakthrough point is a practicable, effective approach; that the Party's collective leadership system and democratic centralism should be perfected and the regular reporting system should be set up that the Standing Committee of the Political Bureau of the Central Committee reports regularly to the Political Bureau of the Central Committee, which reports regularly to the plenary session of the CPC Central Committee; that the working rules and the Party life meeting system should be established for the Political Bureau of the Central Committee, the Standing Committee of the Political Bureau of the Central Committee and the Secretariat of the Central Committee to institutionalize collective leadership and strengthen the supervision and constrains of Party leaders; that the intra-Party electoral system should be reformed and improved, with rules laid down for the nomination procedure of intra-Party election and for multi-candidate election; and that Party members' democratic rights in line with the Party Constitution should be conscientiously ensured and, to serve this end, concrete provisions be formulated so as to give Party members a better knowledge of intra-Party affairs and opportunities of direct participation.[17]

After the 13th CPC National Congress, the system of Party congresses with fixed terms, regarded as the most important means to advance intra-Party democracy, was truly on the agenda. Since 1988, the Organization Department of the CPC Central Committee agreed for the first time to pilot the system successively in twelve counties, county-level cities, and districts of five provinces, including Shaoxing City, Jiaojiang City of Taizhou, Yongjia County and Rui'an City in Zhejiang; Lindian County and Zhaodong City in Heilongjiang; the Mining Area of Datong, Hongtong County, Yuci District of Jinzhong City and Heshun County in Shanxi; Xinji City in Hebei; and Hengshan County in Hunan.[18] The purpose of these pilot programs was to change the operating mechanism of intra-Party power and expand intra-Party democracy. However, very few of them persevered and quite a few went nowhere. "All of them shared one common problem: they sank into a situation promising a breakthrough that did not happen. That is, there was no substantial progress in scientifically dividing up the power of the Party committee, reforming the leadership mechanism combining legislative and executive powers, and changing the operating mechanism of intra-Party power. Eventually the pilot programs slid into stagnation due to the lack of motive power and became formalistic without a clear direction. Therefore, they automatically aborted because Party members and officials and common people lost interest in them."[19] Before the 16th CPC National Congress in 2002, only five counties, cities, and districts, including Shaoxing, Jiaojiang, and Rui'an in Zhejiang, and the Yuci District of Jinzhong City and Heshun County in Shanxi, were still continuing the pilot program; the other seven counties, cities, and districts all aborted it.

In 2002, the report of the 16th National Congress stated that intra-Party democracy is the life of the Party and plays an important exemplary and driving role for the people's democracy; that the system of intra-Party democracy fully reflecting Party members' and Party organizations' will should be established and improved, on the basis of ensuring Party members' democratic rights, with the improvement of the Party congress and Party committee systems as a focus and system and mechanism reform as a means; that the discussion and decision-making mechanism inside the Party committee should be improved to give better play to the role of its plenary session; that the intra-Party electoral system should be reformed and improved; and that the intra-Party briefing system, the information reporting system, and the opinion soliciting system for major decisions should be established and improved. Special emphasis is placed on expanding the experiment with the system of Party congresses with fixed terms at cities and counties and actively exploring the means and forms of giving play to the role of delegates to Party congresses when the congresses are closed. The report of the 16th CPC National Congress encouraged many counties (county-level cities and districts) in Guangdong, Jiangsu, Zhejiang, Sichuan, Hubei, Jilin, Shandong, and Guangxi to launch fresh practices in expanding intra-Party democracy. For instance, the Organization Department of the CPC Provincial Committee of Sichuan promulgated in March 2003 the *Opinions on the Piloting of Party Congresses with Fixed Terms in Cities and Counties (County-Level Cities and Districts)*, which directs the piloting in seventeen cities, counties, and districts. In the new round of piloting, apart from implementing the system of Party congresses with fixed terms and the annual meeting system of Party congresses, they also carried out many institutional innovations such as direct election of delegates to Party congresses, the definition of the power relations between the Party congress, plenary session, and villages' committee. The mechanisms which enable delegates to Party congresses to function on an everyday basis were designed. The modes of Jiaojiang, Ya'an and Luotian gradually took shape.

Apart from instituting measures to improve the Party congress system, implement the tenure system for delegates to Party congresses, pick some counties (county-level cities and districts) to pilot the system of Party congresses with fixed terms, reform intra-Party electoral system, and improve the candidate nomination procedure and electoral means, the report of the 17th CPC National Congress officially acknowledged the intra-Party democracy practices in Ya'an. All these measures are decisions made on the basis of the experience from the pilot program.[20]

Apart from requiring that the system of Party congresses with fixed terms continue to be piloted in counties (county-level cities and districts), the report of the 18th CPC National Congress also requires raising the proportion of delegates from among workers and farmers to Party congresses, the tenure system for delegates to Party congresses implemented and improved, the Party congress proposal system practiced, the intra-Party electoral system improved, multi-candidate nomination and election standardized, the decision-making and oversight role of plenary sessions of Party committees strengthened, the procedural rules and decision-making procedures of their standing committees improved, the mechanism improved for local Party committees discussing and making decisions on major issues and appointing important officials, and the system for Party members to assess the performance of leading bodies of community-level Party organizations on a regular basis improved. Party members are entitled to sit in and audit meetings of community-level Party committees and for delegates to Party congresses to attend relevant meetings of Party committees at the same levels.

Ya'an intra-Party democracy practice[21]

The 16th CPC National Congress decides to "expand the experiment with the system of Party congresses with fixed terms at cities and counties and actively explore the means and forms of giving play to the role of delegates to Party congresses when the congresses are closed". Based on this decision, directed by the Organization Department of the CPC Provincial Committee of Sichuan and the CPC Municipal Committee of Ya'an, Ya'an City started to pilot the system of Party congresses with fixed terms and the annual meeting system of Party congresses and carry out a series of supporting reforms in Yucheng District and Yingjing County in December 2002. Now after more than ten years' practice, the effort has achieved phased results and gradually formed the Ya'an mode of intra-Party democracy. In early September 2009, we conducted a special field interview in Ya'an.

Main contents of the Ya'an practice

Direct election of delegates to Party congresses

The direct election of delegates to Party congresses of Yucheng District follows an eight-step procedure i.e., "registration – preliminary recommendation of candidate delegates – preliminary examination – nomination of delegates candidates – qualification examination – public notification – election of delegates – public notice". Party members cast secret ballots to determine delegates to Party congresses via multi-candidate election. Yingjing County follows a ten-step procedure to elect delegates to Party congresses i.e., "voluntary self-registration – nomination by voting at the Party branch meeting – nomination of the electoral unit by voting – organization inspection – examination of the county electoral committee – public notification – competitive promises – election – issuing certification – public notice". Party members directly elect delegates to Party congresses via secret voting and multi-candidate election. Whereas all Party members of Yucheng District elect delegates to Party congresses directly, Yingjing County combines direct and indirect elections – direct election at the county level of governmental departments and indirect election at the town and township level. Such direct and competitive elections give the right of electing delegates to Party members and ensure Party members' rights to know, participate in, choose, and supervise the election of delegates to Party congresses.

The structural system for delegates to Party congresses and committee members[22]

The structural system for delegates to Party congresses means that the number of Party delegates is determined by the division of constituencies and the number of Party members. There should be at least one delegate in each constituency. If a delegate transfers out of his constituency or his status as a delegate to Party congresses is terminated for other causes, he will automatically be disqualified as a Party delegate. His slot will be re-filled accordingly via by-election in his previous constituency. In this way, the issue of incongruity between delegates to Party congresses and constituencies caused by work transfer is resolved. The structural system for district/county Party committee members is also implemented. There are no more alternate committee members. The mechanism for committee members' dynamic exiting and oriented supplementing is set up to ensure the broad representativeness and relative stability of district/county Party committee members and give better play to the decision-making role of the committee between plenary sessions. The implementation of the structural system and dynamic management standardizes and ensures the stability of the number and structure of delegates to Party congresses and district/county Party committee members, thereby laying a solid foundation for the system of Party congresses with fixed terms.

Straightening out the relations among the Party congress,
plenary session, and standing committee

After the launch of the tenure system for delegates to Party congresses, Yucheng District and Yingjing County adjust and streamline the relations between the Party congress, the plenary session of Party committee, and the standing committee, which have been unclear. The Party congress produces the plenary session, which produces the standing committee. The latter two are responsible to the Party congress; and rules are laid down so that the standing committee reports to the plenary session and the plenary session reports to the Party congress on a regular basis. Yingjing County has also formulated rules for the power execution of the plenary session; the standing committee is required to research the opinions of the plenary session with care, thoroughly resolve the existing problems, and make a report at the next plenary session. The power of the plenary session is greatly enhanced particularly on sensitive matters such as the appointment of leading officials. All officials above deputy section chief must be nominated by the standing committee and decided by ballot at the plenary session. Among the 2009 public credit rankings in official selection and appointment in Ya'an, Yingjing County ranked first.

Stepping up the combination of strengths, multiparty
cooperation, and political consultation

After the implementation of the system of Party congresses with fixed terms, the counties and districts convene the Party congress every year, followed by a session of the People's Congress and the Chinese People's Political Consultative Conference. Some worry that the operational costs might be too high, the efficiency be affected, and the Party congress with a fixed term deals an impact on the People's Congress system. Therefore, on the basis of strengthening the functions of the Party congress and basically completing the adjustments required, further efforts are made to explore the coordination between the Party congress, the Chinese People's Political Consultative Conference, and the people's congress and properly define their relations.

Yucheng District makes the head of the district Party committee the chairman of the standing working committee of the Party congress, the head of the Party members' group of the district people's congress the chairman of the standing supervision committee of the Party congress, and the head of the Party members' group of the district committee of Chinese People's Political Consultative Conference the chairman of the decision-making consultation committee of the Party congress. In other words, they are made heads of the three organs within the Party congress. In this way, a coordination mechanism is set up for the leading groups. Such a design also lays the function for the coordination of the relations between the Party congress, People's Congress and Chinese People's Political Consultative Conference so that the three can effectively coordinate with each other and the strengths of different political organs are combined to give play to the Party's role of commanding the whole situation and coordinating all parties involved.[23]

Now, to better enable the Chinese People's Political Consultative Conference (CPPCC) to perform its functions of democratic consultation and supervision and lay special emphasis upon the principle of "placing consultation before decision making", Yingjing County has creatively invited personnel from the CPPCC, non-communist parties and federations of industry and commerce to be present at the Party congress, and continuously strengthened the function of the CPPCC and its component units, thereby giving full play to their role of political consultation and participation in the deliberation and administration of state affairs, and promoting the scientific decision making of the Party congress.

Setting up the Party delegate liaison office

To ensure that delegates to Party congresses can better perform their duties and the Party congresses continuously handle everyday affairs, Yucheng District and Yingjing County both set up a Party delegate liaison office – an organ at section level under the organization department of the Party committee. Its main responsibilities are to make arrangements for the meetings, contacting delegates, organizing investigations and researches, collecting delegates' opinions and feeding them back to the plenary session, standing committee, and Party commissions for discipline inspection.

Establishing the system enabling Party delegates to play their role between sessions

To give better play to delegates to Party congresses, it is necessary to actively explore the means and forms which enable delegates to function between the sessions.

1 *Implement the ties-establishing system.* Every member of the district/county Party committee establishes ties with Party delegates (every member of the district Party committee in Yucheng District with three delegates to Party congresses and one Party branch, and every member of the county Party committee or the county commission for discipline inspection in Yingjing County with three to five delegates to Party congresses); every Party delegate establishes ties with three Party members, and every Party member with three common families.

2 *Build the Party delegate proposal-making system.* Delegates to Party congresses have actively carried out investigations and researches on Party construction, economic development, and other major social affairs. This is a process of going deeper into the masses so that they can present the people's wishes to the agenda of the standing committee in the form of proposals.

3 *Implement the Party delegate inspection system.* Every group of delegates in Yingjing County inspect the implementation and execution of the resolutions and decisions of the Party committee and its executive bodies on either a regular or irregular basis, make inspection tours on practical problems

concerning the people's vital interests and hear opinions extensively through delegate symposiums and symposiums of Party members from the community-level units.

4   *Implement the proposal handling system.* In the case of Yingjing County, Party delegates' proposals inspected by the county Party delegate liaison office are forwarded in a timely fashion to the departments concerned, which are required to deliver the results of their measures in writing to the Party delegates in question within the prescribed time and ask for their opinions on the results. As for major proposals with overall impact, the liaison office collects them and, after handing them over to the leading group of Party delegates' activities for inspection and discussion, submits them in writing to the standing committee for deliberation. The liaison office is also responsible for forwarding the proposals and supervising their implementation.

Work report review and supervision system

The work report review system is established, which requires Party committee members to deliver work reports to the delegates to Party congresses and the delegates to deliver work reports to Party members. Every year, the delegates to the district Party congress and members of the district Party committee and Party commissions for discipline inspection in Yucheng District are required to deliver work reports to Party members and representatives in the respective constituencies. Work report evaluation meetings are convened; the results for Party committee members are reported to Party delegates and they will serve as an important basis for the performance assessment of district leaders. Yingjing County sets up and improves the working rules for delegates to county Party congresses, which authorize them to hear important meetings such as the meetings of the standing committee and the plenary sessions of the county Party committee; and to participate in major work as supervisors. In this way, the oversight of delegates to Party congresses over the Party committee shifts from supervision after the affairs to that throughout the whole process; from the supervision over the Party committee as a whole to that over Party committee members and Party and government officials. Moreover, through the annual work report arrangement for delegates to Party congresses, their duty fulfillment is also overseen.

Effects of the Ya'an practice

Chinese democratic politics develops along such a path that intra-Party democracy drives the people's democracy. Therefore, how intra-Party democracy fares determines the success or failure of the people's democracy. Considering that cooperative-harmonious democracy stresses the combination of freedom and authority, the future developments of democracy within the Communist Party of China must establish a virtuous cycle between the leadership of the Party (collective authority) and the democracy for Party members (freedom for Party members) through cooperative game between the two, because intra-Party democracy means prominence given to Party members' rights. However, if the relationship between Party members' individual freedom and the leadership of the Party organization cannot be handled properly, conflict will arise between the two. Judging by the survey and interviews in Ya'an, on the one hand, Ya'an's practice of intra-Party democracy demonstrates the vitality and responsibilities of Party members as individuals; on the other, it also strengthens the Party's authority and, to some extent, embodies the thought of cooperative game.

Party members' rights are ensured and Party member awareness is strengthened

After the launch of the system of Party congresses with fixed terms, Ya'an has changed the past situation that Party delegates attended one meeting every five years. The system of Party congresses with fixed terms not only ensures the democratic rights of Party members and Party delegates, but enhances their sense of responsibility, honor, and mission and, particularly through competitive elections, enhances Party members' and Party delegates' awareness of their identities.

First, Party members' desire to participate is whipped up. As a result, the Party member awareness is enhanced. If a Party delegate is elected once, he will strive to be elected for a second time. To serve this end, he pays constant attention to his speech and behavior so that they comply with the requirements on Party members and on good Party members. Therefore, their desire to participate and their Party member awareness are strengthened. (J²⁴)

Delegates to Party congresses have to deliver work reports to Party members in their constituency on an annual basis. This strengthens Party delegates' Party member awareness. (S)

The Party committee's decision making becomes more scientific and democratic

The measures, including the Party delegate proposal system, the CPPCC participation system, and the ties-establishing system, linking Party committee members to Party delegates, Party delegates to Party members, and Party members to the people bring the Party's major decisions closer to reality and make Party committee decisions more scientific and democratic.

Every year, delegates to Party congresses are subject to Party members' appraisal. So they are encouraged to bring Party members' good advice to meetings and are required to communicate with community-level Party members. It is thus easier for community-level Party members' advice to move upward, and the Party organizations can hear more truths before they make decisions. The more truths they hear, the more likely they are to make right decisions. (J)

Before a session of the Party congress is convened, the work report of the county Party committee needs to be drawn up. So members of the county committee of the CPPCC are not merely present at plenary sessions of the Party committee; but when we are drawing up the work report of the county Party committee, we hear their opinions every year. After a draft is formed, some insightful members with ideas are gathered together so that we can hear their suggestions and opinions. The CPPCC committee boasts a lot of talented people. Therefore, by fully soliciting their opinions, we can further improve the work report of the county Party committee. When they are present at the Party congress, county leaders take part in group discussions of the county committee of the CPPCC to see if the members of the county committee of the CPPCC have good advice so that they can execute scientific and democratic decision making. (Z)

The presence of members of the CPPCC county committee at the Party congress has many merits. Since they can hear the work reports of both the Party committee and county commission for discipline inspection, they can thus offer consultation on and supervise not only government affairs, as they did in the past, but also the decisions by the county Party committee. Their presence at the Party congress is beneficial to the construction of the ruling party itself and to its democratic decision making and can better embody the spirit of multiparty cooperation. (M)

Party delegates' and leaders' sense of responsibility and responsiveness are improved

As the implementation of the work report review system embodies the principle "I am responsible to the people who elected me", Party delegates' and leaders' sense of responsibility and responsiveness are improved.

Votes are cast and satisfaction surveys conducted based on whether the promises made by delegates to Party congresses when they take part in the election. If they cannot reach a certain approval rating, they will be disqualified. The members of the standing committee of the county Party committee deliver work reports to the plenary session; and the members of the county Party committee to delegates to Party congresses. Delivering work reports is on the agenda on every plenary session. Now the county Party committee consists of thirty-five members. Some of them deliver their work reports orally and others submit work reports in writing. Delegates to Party congresses assess the work of every member and use the results as the basis for our year-end evaluation. So the evaluation matters very much. (Y)

Being a Party delegate means not only honor and glory, but also responsibility. They should set an example for Party members to follow. The annual work report system can further whip up their sense of responsibility in work. (X)

The vitality of community-level Party organizations is stimulated

The piloting of the system of Party congresses with fixed terms stimulates Party members' initiative and enthusiasm, and the activities of Party delegates between sessions of the Party congress also enrich the intra-Party political life and enable the Party delegates to participate in the making of major decisions within the

Party. This is a new measure of developing intra-Party democracy, which also improves the atmosphere of intra-Party democratic politics. Party delegates' inspections and surveys and proposals provide new approaches to developing intra-Party democracy and effectively stimulate the vitality of community-level Party organizations.

The status of Party delegates is raised, and their rights protected. (L)

After the system of Party congresses with fixed terms is piloted, intra-Party democracy is demonstrated. It can give play to Party members' role and enhance their initiative to the greatest extent, concentrate their wisdom and thus help the ruling party to avert mistakes. (N)

The legitimacy of the Party's ruling status is consolidated

The system of Party congresses with fixed terms not only whips up Party delegates' enthusiasm and taps the vitality of community-level Party organizations, but also finds an echo and strong approval among all social strata. It combines the strengths of the people from different circles and different sectors of society, improves the relationship between the Party and the masses, between officials and common people, betters the Party's image, increases Party organizations' solidarity, and consolidates the legitimacy of the ruling status.

Now many officials have done fairly well in being responsible to superiors but fallen short in being responsible to subordinates. This is where the conflict between the people and the government lies. The system of Party congresses with fixed terms changes this situation to a certain extent. (J)

At every Party congress, we delegates to Party congresses will make some proposals. After the meeting, the Party delegate liaison office will classify them and forward them to the authorities concerned, together with the requirement that they must respond within a specified period of time to the delegates who have made the proposals and suggestions. To their response we will attach a table, a questionnaire to find out whether the delegates are satisfied with the response. If they are not, the proposal in question has to be dealt with again. (Z)

I am a Party delegate myself. I feel that the system of Party congresses with fixed terms consolidates the core leadership of the Party. (S)

Existing problems

Understanding of intra-Party democracy needs to be deepened

The piloting the system of Party congresses with fixed terms in Ya'an indicates that certain Party members' and officials' understanding and perception of intra-Party democracy are yet to be deepened. Some even think that the system on which so much money and energy have been spent is merely a formality with little significant meaning and that the money and energy expended would generate more returns if invested in economic construction.

Party delegates' abilities have yet to be improved

In the process of work, there exist some problems. So far, Party delegates' aware-ness of political participation and their qualities have yet to be further improved. Though some of them have the desire to participate, they make no proposal at the meeting. It is possible that they wish to, or have one idea but cannot express it or cannot express it properly. So they simply refrain from making it. (N)

The guarantee mechanism has yet to be perfected

In each of the two pilot programs in Yucheng District and Yingjing County, a Party delegate liaison office is established to be responsible for contacting delegates to Party congresses regularly, organizing their inspections, handling their proposals, and overseeing the departments concerned to deal with them. However, Party delegates' exercise of power is only guaranteed by one article, i.e., "If delegates to Party congresses attend a session or an activity during two sessions, all units concerned shall commit enough time." The difficulties the delegates may face in their fulfillment of duties have been underestimated, and relevant guarantee provi-sions on funds, etc. are absent.

We ourselves are somewhat perplexed about the ongoing pilot program. After one session of the Party congress is closed, our resumption of work has been faced with a bottleneck at town and township level. How can we further our work? Depu-ties to the People's Congress and members of the CPPCC county committee have the guarantee of law and regulations and funds when they exercise power and carry out their work, but we have none of those in this regard. (S)

When our Party delegates conduct investigations and surveys, they don't have the money needed. To give full play to the role of Party delegates, I think they should be able to get hold of some working funds. With financial support, they can do investigation or research. With some money allotted to them and with the annual work report system, they are certain to be under pressure and the pressure motivates them to give play to their wisdom and talent. Now that being a Party delegate means responsibility, he or she is entitled to some funds, which enable them to better perform the duties. (N)

Reflections on the future development of intra-Party democracy

The pilot programs of intra-Party democracy across China, particularly the prac-tice in Ya'an, are constructive in both institutional innovation and effect. However, the success of these pilot programs alone cannot serve as an important indicator for evaluating Chinese political system reform and democratic development. To advance intra-Party democracy with the system of Party congresses with fixed terms as a breakthrough point and drive the people's democracy with intra-Party democracy, understanding needs to be furthered and more extensive practices are called for. At least theoretically the future development of intra-Party democracy is still faced with some issues worth discussing.

1   The full implementation and sustainability of the piloting of intra-Party democracy need to be watched. "Democracy" and "centralism" have been a recurring topic within the Party. This in itself shows that the Communist Party of China needs democracy, and the crux of the problem lies in how to avoid excessive concentration. In contemporary China, the Party is not only the stabilizer of the entire political system, but also the only player that can dominate the mending of the political system without jeopardizing the political system itself.[25] If the practices of intra-Party democracy help make decision making more scientific and more democratic and are beneficial to the political stability of multiparty cooperation, the development of intra-Party democracy is something to be expected. However, democracy is a double-edged sword. If its extension incurs political instability and threatens the Party's ruling status, it is hard not to restrict it.

2   Can intra-Party democracy drive the people's democracy? Historically speaking, a party which advances democratic politics may not necessarily be a pro-democracy party. On the contrary, the democratic process is more often advanced by undemocratic parties. The democratic transformation in the Taiwan region is a case in point. Of course this does not mean that democracy within a party is not important. If the ruling party leads in practicing democracy, streamlines the ruling relations within the party, stimulates its vitality, and strengthens its governance capabilities, it will be more confident to advance the people's democracy and the process of national democratization. Therefore, in China intra-Party democracy is one of the crucial political reforms for the democratic development.

3   The reform of intra-Party democracy needs to be incorporated into a broader theoretical framework of democracy. Starting from 1988, the reform of intra-Party democracy, or the piloting of the system of Party congresses with fixed terms, has been going on for twenty-five years. In the field of political system reform, "crossing the river by feeling the stones" and "it doesn't matter whether the cat is black or white, as long as it catches rats" are approaches with limitations; political reform is unlike economic reform in that the former must be guided by some theories. Sporadic reform is not only of limited effect, but also certain to encounter great resistance and serious problems. For instance, villagers' autonomy, which has been advocated for many years, has hit a wall and the bottleneck cannot be overcome by pushing forward elections. It is the same with the reform of intra-Party democracy, which will eventually cause a shift in the political system of China; the risks of reform and the uncertainty of interests will cause the ruling party to vacillate on this matter. How to define the levels of the reform through a global development framework of democratic theory and progress gradually is a question that must be considered in the development of Chinese democratic politics. The development framework of cooperative-harmonious democracy we have proposed is not mature, but we, to say the least, believe that it represents the direction toward which we should direct our effort.

Summary

Cooperative-harmonious democracy stresses the balance between individuality and collectivity, between freedom and authority, between right and power. Through our investigation of the practices of intra-Party democracy in Ya'an, Sichuan, from the perspective of the theory on cooperative-harmonious democracy, fairly good interaction can be achieved between the Party's authority and individual Party members' rights. Party members hope to achieve their value through the exercise of rights; by means of diversifying the forms of intra-Party democracy, the Party's authority is further strengthened. However, further improvements need to be made in institutional design and guarantee.

Notes

1 Part of this chapter has been published. See Ma Ben and Peng Zongchao, *Appraisal and Review of Practices of Intra-Party Democracy: A Case Study of Ya'an. Study & Exploration*, 2011, 9.
2 *Decision of the CPC Central Committee on Major Issues Pertaining to Strengthening and Improving Party Construction in the New Circumstances*, http://qzlx.people.com.cn/n/2013/0530/c364581–21669817.html.
3 Special correspondent Zhong Zuxuan, "Improve the Party's Solidarity, Unification and Innovative Vigor – New Developments in the Party's Organization System and Intra-Party Democracy", *China Organization and Human Resources News*, October 29, 2012.
4 See Peng Suining, Hou Deling, Peng Yangqing, Ma Guoxiang, Wu Xianxi, Qiu Ruoyu and Wang Yingsheng, "The System and Practice Stimulating Democratic Vitality within the Party – An Investigation and Reflection of the Piloting of the System of Party Congresses with Fixed Terms in Ya'an City, Sichuan Province", *Theory and Reform*, 2003, 2. Pei Zeqing, "Innovation in Intra-Party Democracy – The Experiment with the System of Party Congresses with Fixed Terms in Ya'an City, Sichuan Province and Its Revelations", *Journal of the Party School of the CPC Sichuan Provincial Committee*, 2004, 1.
5 Gao Fang, "How Was the Democracy within the Communist Party of the Soviet Union Destroyed?", *Journal of the School of Administration of Jiangsu*, 2004, 4: 69–76.
6 Gao Fang, *Heartbeats of the Reform of Chinese Political Reform*. Chongqing: Chongqing Publishing House, 2006.
7 Hu Wei, "Intra-Party Democracy and Political Development: Exploiting the Resources of Chinese Democratization within the Existing System", *Fudan Journal* (Social Sciences Edition), 1999, 1: 1–11.
8 Wang Guixiu, "Direction and Path of the Development of Intra-Party Democracy", *Leaders' Friend*, 2003, 3: 20–22.
9 Cai Xiao, "Advancing the System of Intra-Party Democracy as a Whole", *Outlook Weekly*, 2007, 14: 44–45.
10 Zheng Yongnian, *The China Mode: Experience and Plight*. Hangzhou: Zhejiang People's Publishing House, 2010, 57–84.
11 Zheng Yongnian, "Where Will Intra-Party Democracy in China Go?", http://comments.caijing.com.cn/2012–05–29/111865448.html (February 17, 2013)
12 Wang Changjiang and Zhou Hongyun (eds.), *Innovations of the System of Intra-Party Democracy*. Beijing: Central Compilation and Translation Press, 2007.
13 Wang Changjiang, "We Should Feel Pressed to Step up Innovation in Intra-Party Democracy", *Study Times*, July 25, 2011.
14 Ren Jiantao, "Intra-Party Democracy May Start with the 'Three Implements'", *Yan-Huang Historical Review*, 2012, 12.

15 Zeng Jingzhong, "The Eighth CPC National Congress and Intra-Party Democracy", *CPC History Studies*, 1996, 4: 18–24.

16 Hu Deping, "Comrade Hu Yaobang before and after the Great Discussion on Standards for Truth", *Decision and Information*, 2008, 5: 16–25.

17 See Zhao Ziyang, *March on the Path of Socialism with Chinese Characteristics, – Report at the 13th National Congress of the Communist Party of China*. Beijing: People's Publishing House, 1987.

18 Shen Haixiong and Cai Guozhao, "Unveiling the History of Piloting the Reform of Party Congresses", *Oriental Outlook*, 2008, 3.

19 Xue Kai, "Scholars Say the System of Party Congresses with Fixed Terms Is a New Breakthrough in Intra-Party Democracy", *China Comment* (Internal Edition), 2003, 10(3).

20 "Ouyang Song, Head of CPC Central Committee Organization Department, Briefs on Party Building and Strengthening the Ranks of Party Officials", china.com.cn, http://www.china,com.cn/zhibo/2007–10/17/content_9060556.htm.

21 Major part of this section has been published. See Ma Ben and Peng Zongchao, "Appraisal and Review of Practices of Intra-Party Democracy: A Case Study of Ya'an", *Study & Exploration*, 2011, 5.

22 The structural system means that delegates to Party congresses are classified into sector-specific ones and fixed-structure ones. Delegates are elected by sector in cities and by administrative division at township and town level in rural areas.

23 Initially, Yucheng District piloted the three-committee architecture of the Party congress, which were respectively the supervision committee, the delegate work committee, and the decision-making consultation committee. The decision-making consultation committee was the Party congress's organ of decision-making consultation, responsible for organizing experts, scholars, and personnel of other circles to conduct surveys and researches, offering basis and reference for scientific decision-making and evaluating decisions. The delegate work committee was mainly responsible for everyday management and service of delegates, handling and overlooking proposals, organizing activities, directing the supplementary elections of delegates and organizing evaluations. In brief, it provided organization guarantee for the other two committees. The members of the supervision committee were generated via multi-candidate election among the non-members of the district Party committee and the commission for discipline inspection. It was mainly responsible for supervising the duty fulfillment of the members of the Party committees and Party commissions for discipline inspection, organizing evaluations, delivering admonishing or encouraging talks, and making dismissal proposals. As designed, the post of the chairman of the supervision committee was held concurrently by a deputy chairman of the people's congress and that of the chairman of the decision-making consultation committee by a deputy chairman of the people's political consultative conference. However, this three-committee architecture has been recalled because the supervision committee and the Party commissions for discipline inspection somewhat overlapped in functionality. "Two possibly conflicting organs are not allowed to coexist within one party." Also see He Zhongzhou, "The System of Party Congresses with Fixed Terms Drives the People's Democracy – The Democratic Experiment in Ya'an", *China News Weekly*, 2007, 44.

24 J. is the series number of interviewee in our field interview in Ya'an City in 2009. The single capital letters in brackets following each paragraph in italicization will be also the series numbers of interviewees.

25 Lewin Moshe, *The Gorbachev Phenomenon: A Historical Interpretation*. Berkeley: University of California Press, 1988, 133.

10 Conclusion and recommendations

China's peaceful development and the realization of the Chinese Dream must be supported by a democratic political system with its own characteristics. Likewise, the building of a harmonious society would be impossible without the development of democracy. The idea that only the Western model of democracy is the final solution ("even if Emperors Yao and Shun lived today, they would undoubtedly lose no time in adopting the Western system and put it into practice without a single day's delay"[1]) would not only undermine our tradition, but also create barriers for the actual development of democracy. Tradition often resists a total revamp with a tenacious vitality. In fact, the American democracy is different from the British, and the French democracy also differs from the American. Each nation has tried to seek support in her own culture during the construction of her democracy. Among the Western countries, none of the latecomers to democratization has copied the model of any other country; instead, they have all opted for creative incorporation and reconstruction based on their own cultural traditions. The difference between democracies lies in nothing but their cultural foundations.

Therefore, Chinese democracy should transcend both the traditional socialist model of democracy and the worship of Western liberal democracy. We should develop a model of cooperative-harmonious democracy with real Chinese characteristics based on what can be learned from other models, with a combination of respect for our traditional culture and the step-by-step approach of modern cooperative game. To this end, the following should be our main considerations:

1   Make full use of cooperative-harmonious and people-oriented thought in our traditional culture. Unlike the stress on competition in Western countries, cooperation and harmony have always been regarded as the highest values and ideals in the Chinese tradition. It can be said that these two concepts highlight Chinese characteristics and epitomize China's difference from Western nations in values. Because of this, in building the Chinese model of democracy, we do not need the same blueprints and institutional designs as those of Western countries; instead, we should try to incorporate the people-oriented and cooperative-harmonious thought into the design of contemporary Chinese democracy so that democracy could really be rooted in the fertile soil of our traditional culture and fully reflect Chinese characteristics.

Otherwise, if the essence of our traditional culture is abandoned, even such a good thing as democracy would go wrong.

2 Future design of democratic institutions should reflect the philosophy of cooperative game. In the future, when considering the design of specific democratic institutions and the planning of the stages of democracy, be it electoral democracy, deliberative democracy, or democracy within the Party, we need to focus on striking a balance between competition and cooperation; we should give all stakeholders and political forces an opportunity for communication and negotiation to prevent polarized competition. We should promote social consensus and harmony through resolving serious conflicts of interest and differences in opinions by institutional means wherever possible.

3 Persist in the combination of the Party's leadership, the people's role as the master of the country, and the rule of law. Cooperative-harmonious democracy cannot be accepted and approved of unless it is combined with the existing democratic system. How to unify the three elements would determine the future of cooperative-harmonious democracy. In fact, the perspective of cooperative-harmonious democracy would give a new interpretation of the three: the Party's leadership means authority, the people's role as the master of the country represents the popular will, and the rule of law provides institutional arrangement and support. What is stressed in cooperative-harmonious democracy is an appropriate degree of combination of and balance between the Party's leadership (authority) and the people's role as the master of the country (the popular will) through the rule of law (institutional constraints).

4 While continuing to adhere to and improve the CPC's leadership, gradually give full play to the democratic parties' role in the deliberation and administration of state affairs. We may consider restoring the coalition government by the CPC and the other democratic parties in history. With the change of the times and the growth of various political forces, we should, under the current party system, gradually enlarge the scope of the deliberation and administration of state affairs by democratic parties; we should keep drawing upon Mao Zedong's important idea of "coalition government" and the good practice of multiparty coalition in the early years of the People's Republic of China. This requires us to design a more inclusive party system, gradually increase opportunities for democratic parties to participate in coalition government, and enhance their ability to do so. This would truly help to avoid the defects of both the one-party system and the multiparty system, and further improve the other parties' ability to take part in political affairs and increase the degree to which they can do so.

5 Attach great importance to reforming and improving horizontal and vertical state power relationships. Horizontally, we must adhere to and improve the CPC's leadership of state organs, gradually straighten out the relationship between the two, maintain the Party's self-discipline, and make sure that the Party always works within the boundaries of the Constitution and other

laws. We should adhere to the institution of the People's Congress and the principle of democratic centralism, preserve and enhance the status and role of the People's Congress as the sole organ of state power, intensify its supervision and restraint of the executive and judicial branches of the government, and guard against the abuse of power and corruption. Vertically, we should adhere to the unitary system yet adopt a certain measure of decentralization and local autonomy in order to give full play to the roles of local governments and grassroots organizations.

6   Gradually expand orderly political participation by Party members and citizens and propel the progress of electoral democracy and deliberative democracy based on the People's Congress system. With the deepening of the reform and opening up, the traditional political structure in which state and society are highly unified has begun to totter; the old mono-interest structure is giving way to a poly-interest structure, and citizens' sense of participation is awakening. This has led us to believe the following to be true: (a) we need to intensify the reform and development of election and democracy within the Party, and, in good time and from a strategic perspective, consider how to steadily raise the level at which the direct election of deputies to the People's Congress can be applied[2]; we should also implement equal representation of urban and rural areas completely, reform and improve People's Congress–related institutions for meetings, agendas, and the exercise of power, in order to expand electoral democracy more effectively; (b) we should continue to vigorously propel the reform for consultative democracy in the institutions for multiparty cooperation and political consultation, hearings,[3] and dialogues between officials and the masses; we should also draw on foreign countries' practices for citizens' direct participation, including deliberative democracy, voting by citizens, and e-democracy; citizens should be allowed to have real rights of participation, information, supervision, and expression, so that public governance, instead of being the monopoly of the elite, would become open to the public. This would make our public policies more legitimate and improve the quality of democratic governance.

Undoubtedly, the construction of cooperative-harmonious democracy would be an enormous and progressive project of the entire society. It involves many aspects of the political structure and public governance, and cannot succeed overnight. We need to draw on the lessons of democratic transition and institutional change at home and abroad, and move forward in a proactive, stable, and systematic way while trying to implement the fundamental principles of cooperative-harmonious democracy and making full use of all favorable factors from every quarter. We are convinced that the building of a cooperative-harmonious democracy model that transcends both the existing model of democracy and the worship of Western liberal democracy will shape China's future. Though the building of a model of democracy is not a skill of free innovation and design, neither is it like a sapling that, once planted, will keep growing while we slumber. Each stage of it is imprinted with the effects of human reason and requires voluntary effort as well as top-level design and strategic planning. The building of a cooperative-harmonious democracy model in China would be impossible without the power of reason and the guidance of top-level strategy. To combine tradition and reality, bring human reason and imagination into full play, conduct a prospective search for a Chinese model of democratic development, and come up with new vision – all these call for a profound revolution in thought and ideological liberation, which in turn requires politicians and scholars to think and work together. We hope that this book could offer a new way to analyze and think about the development of democracy, social cooperation, and harmonious governance in China.

Notes

1 Guo Songtao, *Guo Songtao's Diary* (III). Changsha: Hunan People's Publishing House, 1981, 814.
2 See Peng Zongchao, *Civic Authorization and Representative Democracy: A Comparative Study of the Direct Election of People's Representatives*. Zhengzhou: Henan People's Publishing House, 2002.
3 See Peng Zongchao, *Public Hearing Systems in China: Transparent Policy-Making and Public Governance*. Beijing: Tsinghua University Press, 2004.

Bibliography

Ackerman, Bruce & James S Fishkin, "Deliberation Day", *Public Opinion Quarterly*, 2004, 68(4).

Alexandra, Barahona De Brito, Carmen Gonzalez Enriquez & Paloma Aguilar, *The Politics of Memory and Democratization*. Oxford: Oxford University Press, 2001.

Almmond, Gabriel A & Sidney Verba, *The Civic Culture: Political Attitudes and Democracy in Five Nations*, Ma Dianjun, Yan Huajiang & Zheng Xiaohua (trans.). Hangzhou: Zhejiang People's Publishing House, 1989.

Arblaster, Anthony, *Democracy*, Sun Rongfei, Duan Baoliang and Wenya (trans.). Changchun: Jilin People's Publishing House, 2005.

Aristotle, *Politics*, Wu Shoupeng (trans.). Beijing: The Commercial Press, 1965.

Bai, Lin, "Vladimir Lenin's Idea of Democracy and Its Realistic Significance", *Chinese Cadres Tribune*, 1990, 7.

Bai, Yihua, *Reforming and Exploring China's State Power at the Community Level*. Beijing: China Society Press, 1995.

Barber, Benjamin, *Strong Democracy*, Peng Bin & Wu Runzhou (trans.). Changchun: Jilin People's Publishing House, 2006.

Bell, Daniel A (Canada), *Beyond Liberal Democracy*, Li Wanquan (trans.). Shanghai: Shanghai Joint Publishing Company, 2009.

Ben, Ma & Peng Zongchao, "Integration of Deliberative Democracy and Ballot Democracy: Models of Democratic Development in China", *Theoretical Studies*, 2009, 4.

Ben, Ma & Peng Zongchao, "Appraisal and Review of Practices of Intra-Party Democracy: A Case Study of Ya'an", *Study & Exploration*, 2011, 9.

Berman, James, *Public Deliberation: Pluralism, Complexity and Democracy*, Huang Xianghuai (trans.). Beijing: Central Compilation and Translation Press, 2006.

Bohman, James & William Rehg, *Deliberative Democracy: Essays on Reason and Politics*, Chen Jiagang, Lin Li, Yu Hongqiang, Zhou Yanhui, Hao Wenjie, Xu Xingjian, Wang Wenzi, Chen Zhigang, Xu Huan & Zhang Caimei (trans.). Beijing: Central Compilation and Translation Press, 2006.

Cai, Xia, "Advancing the System of Intra-Party Democracy as a Whole", *Outlook Weekly*, 2007, 14.

Chen, Jiagang, *Deliberative Democracy*. Shanghai: Shanghai Joint Publishing Company, 2004.

Chen, Shengyong & He Baogang (eds.), *The Development of Deliberative Democracy*. Beijing: China Social Sciences Press, 2006.

Chua, Amy, *World on Fire: How Exporting Free Market Democracy Breeds Ethnic Hatred and Global Instability*. Beijing: Encyclopedia of China Publishing House, 2005.

Colomer, Josep M, *Game Theory and the Transition to Democracy*. Aldershot, UK: Edward Elgar, 1995.

Colomer, Josep M, *Strategic Transitions: Game Theory and Democratization*. Baltimore, MD: The Johns Hopkins University Press, 2000.

Cui, Zhiyuan, *Game Theory and Social Sciences*. Hangzhou: Zhejiang People's Publishing House, 1988.

Dahl, Robert A, *Polyarchy: Participation and Opposition*. New Haven: Yale University Press, 1971.

Dahl, Robert, *On Democracy*, Li Baiguang & Lin Meng (trans.). Beijing: The Commercial Press, 1999.

Donne, John, *The History of Democracy*, Lin Meng, Li Zhi, Lü Fang, Han Li, Gao Wang, Fan Xianrui, Chen Liyan, Shang Hongri & Chen Juan (trans.). Changchun: Jilin People's Publishing House, 1999.

Dryzek, John S (Australia), *Deliberative Democracy and Beyond: Liberals, Critics, Contestations*, Ding Kaijie (trans.). Beijing: Central Compilation and Translation Press, 2006.

Du, Weiming, "Cultural Implications of the Rise of Confucianism in East Asia". *Dialogue and Innovation*. Guilin: Guangxi Normal University Press, 2005.

Dworkin, Ronald, "Hart's Postscript and the Character of Political Philosophy", *Oxford Journal of Legal Studies*, 2004, 24.

Elster, Jon, *Deliberative Democracy*. Cambridge: Cambridge University Press, 1998.

Field, Bonnie N & Kerstin Hamann, *Democracy and Institutional Development: Spain in Comparative Theoretical Perspective*. Basingstoke: Palgrave Macmillan, 2008.

Gaetano, Mosca, *The Ruling Class*, Jia Hepeng (trans.). Nanjing: Yilin Press, 2002.

Gallie, W B, "Essentially Contested Concepts", *Proceeding of the Aristotelian Society*, 1955–1956, 56.

Gan, Chunsong, *Confucianism Institutionalized*. Shanghai: Shanghai People's Publishing House, 2006.

Gao, Fang, "Lenin on the Theory and Practice of Socialist Democracy", *Nanjing Journal of Social Sciences*, 1995, 1.

Gao, Fang, *Politics and Political System Reform*. Beijing: China Book Press, 2002.

Gao, Fang, "How Was the Democracy within the Communist Party of the Soviet Union Destroyed?", *Journal of the School of Administration of Jiangsu*, 2004, 3.

Gao, Fang, *Voices of China's Political System Reform*. Chongqing: Chongqing Publishing House, 2006.

Gao, Fang, "Accelerating the Reform of the Political System to Improve the Chinese Model of Democracy", *Journal for Party and Administrative Cadres*, 2007, 10.

Gao, Fang, "Political Reform is Expected to Catch Up – To Effectively Implement the Concept of Socialist Democracy with Chinese Characteristics", *People's Forum*, 2012, 33.

Gastil, John & Peter Levine, *The Deliberative Democracy Handbook: Strategies for Effective Civic Engagement in the Twenty-First Century*. San Francisco: Jossey-Bass, 2005.

Gunther, Richard, Giacomo Sani & Godie Shabad, *Spain after Franco: The Making of a Competitive Party System*. Berkeley: University of California Press, 1988.

Guo, Daojiu, *Society as a Restraining Force against Power: A New Perspective on Democracy*. Tianjin: Tianjin People's Publishing House, 2005.

Guo, Qiuyong, *Three Contemporary Democratic Theories*. Taipei: Linking Publishing Company, 2001.

Guo, Zhenglin, "Levels, Motives and Social Benefits: Contemporary Chinese Farmers' Political Participation", *Sociological Studies*, 2003, 3.

Guo, Zhonghua, "Monitory Democracy as the Trend of Democracy in the Contemporary Development – An Interview with Famous Scholar John Keane", *Social Science News*, April 7, 2011.

Gutmann, Amy & Dennis Zhompson, *Why Deliberative Democracy?* Princeton: Princeton University Press, 2004.

Habermas, Jürgen, *Between Facts and Norms-Contributions to a Discourse Theory of Law and Democracy*, Tong Shijun (trans.). Beijing: SDX Joint Publishing Company, 2003.

Hall, David & Roger Thomas Ames, *The Democracy of the Dead: Dewey, Confucius, and the Hope for Democracy in China*. Nanjing: Jiangsu People's Press, 2004.

He, Qing, *Utopia of Democracy*. Hong Kong: Ming Pao Publications, 1994.

He, Xinquan, *Confucianism and Modern Democracy*. Beijing: China Social Sciences Press, 2001.

Herr, Ranjoo Seodu, "Confucian Democracy and Equality", *Asian Philosophy*, 2010, 20(3).

Holmstrom, Bengt, "Moral Hazard in Team", *Bell Journal of Economics*, 1982, 13.

Hong, Yunshan, "On Lenin's Ideas of Democratic Centralism", *Studies on Marxism*, 1985, 2.

Hu, Deping, "Comrade Hu Yaobang before and after the Great Discussion on Standards for Truth", *Decision and Information*, 2008, 11.

Hu, Jintao, *Firmly March on the Path of Socialism with Chinese Characteristics and Strive to Complete the Building of a Moderately Prosperous Society in All Respects: Speech at the 18th CPC National Congress*. Beijing: People's Press, 2012.

Hu, Wei, "Intra-Party Democracy and Political Development: Exploiting the Resources of Chinese Democratization within the Existing System", *Fudan Journal* (social sciences edition), 1999, 1.

Huang, Junjie & He Jipeng, *Cultural Development of Taiwan toward the twenty-first Century*. Taipei: National Taiwan University Press, 1999.

Huang, Weiping, "The Reform of the Election of Chinese Township Heads: Significance and Predicament", *Marxism and Reality*, 2001, 5.

Huang, Xiaohui & Chen Cheng, "Comparison between Majoritarian Democracy and Consensus Democracy of their Argument Logic and Efficiency of State Power Control: Discussions on the Path of Reforming China's State Power Control Mechanism", *Journal of Fujian Normal University* (philosophy and social sciences edition), 2008, 2.

Huang, Zongxi, *Waiting for the Dawn*. Beijing: Zhonghua Book Company, 1985.

Huntington, Samuel, *No Easy Choice: Political Participation in Developing Countries*, Wang Xiaoshou (trans.). Beijing: Huaxia Publishing House, 1989.

Jiang, Yihua, *Ways to Freedom and Democracy*. Taipei: Linking Publishing Company, 2001.

Jin, Taijun, "Prudence Is Needed in the Introduction of Direct Election of Township Heads", *Study Monthly*, 2007, 2.

Jin, Yaoji, *Dilemma and Development of the Chinese Democracy*. Taipei: China Times Publishing Co., 1984.

Kang, Xiaoguang, "Further Discussion on 'Incorporation of Politics into Administration': Political Development and Stability of the Chinese Mainland in the 1990s", *Twenty-First Century* (online edition), 2002, 8.

Karatnycky, Adrian, "Muslim Countries and the Democracy Gap", *Journal of Democracy*, 2002, 13(1).

Keane, John, *The Life and Death of Democracy*. New York and London: W.W. Norton & Company, 2009.

Keane, John, Monitory Democracy and Media-saturated Societies. Griffith REVIEW Edition 24: Participation Society, 2009.

Leslie, Lipson, *The Democratic Civilization*. Hong Kong: Xinzhi Press, 1972.

Li, Eric X, "The Life of the Party: The Post-Democratic Future Begins in China", *Foreign Affairs*, 2013, 92(1).

Li, Fan, *Reform of the Electoral System in China*. Shanghai: Shanghai Jiao Tong University Press, 2005.

Li, Fan, Shou Huisheng, Peng Zongchao & Xiao Lihui, *Innovation and Development: Reforms in the Election of Township Heads*. Beijing: Orient Press, 2000.

Li, Tieying, *On Democracy*. Beijing: China Social Sciences Press, 2001.

Li, Tieying, "Some Issues of Democratic Theory", *Social Sciences in China*, 2001, 1.

Liang, Qichao, *History of Pre-Qin Thoughts on Politics*. Shanghai: Oriental Press, 1996.

Liang, Shuming, *The Substance of Chinese Culture*. Shanghai: Xuelin Press, 2000.

Liang, Shuming, *Eastern and Western Culture and their Philosophy*. Beijing: Commercial Press, 2004.

Lijphart, Arend, "Consociational Democracy", *World Politics*, 1969, 21(2).

Lijphart, Arend, *Democracy in Plural Societies: A Comparative Exploration*. New Haven: Yale University Press, 1977.

Lijphart, Arend, *Democracies: Patterns of Majoritarian and Consensus Government in Twenty-One Countries*. New Haven and London: Yale University Press, 1984.

Lijphart, Arend (US), *Patterns of Democracy: Government Forms and Performance in Thirty-Six Countries*, Chen Qi (trans.). Beijing: Peking University Press, 2006.

Lin, Meng, "On the Classical and Modern Democracies – A Historical Perspective of the Study of Democracy", PhD. Diss., School of Government of Peking University, 2001.

Lin, Shangli, "Deliberative Democracy: Pondering the Development of China's Democracy", *Academic Monthly*, 2003, 4.

Linz, Juan J & Alfred Stepan, *Problems of Democratic Transition and Consolidation: Southern Europe, South America, and Post-Communist Europe*. Baltimore: The Johns Hopkins University Press, 1996.

Lipset, Seymour M, "Some Social Requisites of Democracy: Economic Development and Political Legitimacy", *American Political Science Review*, 1959, 53(1).

Lipset, Seymour M, *Political Man: The Social Bases of Politics*. New York: Doubleday, 1960.

Liu, Huiping & Zhang Shiying, "A Study of the Reputation Theory-Based Dynamic Incentive Model for Chinese Managers", *Chinese Journal of Management Science*, 2005, 4.

Liu, Taoxiong & Zhou Bihua, "Democratic System in the Perspective of Responsibility: A Basic Model", *Comparative Economic and Social Systems*, 2012, 1.

Liu, Xirui, "The Established Model of Democracy in China", *People's Tribune*, 2007, 4.

Liu, Xirui, "Integration: The Essence and Destination of Chinese Democracy", *People's Tribune*, 2009, 1.

Liu, Xirui, "Integrationism: Essentials of Chinese Democratic Model – On the Relations of the Chinese Democratic Model with the Western Representative System", see Huang Weihua and Wang Yongcheng (ed.), *Research Reports on the Politics of Contemporary China*, Social Sciences Academic Press, 2010.

Liu, Zehua, *A History of Chinese Political Thoughts (From Sui to Qing Dynasties)*. Hangzhou: Zhejiang University Press, 1996.

Liu, Zehua, *A History of Chinese Political Thoughts (Pre-Qin Times)*. Hangzhou: Zhejiang University Press, 1996.

Locke, John, *Second Treatise of Government*, Ye Qifang & Qu Junong (trans.). Beijing: The Commercial Press, 1997.

Lü, Buwei, *The Annals of Lü Buwei* (photocopy). Shanghai: Shanghai Ancient books Publishing House, 1989.

Lupia, Arthur & John G Matsusaka, "Direct Democracy: New Approaches to Old Questions", *The Annual Review of Political Science*, 2004, 7.

Magone, Jose M, *Contemporary Spanish Politics*. New York: Routledge, 2004.

Michels, Robert, *Political Parties: A Sociological Study of the Oligarchical Tendencies of Modern Democracy*, Ren Junfeng, Xie Yue, Liu Wenfu & Cheng Zhuru (trans.). Tianjin: Tianjin People's Publishing House, 2003.

Mill, John Stuart (UK), *Representative Government*, Wang Xuan (trans.). Beijing: The Commercial Press, 1997.

Montesquieu, Charles de Secondat, *The Spirit of Laws* (Vol. I and II), Zhang Yanshen (trans.). Beijing: The Commercial Press, 1982.

Moscovici, Serge, *L'age des foules*, Xu Liemin (trans.). Nanjing: Jiangsu People's Publishing House, 2003.

Mou, Zongsan, *Dao of Politics and Dao of Governance*. Guilin: Guangxi Normal University Press, 2006.

Mu, Yifei, *The Democratic Forum: A Creation by the People of Wenling*. Beijing: Central Compilation and Translation Press, 2005.

Myerson, Roger B, *Game Theory: Analysis of Conflict*, Fei Jianping & Yu Yin (trans.). Beijing: Economic Press of China, 2001.

North, Douglas, *Institutions, Institutional Change and Economic Performance*. Shanghai: Shanghai Joint Publishing Company, 1994.

Ogden, Suzanne, *Inklings of Democracy in China*. Cambridge: Harvard University Press, 2002.

Omar, G, "Encarnacion: Spain after Franco: Lessons in Democratization", *World Policy Journal*, 2001, 2.

Pan, Wei, *The Rule of Law and the "Democracy Worship"*. Hong Kong: Hong Kong Social Sciences Publishing House, 2003.

Pareto, Vilfredo, *The Rise and Fall of Elites*, Liu Beicheng (trans.). Shanghai: Shanghai People's Publishing House, 2003.

Pateman, Carole (US), *Participation and Democratic Theory*, Chen Yao (trans.). Shanghai: Shanghai People's Publishing House, 2006.

Pei, Minxin, "Will Confrontation Cause Unrest in China?", *Apple Daily*, September 8, 2004.

Pei, Zeqing, "Innovation in Intra-Party Democracy – The Experiment with the System of Party Congresses with Fixed Terms in Ya'an City, Sichuan Province and Its Revelations", *Journal of the Party School of the CPC Sichuan Provincial Committee*, 2004, 1.

Peng, Huai'en, *The Theory of Elitist Democracy*. Taipei: Cheng Chung Book Co., Ltd, 1983.

Peng, Suining, Hou Delin, Pei Zeqing, Ma Guoxiang, Wu Xianxi, Qiu Ruoyu & Wang Yinsheng, "The System and Practice Stimulating Democratic Vitality within the Party – An Investigation and Reflection of the Piloting of the System of Party Congresses with Fixed Terms in Ya'an City, Sichuan Province", *Theory and Reform*, 2003, 2.

Peng, Zongchao, *Authorization by Citizens and Representative Democracy: A Comparative Study of Systems for the Direct Election of People's Deputies*. Zhengzhou: Henan People's Press, 2002.

Peng, Zongchao, *Public Hearing Systems in China: Transparent Policy-Making and Public Governance*. Beijing: Tsinghua University Press, 2004.

Peng, Zongchao & Li Ming, "A New Perspective on China's Public Budgeting Reform: Cases and Approaches of 'Cooperative-Harmonious Democracy'", *Reform*, 2008, 9.

Peng, Zongchao, Ma Ben & Xu Jiajun, "Cooperative-Harmonious Socialist Democracy: A Model of Chinese Democracy", *Comparative Economic and Social Systems*, 2010, 3.

Pereira, Anthony W, "Will Democratic Politics Necessarily Lead to Prosperity: Also on 'Transitionism'", *Digest of Social Sciences*, 2001, 8, 10–12.

Pi, Weibing, *The Pursuit in Political Ethics as Reflected in "Harmony Is Precious" – A Study of Pre-Qin Confucian Political Ethics in the Context of "Harmony"*. Shanghai: Shanghai Joint Publishing Company, 2007.

Przeworski, Adam, "Democracy as a Contingent Outcome of Conflicts". Jon Elster & Rune Slagstadeds (eds.). *Constitutionalism and Democracy*. Cambridge: Cambridge University Press, 1988.

Przeworski, Adam, Jose Antonio Cheibub, Miachael E Alvarez and Fernando Limongi, *Democracy and Development: Political Institutions and Material Well-being in the World, 1950–1990*. Cambridge: Cambridge University Press, 2000.

Przeworski, Adam, *Democracy and the Market: Political and Economic Reforms in Eastern Europe and Latin America*. Beijing: Peking University Press, 2005.

Pu, Xingzu, *Political System of the People's Republic of China*. Shanghai: Shanghai People's Publishing House, 1999.

Qian, Mu, *The Success and Failure of Political System in Chinese Dynasties*. Beijing: SDX Joint Publishing Company, 2005.

Qin, Haibo, "On the Democratic Reform in Spain (1975–1986)", *World History*, 2006, 3.

Rawls, John, *A Theory of Justice*, He Huaihong, He Baogang & Liao Shenbai (trans.). Beijing: China Social Sciences Press, 1997.

Rawls, John, *Political Liberalism*, Wan Junren (trans.). Nanjing: Yilin Press, 2000.

Ren, Jiantao, "Intra-Party Democracy May Start with the 'Three Implements'", *Yan-Huang Historical Review*, 2012, 12.

Rousseau, Jean-Jacques, *The Social Contract*, He Zhaowu (trans.). Beijing: The Commercial Press, 1980.

Ruan, Yuan (Qing dynasty), *Commentaries and Notes on the Thirteen Classics* (photocopy). Beijing: Zhonghua Book Company, 1980.

Sabine, George Holland, *A History of Political Theory* (Vol. I & II), Sheng Kuiyang & Cui Miaoyin (trans.). Beijing: The Commercial Press, 1986.

Sanders, Lynn M, "Against Deliberation", *Political Theory*, 1997, 25(3).

Sartori, Giovanni (US), *Theory of Democracy Revisited*, Feng Keli & Yan Kewen (trans.). Beijing: Oriental Press, 1998.

Schumpeter, Joseph, *Capitalism, Socialism and Democracy*, Wu Liangjian (trans.). Beijing: The Commercial Press, 2000, 395–396.

Sen, Amartya, "Democracy as a Universal Value", *Contemporary China Studies*, 2000, 2.

Shang, Xuefeng & Xia Dekao (trans.), *The Discourses of the States* (annotated edition). Beijing: Zhonghua Book Company, 2007.

Shen, Haixiong & Cai Guozhao, "Unveiling the History of Piloting the Reform of Party Congresses", *Oriental Outlook*, 2008, 3.

Sheng, Huaren, "Carry out the Election of Deputies to the People's Congress at the County and Township Levels According to Law", *Qiushi*, 2006, 6.

Shi, Tianjian & Maya, "Demystify Democracy", *Open Times*, 2009, 6.

Sunstein, Cass R, "Deliberative Trouble? Why Groups Go to Extremes", *The Yale Law Journal*, 2000, 110(1).

Takashi, Katou (Japan), *Politics and People*, Tang Shiqi (trans.). Beijing: Peking University Press, 2003.

Tan, Yuanping, *Chinese Political Thoughts – Confucianism and Democratization*. Taipei: Yang-Chih Book Co., Ltd., 2004.

Tang, Tsou, *Twentieth Century Chinese Politics: From the Perspectives of Macro-History and Micromechanism Analysis*. Hong Kong: Oxford University Press, 1994.

Thorley, John, *Athenian Democracy*, Wang Qiongshu (trans.). Shanghai: Shanghai Translation Publishing House, 2001.

Tong, Zhiwei, "Prudence Is Needed in the Re-Justification of Unconstitutional Reform: The 'Experiments' of Direct Election of Township Heads in the Past Few Years", *Jurists*, 2007, 4.

Vanhanen, Tatu, *The Process of Democratization: A Comparative Study of 147 States, 1980–1988*. NewYork: Taylor & Francis, 2000.

Wang, Changjiang, *Innovations of the System of Intra-Party Democracy*. Beijing: Central Compilation and Translation Press, 2007.

Wang, Changjiang, "We Should Feel Pressed to Step up Innovation in Intra-Party Democracy", *Study Times*, July 25, 2011.

Wang, Guixiu, "Origin and Implications of Democratic Centralism", *Theory Front*, 2002, 8.

Wang, Guixiu, "Direction and Path of the Development of Intra-Party Democracy", *Leaders' Friend*, 2003, 3.

Wang, Guohong, *Research on Marxist Democratic Theory*. Beijing: Party School of the Central Committee of CPC, 2007.

Wang, Huning, *Logic of Politic*. Shanghai: Shanghai People's Publishing House, 2004.

Wang, Shaoguang, *Four Discourses on Democracy*. Shanghai: SDX Joint Publishing Company, 2008.

Wang, Zhengxu & Dragan Pavlicevic, "Citizens and Democracy: Shi Tianjian's Contribution to China Studies and Political Science", *Open Times*, 2011, 9.

Wang, Zhenhai, *Democracy and Chinese People*. Beijing: China Radio Film & TV Press, 1989.

Wu, Jiangxiang, "The Rise of China During Democratization". Gao Quanxi (ed.). *Great Nation*. Beijing: Peking University Press, 2004 (1).

Xiao, Bin & Guo Zhonghua, *Sun Yat-sen University Political Science Review*. Guangzhou: Sun Yat-sen University Press, 2005.

Xiao, Gongquan, *A Chinese History of Political Thoughts*. Shenyang: Liaoning Education Press, 1998.

Xin, Xiangyang, "Jiang Zemin's Thoughts on Political Reform", *Contemporary World and Socialism*, 2007, 2.

Xu, Guoxian, "Political Costs of Democracy", *Journal of Social Sciences and Philosophy*, 2005, 6.

Xu, Xianglin, "Goal-Setting and Strategy-Choosing of Political Reform Policy", *Journal of Social Sciences of Jilin University*, 2004, 6.

Xu, Yatang, *People-Oriented Governance*. Taipei: The Commercial Press, 2005.

Xue, Kai, "Scholars Say the System of Party Congresses with Fixed Terms Is a New Breakthrough in Intra-Party Democracy", *China Comment* (internal edition), 2003, 10–3.

Xun, Yue, *On Lessons*. Shanghai: Shanghai Guji Publishing House, 1990.

Yan, Jirong, "Theoretical Construction of Chinese Democracy", *Comparative Economic and Social Systems*, 2010, 3.

Yang, Chenggang, "Strategic Thinking of Deng Xiaoping's Political Reform", *Journal of Wuhan University of Technology* (social science edition), 2002, 5.

Yang, Xuedong, He Zengke & Lai Hairong, *Grassroots Democracy and Innovation in Local Governance*. Beijing: Central Compilation and Translation Press, 2004, 51–108.

Yu, Keping, *Incremental Democracy and Good Governance*. Beijing: Social Sciences Academic Press, 2005.

Yu, Keping, "Marx on the General Concept, Universal Values and Common Form of Democracy", *Marxism and Reality*, 2007, 3.

Zakaria, Fareed, "The Rise of Illiberal Democracy", *Foreign Affairs*, 1997, 76(6).

Zakaria, Fareed, *The Future of Freedom: Illiberal Democracy at Home and Abroad*. New York: W.W. Norton, 2003.

Zeng, Jingzhong, "The Eighth CPC National Congress and Intra-Party Democracy", *CPC History Studies*, 1996, 4.

Zhang, Liwen, *Theory of Harmony and Cooperation – A Conception of the twenty-first Century Cultural Strategy*. Beijing: China Renmin University Press, 2006.

Zhang, Minggui, *Theory of Democracy*. Taipei: Wu-Nan Book Inc., 2002.

Zhang, Weiying, *Game Theory and Information Economics*. Shanghai: Shanghai People's Press, 1996.

Zheng, Yifan, "Centralism, Democratic Centralism and the Workers' Democracy – The Development of Organizing Principles within the Party during Lenin's Time", *Journal of Party School of the Central Committee of CPC*, 2009, 5.

Zheng, Yongnian, "Rethinking China's Democracy for a Faster and Better Democracy", Zaobao.com, February 27, 2008.

Zhong, Zuxuan, "Improve the Party's Solidarity, Unification and Innovative Vigor – New Developments in the Party's Organization System and Intra-Party Democracy", *China Organization and Human Resources News*, October 29, 2012.

Zhou, Daoji, "Analysis and Review of Chinese People-Oriented Thought", *Selected Reportage IV*, Institute of the Three Principles of the People, Academia Sinica, 1985.

Index

For Product Safety Concerns and Information please contact our EU
representative GPSR@taylorandfrancis.com
Taylor & Francis Verlag GmbH, Kaufingerstraße 24, 80331 München, Germany

www.ingramcontent.com/pod-product-compliance
Lightning Source LLC
Chambersburg PA
CBHW062026270326
41929CB00014B/2331